Infant Crafts
for school and home

Infant Crafts
for school and home

Margaret Norton

BLANDFORD PRESS

First published in 1975
by Blandford Press Ltd,
167 High Holborn, London WC1V 6PH

© Blandford Press Ltd 1975

ISBN 0 7137 0671 6

Printed in Great Britain by
Unwin Brothers Limited
The Gresham Press
Old Woking Surrey
A member of the Staples Printing Group

Contents

Introduction

This is a book for parents, teachers and children up to the age of eight or nine. The suggestions are intended to stimulate ideas in various media, and allow for as much creativity by the child as possible. For example, if form or material are fixed, allow choice of colour and decoration. For most of the craft work suggested each child needs a good pair of sharp scissors, and access to a small stapler and various adhesives. Templates needed by younger children can be cut from waste card. A template is a cut-out shape round which a child may draw. When a design (flower, bird, etc.) is too difficult or too large for a child to draw, or when several shapes must be identical, a template should be prepared to provide the required outline. The templates in this book are not full size.

I   Hats

Make with crêpe paper, newspaper, cake frills, doylies, sugar paper, or cartridge, and decorate with beads, buttons, ribbons, paper strips, earrings etc.

Most hats begin with the length of the headband. This is marked X in the drawings.

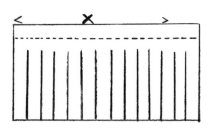 

Bonnet: fold on the dotted line to strengthen the band. Fit round the head, overlap and fasten. Gather up the top. Streamers of ribbon or crêpe may be added.

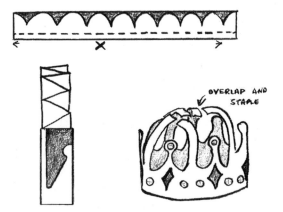

Crown: fold at the dotted line for a simple crown, or more complicated, fold in a concertina fold as illustrated, and cut out a shape, such as the one suggested, which leaves pieces to overlap on the top of the head. Decorate with foil, buttons and beads.

9

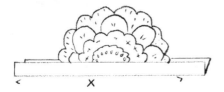

Bonnet: insert doylies, tissue circles or **coloured** foil into the folded hatband.

Helmets: see Section 4 on Masks and Faces, p. 43.

Soldier's Hats:

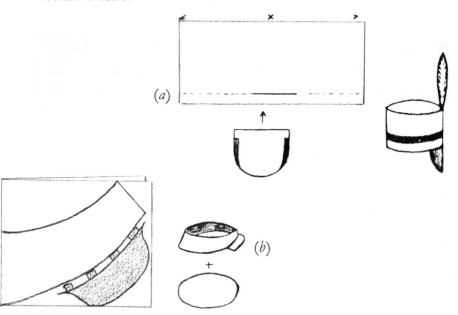

(*a*) The brim is inserted into the slit on the fold. Decorate with paper or a feather, and pieces of large jewellery for badges.

(*b*) The brim and band are cut from a large folded paper. Only one brim is required. Overlap the hat at the front. The brim is taped to the band.

(*c*) *Officer's Cap:* fold the band on the two lines inwards, overlap and staple. Score the brim in a shallow curve, and cut slits to the curve. Staple to the inner hatband. Cut a crown and fasten to the folded-in tabs.

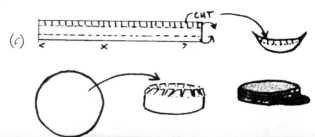

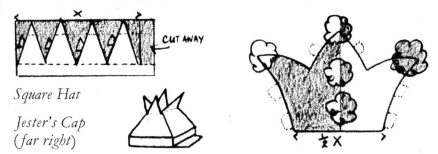

Square Hat

Jester's Cap
(far right)

Square Hat: fold the hatband. Tabs can be cut to glue the sides together, or they can be taped. A brim can be made by cutting two corners, and bending down the side.

Jester's Cap: make multicoloured in crêpe or sugar paper. Cut two, allow tabs for fixing if required. Decorate with tissue pompoms or bells. Strengthen by the insertion of a broad hat-band.

Robin Hood Hat: fold corners down as indicated. Slit fold to dotted line and fold up edges to make a hat-band. Fold on lines as shown. Glue or staple to secure. Fringe the back to make a feather.

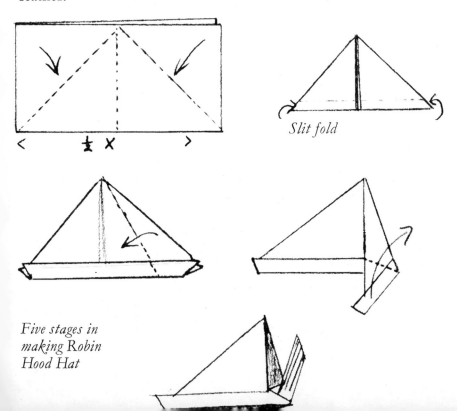

Slit fold

Five stages in making Robin Hood Hat

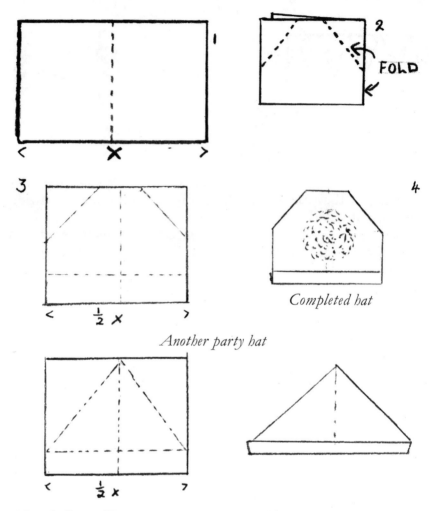

Completed hat

Another party hat

Simple Party Hat: use crêpe paper. Fold on the dotted lines—two ways are shown. Fasten back the folded triangles, fix onto folded headband and decorate. See also p. 17.

Chef's Hats:

(a) A white crêpe circle stapled or glued to a headband.

(b) Three superimposed circles, glued on to a hatband (like that of the officer's cap on p. 10). Attach strings to tie.

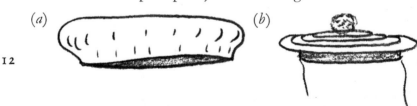

(a)   (b)

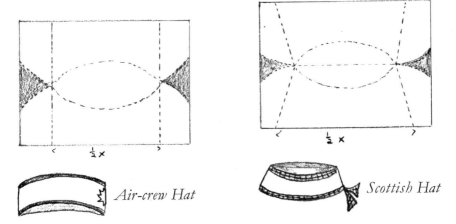

Air-crew Hat

Scottish Hat

Air-crew Hat: use a large sheet of very stiff paper. Score and cut as indicated. Staple the end flaps.

Scottish Hat: score in the curves as before, and reverse score down the centre. Staple the end flaps.

Hats based on circles

A quarter circle makes a tall thin cone, suitable for a witch's hat, and a semi-circle gives a wider cone.

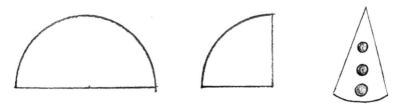

These are hats where the brim is made by scoring.

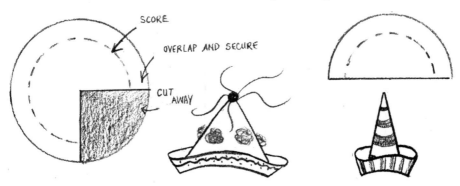

Make in stiff paper, or soft paper over a stiff base.

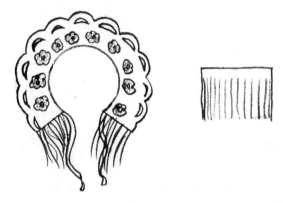

Fasten fringed paper or ribbon at the ends. Decorate with sequins, doylies etc.

Made from a full circle of stiff paper

Bonnet: turn in the folds and glue. Decorate with doylies, lace etc.

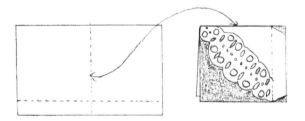

Admiral's Hat: this is rather difficult for young children to make. A large square of stiff paper is required. Make the diagonal folds, turn the paper over and make the crossways folds. Open out. Shape 3 is formed by pushing the sides gently inwards.

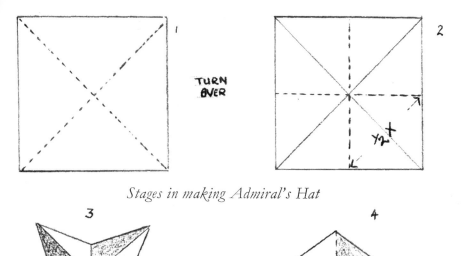

Stages in making Admiral's Hat

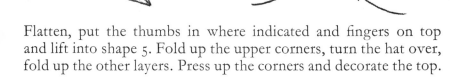

Flatten, put the thumbs in where indicated and fingers on top and lift into shape 5. Fold up the upper corners, turn the hat over, fold up the other layers. Press up the corners and decorate the top.

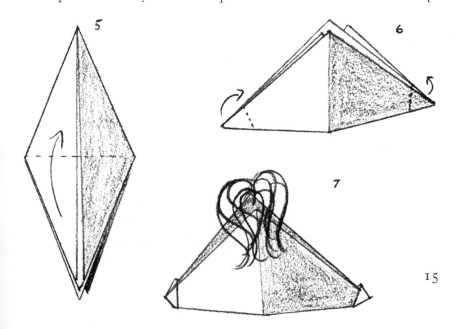

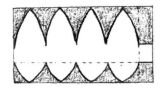

Petal Hat: cut as indicated, overlap the tab and secure, and tape the points at the top.

Red Indian Headdress: there are several ways of making this. Use ink-dyed feathers fixed in a headband of stiff paper or corrugated paper, or fabric, or paper feathers made of fringed crêpe stiffened with wire, paper, milk straws or cardboard.

One headdress can be made as a whole in stiff paper as drawn. Extra support for the feathers is given by two long strips of paper or ribbon woven between the feathers. Add streamers over the ears.

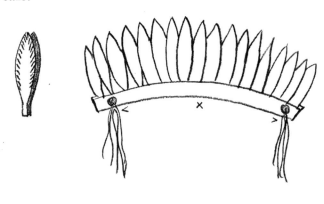

Made to a fold

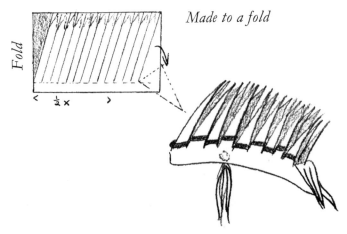

Party Hat: this is an origami traditional design, requiring a large square.   (Crêpe paper is too small.)

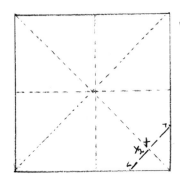

A large sheet of newspaper (60 cm square) will make a hat to fit a child.

Fold crossways, and then diagonally (1). Turn under the corners as in Stage 2. Fold the top corners to the centre fold (3). Fold up one piece, which may be glued now or later (4). Turn the hat over. Fold up the two flaps as in 5, leaving one piece. Turn down the two corners of the flaps as drawn in 6. Fold up the remaining piece as shown. Open out the hat and glue at the back, if this has not already been done.

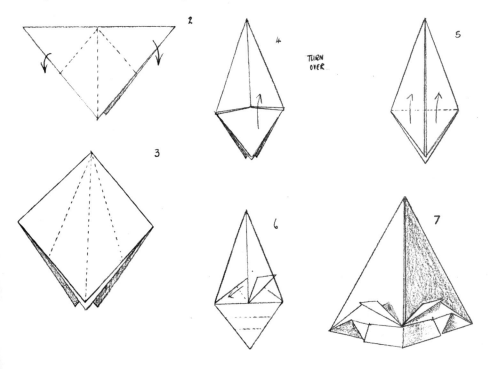

2   Fishes and birds

Fishes

Fishes are popular subjects in out-of-season classroom decoration, and a staple diet for inventive fingers. They can be displayed in such a variety of ways, on friezes, mobiles, models, patterns, etc.

The following variations are in increasing order of difficulty:

(*a*) A simple cut-out, textured or coloured, mounted flat or with the form raised as suggested. Unless a colour scheme must be imposed allow colour and texture to be a free choice by the child. Provide paint, crayons, tissue paper circles or scraps to glue as blobs, seeds, pasta, fabric, metal shapes (such as bottle tops and ring-pull can tops) and buttons. Young children will need a template, and the fish should be as large as possible.

(*b*) A decorated shape with scoring on a curve to raise the form when the fish is mounted. A straight fold may be used by younger children. Two cut and stapled together can be hung in a mobile, and the body stuffed with pieces of newspaper.

(*c*) A simple shape, textured and cut, made in a dark-toned paper, mounted against the light, with Cellophane or tissue glued behind. This makes an impressive display. (See pp. 128–9 for paper textures.)

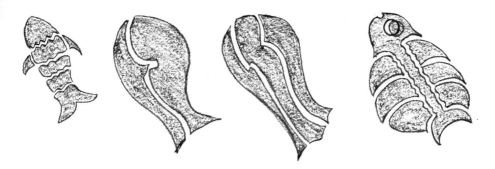

Using a simple shape cut the fish into pieces and fix to a suitable background. The rule is not to add or take away any pieces. Fun at any age.

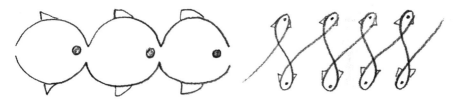

Infant writing patterns can be turned into fish and used as borders, book covers, mats etc.

Fish made to a fold, with or without a template, can have inserts of foil, sticky paper, tissue, strips of paper, ribbon or straws. The fish may be mounted or hung.

Two identical pieces glued round the edges make a mobile fish. Cellophane or tissue can be sandwiched in the middle. Pull it taut when fixing.

The form can be raised by overlapping.

A strip of stiff paper or crêpe can be folded in a concertina fold and inserted to make gill covers and fins.

Find the point of balance of a fish by holding lightly between finger and thumb.

Pieces of wool or paper or raffia make a fancy edge to a paper fish. Cut the holes with a paper punch.

Older children can make a more complicated fish, which is based on a centre fold. Cut the fish out, and fold again as shown. This can be decorated as it is, or cut to form eyes, tail and fins. The front may be slit and overlapped to curve the head, or the tail may be stapled under the gills to plump out the body. If the depth of body is sufficient the bottom edges can be glued together, and strips of raffia or paper added. Find the point of balance of these fish by supporting on a pencil.

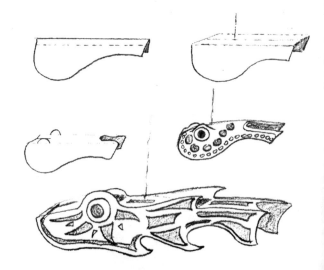

Templates for mobile fish. Cut larger

This is an easy mobile fish, very attractive in coloured sticky paper or wallpaper. Young children will need templates. Two of each shape are cut. The body form is raised by overlapping the radial cut, on each circle, and the tails and fins are sandwiched between them.

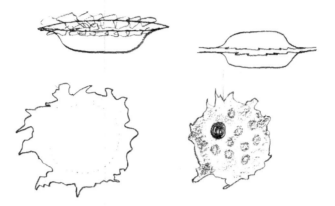

A similar fish, which takes longer to make but is more durable, can be made by pasting torn tissue pieces over a mould, such as a saucer or bowl. Make two and allow to dry. Remove the moulds. Join the two halves of the body together, leaving the torn edges to look like fins. Similarly a balloon may be covered, and decorated to look like a fish or an octopus. These models look very attractive when sprayed with clear polyurethane.

Fish can be hung from a hoop, or against a frieze, using threads supported on wall brackets, or in a box or table top model of an aquarium as shown.

The frieze and model can have additions to the background, such as sand, pebbles, shells, seaweed, crabs, lobsters, made of paper, papier maché, polystyrene etc.

Light enters behind the side pieces, and the top and front can be covered in green Cellophane.

A decorated pelmet can be made to hide the threads.

Older children may need more sober fish for murals involved in a project, such as a harbour scene, life boats, shops, fishing industry, where the fish play a small part in the scene. Fish made of string whorls glued to the shape are very effective. A net can be a real one, or made of loops of string (where no strain is put upon it) or of paper, cut as shown from a folded strip of newspaper or brown paper. Young children can entangle the fish in the loops, and mount them away from the backing paper by glueing to a matchbox.

Folded newspaper to make a net. Fold a large sheet concertina fashion, snip along each fold alternately, as shown. Open out carefully and hang.

Fish made of string glued to a card base.

A very easy fish for a mobile can be made using strips of coloured paper, and all ages of children enjoy these. The form of the fish is made first, and the outline filled in with loops, folds and whorls. The larger the fish the better. Small fish can hang inside larger ones.

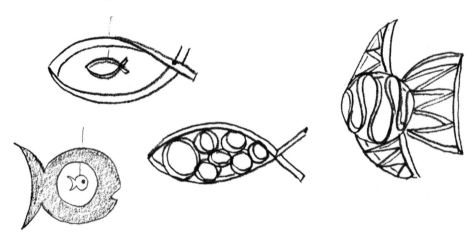

Similarly, solid fish cut in coloured paper can hang inside larger ones which have a circle cut out. This kind look festive at Christmas, and allow older children to be inventive with the basic design. (See also p. 162.)

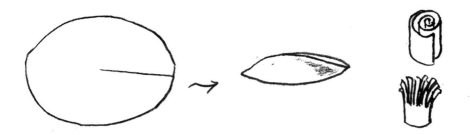

Additional models for underwater displays can be made in a variety of ways, as already suggested. The mussels and pebbles are identical in form, and should be decorated before overlapping to raise the form. A rolled and fringed strip of crêpe or stiff paper makes the sea anemone.

Seaweed can be made in crêpe, cartridge, sponge or polystyrene. The acorn barnacle is cut as shown and then overlapped.

Young children can make a crab from a folded piece of round card or a paper plate. The legs can be made from pipecleaners, fabric etc., and the child can probably suggest his own ideas. A cardboard tube is shown here for the legs.

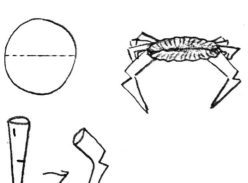

See pp. 28–9 for another way to make a crab.

25

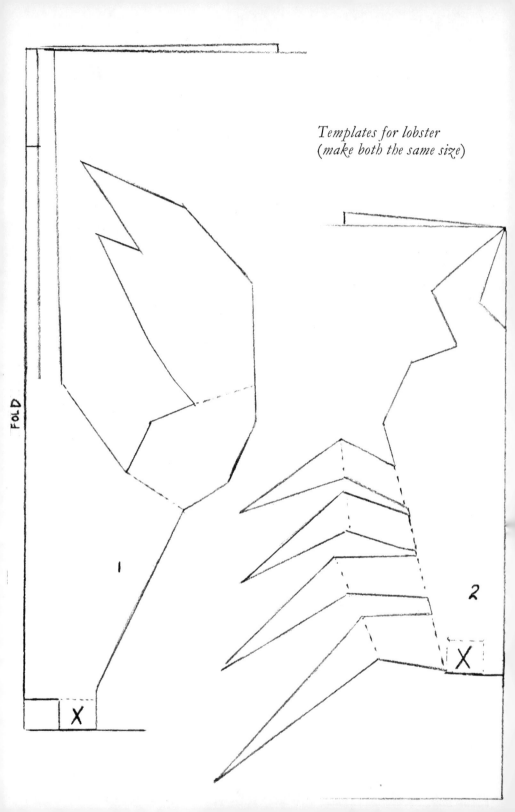

*Templates for lobster
(make both the same size)*

FOLD

1

2

X

X

A lobster can be made from templates. Join pieces 1 to 2 at X (or cut as one piece to the fold). Bend the legs under the body. Bend claws and legs up and down. Part 3 is inserted through the rear slit and fixed under the body. The child decorates the pieces before assembling.

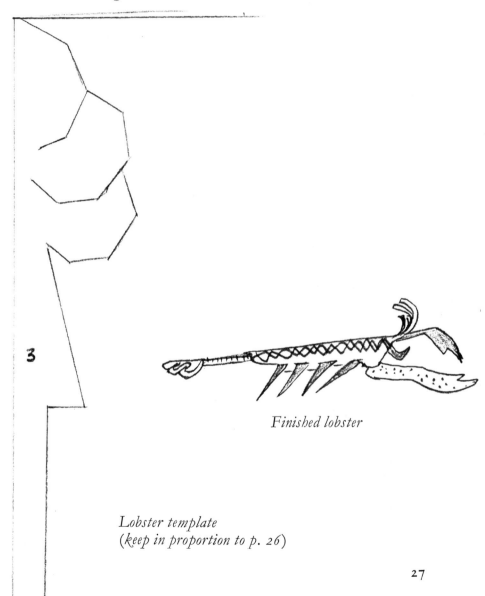

3

Finished lobster

Lobster template
(keep in proportion to p. 26)

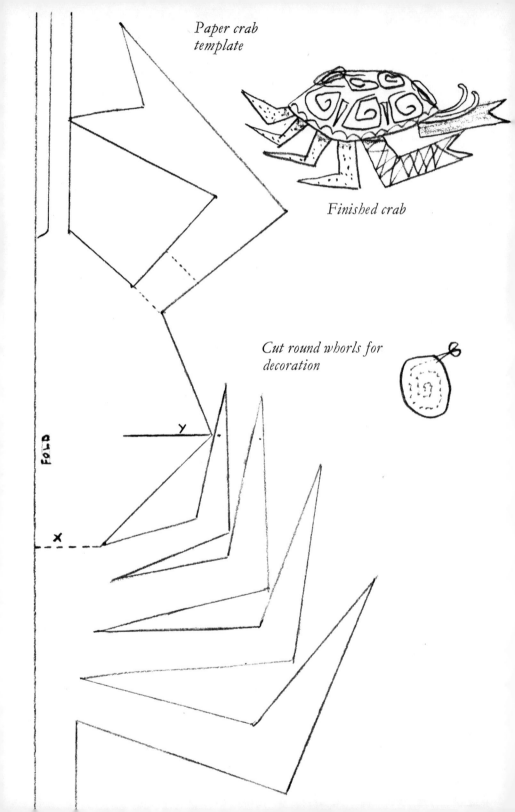

Paper crab
template

Finished crab

Cut round whorls for
decoration

Y

X

FOLD

Another way of making a paper crab from a template and a folded paper is shown. The crab can be freely decorated before folding at X where the legs go under the body.

Cut, overlap and staple at Y.

Fold pincers at dotted lines up and down.

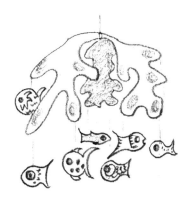 

A mobile support can be made in wire to simulate seaweed. Cover with green tissue and hang fish from it. A hoop is a good shape for round fish. Hang it vertically or horizontally, with crêpe to cover it.

Fish kites

Very young children enjoy making these. They are not difficult to assemble, and the large area is easy to paint. Each kite needs a large folded sheet of newspaper of good quality, tissue, crêpe or ribbon for the streamers, and a strip of brown sticky paper to reinforce the mouth of the fish. The design drawn uses the fold of the paper. This is not vital to the kite, but makes it easier for younger children to cut and glue.

Draw on folded paper and cut. Glue the 2 parts together at edges except for mouth and X⟷X. See over for further instructions

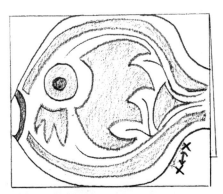

Draw the fish (or a similar large design) on the folded paper as large as possible. Cut it out. Glue the two parts all round the edges except at the mouth and under the tail (between X and X). When the kite is flown, air goes in at the mouth and exits at the tail. Paint both sides of the kite and allow to dry. Reinforce the mouth with tape, keeping it round and open. It should be as strong as possible. Attach streamers to the sides and tail. Thread twine across the mouth and join a long length to the centre of it. This is held by the child. Allow all parts to dry before flying the kite.

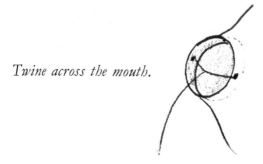

Twine across the mouth.

This is not a long-lasting model, being only as strong as the newspaper. It makes a nice end-product for the large paintings painted by children at play groups. Older children can devise kites with faces, rockets, pigs etc. Any shape will do which is roughly circular and contains two holes, one central at one side and the other below centre opposite.

Birds

Birds, like fish, are inventive and colourful subjects for craftwork. Younger children can use a template and colour or texture a simple cutout, using paint, crayons, seed, buttons, tissue etc.

To raise the form of the bird make a central slit, overlap and staple. Make two and join them together for a mobile. If very large birds are made this way, stuff the body with newspaper.

The body may be scored with a knife or scissor point.

Wings may be stapled to the body. Stiff paper will be required, and the wings can be gently curled over scissors.

Wings may also be fixed by insertion into a slit at the top or across the centre. Concertina-fold wings of crêpe or cartridge are easy to fold and fix.

A simple bird can be made from strips of different colours and lengths. The finished bird can hang in a mobile or be fixed to a frieze.

Birds cut from a folded paper will need cartridge paper. The fold can be at the top or the bottom. Wings are bent down or up. The bird may be decorated with tissue or crêpe pieces overlapped like feathers, or painted or crayoned. Staple or glue the edges where necessary.

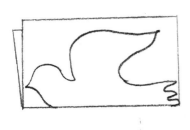 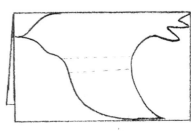

A simple silhouette for a seaside or harvesting frieze where a flock of circling birds is required can be cut in a V shape in paper or polystyrene. The form in paper can be raised by scoring along the wings.

Fantastic and entertaining birds can be made of wire bent into the outline ready for covering in newspaper and tissue. Bare ends of wire are covered first with bits of pasted newspaper, then the pieces of tissue are pasted on. The tissues may be single thickness or overlapped. Spray the finished bird with clear polyurethane. Sequins, buttons, beads may be fixed on to enhance the brilliance of this kind of bird.

Wire framework

Paper tubes and yoghourt cartons can be made into birds, with paint, pipe cleaners, fabric, buttons etc. Young children will need help in fixing the cartons and tubes together.

Owls and robins are popular subjects in fabric and paper collage.

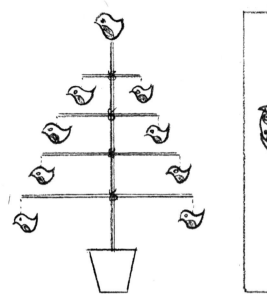

These are three ways of displaying them, two as a hanging
decoration, and the other as a frieze. Leaves or snowflakes can
be added for a seasonal effect. The tree mobile is easily made
from pieces of dowelling tied to a stick. Stand the stick in a
tub of stones. Real branches could be used if available. Bits of
green tissue will simulate spring leaves if necessary, or cutout
autumn leaves could be piled in a heap round the tub with a
few fixed to the branches. The hoop is covered in paper or raffia,
and is large enough to display wire birds. (See also p. 164.)

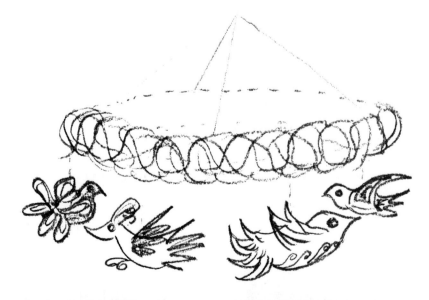

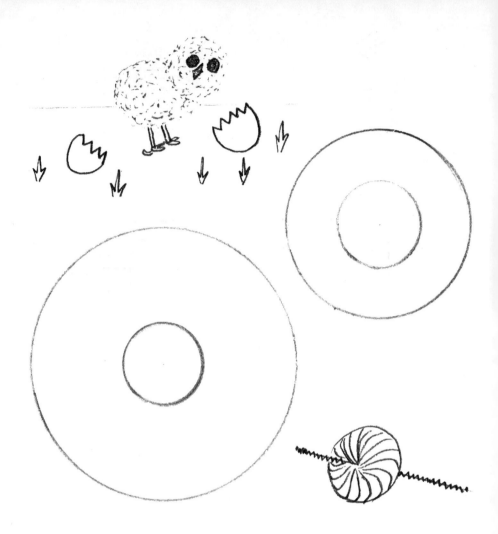

Easter chicks

Young children enjoy making these animals in wool. Two cardboard circles are required for each chick, each with a centre hole. Each disc is wound with thick wool, using a hair clip as a needle. When the centre hole becomes minute, thread a pipe cleaner through the larger disc. This makes the legs of the chick. Tie the ends of the wool. Cut round the circumference of the discs and remove the cardboard after tying threads round the centre. Tie the small ball to the larger for the head.

Bend the legs into feet and twist another half pipe cleaner round each for toes. Cut black eyes and a beak and glue into position. The chick can be stapled to a base. Cut a card eggshell with a tab behind to support it.

An eggshell to fit the chick can be made with a balloon. Blow it up to the required size and stick on pieces of white or coloured tissue paper. Allow it to dry, paint it if necessary, and cut it across the middle.

Large wool balls can make birds and animals with paper or felt feet and features.

The chicks can be used in a group model or an individual Easter model with a chocolate egg in a box.

This background is suitable for a group model. The simple cut-outs can be made in fabric or paper.

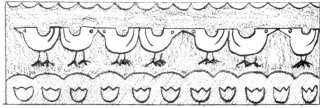

3 Figures

Figure templates

These are suggested templates for figures to be coloured, left as silhouettes or dressed with fabric before mounting on a scene.

Young children find realistic shapes difficult to cut. A stylised shape is easier and provides more opportunity for individual treatment.

These figures stand when cut to a fold.

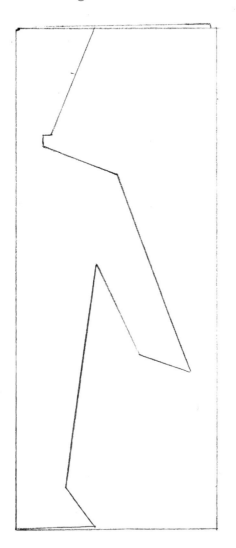
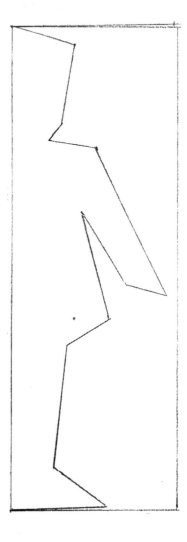

Simple stand-up animals cut to a fold

These are the templates. The animal is drawn on folded cartridge
or card, and the decoration is left to the child. This is a quicker
method of making stand-up animals than the usual one of news-
paper-covered wire which is often a tedious process for younger
children, though the results are more permanent, stronger and
individually creative.

There is an easy reindeer shape in the Christmas section (p. 174).
Children can design individual animals using the starting point
of a folded paper as, for example, in a project on dinosaurs.

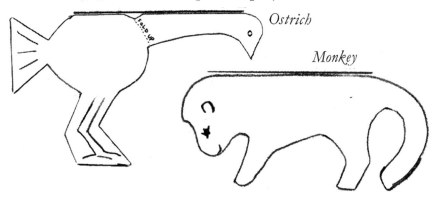

Ostrich

Monkey

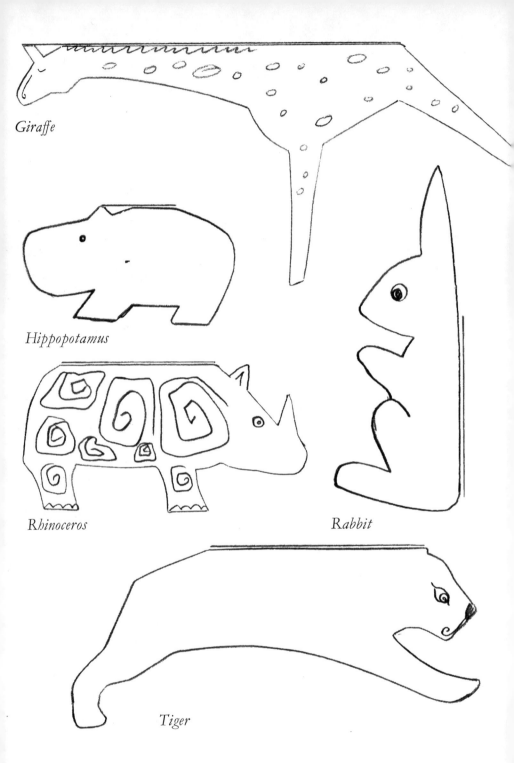

Giraffe

Hippopotamus

Rhinoceros

Rabbit

Tiger

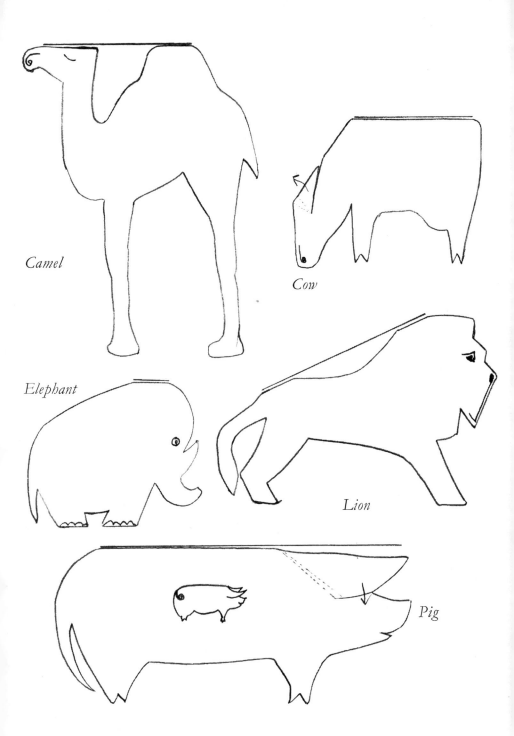

Camel

Cow

Elephant

Lion

Pig

Stand-up people

This is a very easy model suitable for very young children. The figure can be a clown, a soldier, an animal, or whatever they wish. The template has a cut-out which the child uses as the shape of the face. This must not be cut away in his model. Young children tend to draw small faces and the oval helps them to keep the face large.

Crayon or paint before the figure is stapled at the back. Decoration can be fixed on as desired, such as cotton wool for Father Christmas, pipe cleaners for whiskers, paper for curls, wool or wood shavings for hair, twigs for witch's broom.

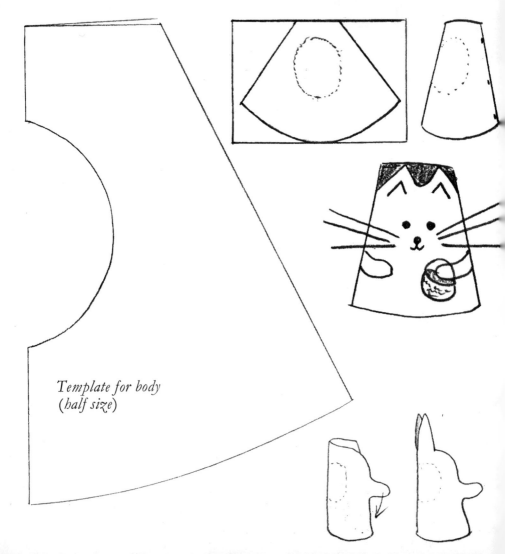

Template for body
(half size)

Older children can add arms to the template, or cut away to make ears.

The model is stapled at the back when the colouring is finished.

Older children can make figures based on a cone. Use a quarter of a circle of cartridge or sticky paper and staple or glue into a cone. A simple Father Christmas can be made by this method. Add a fringed cone with the top cut away, a circle for a nose and a strip for a hat and the figure is complete. Hang from a tree or stand in a snow scene. (See also p. 174.)

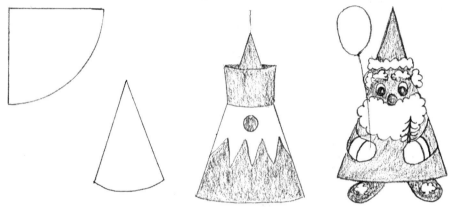

With a larger cone greater details are possible. Use coloured cartridge for the cone and add features in wool, cotton wool, raffia, buttons, wood shavings, paper etc.

This Father Christmas can hang or stand. Feet may be attached to the cone, or the cone may be put over a base.

Make the base by cutting away the top of a cone.

Figures made on a cone can be quite large and detailed. The witch has a small cone for the hat crown, and a circle with an inner circle removed for the brim. The hair is curled paper, wool, or wood shavings. The nose is a triangle, with a centre fold, fixed to a slot in the cone. The arms are a long strip of paper. The broomstick is a twig or rolled tube of paper.

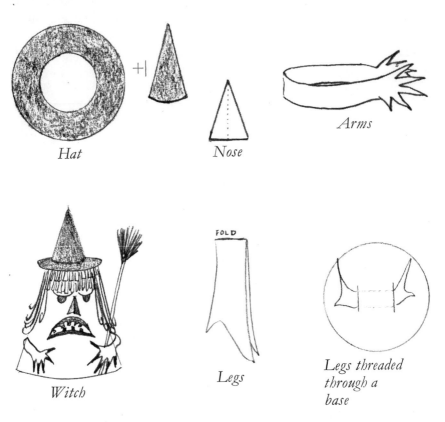

Hat

Nose

Arms

Witch

Legs

Legs threaded
through a
base

The witch can fly by a thread below the hat brim. Attach legs and feet to a circle or oval stapled in the base. The broomstick can be flown or waved in a hand.

Inventive children will put conical cats on the broomsticks, or spiders and bats.

Clowns and animals are good subjects to make from cones.

4 Masks, faces and puppets

Masks and faces

The basic shape of the mask is simple and young children find it easy and exciting to make. The usual difficulty is to make the sides strong enough to last the interest life of the mask. It can be reinforced with tape, or made double as indicated. The mask can be fastened by overlapping the tabs and stapling, or by tying with wool or string.

This basic mask can be decorated with paint, crayon, wool, pipe cleaners, wood shavings, curled paper strips, beads, buttons, or whatever is available, and will make the mask visually exciting.

Pass the string through the holes, over the child's forehead, and tie.

Ears, nose or beak, hair, feathers and so on may be cut with the basic shape. Extra support for the mask can be added by extending the side, or cutting a strip down the fold which then goes over the child's head.

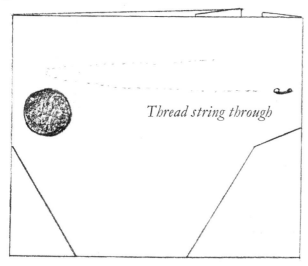

Basic mask in card or paper

Thread string through

Slit the ears, overlap and staple to bend the ear forward or backward.

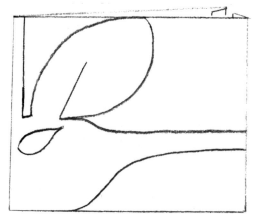

Rabbit's mask

The nose or beak folds down on the dotted line.

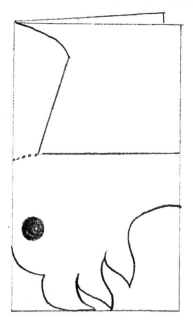

Inventive children will easily devise masks to their own purpose. A few more are suggested below.

Witch's mask

Helmet

Father Christmas

Witch's mask: staple the tops of the hat together, bend over the two tabs at each side and staple together to make the brim. Add hair to the side and hat.

Father Christmas: fold down the hair, fold the moustache up and down in two folds. The nose can be cut as indicated and lifted slightly away from the face.

Helmet with visor: bend the visor down and glue or staple along the front of it.

Heavier masks can be made in two methods from newspaper over a curved mould, such as a catering-size coffee tin.

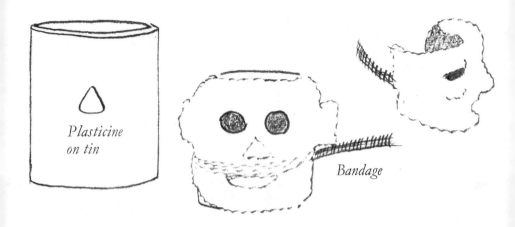

Plasticine on tin

Bandage

1. Prepare a large amount of papier maché (half a bucketful should make six faces). Put a blob of plasticine on the side of the coffee tin where the child's nose will be. Mould the wet maché over the tin in a thin layer over at least half the circumference. Wind a piece of bandage round the tin at below nose level and tie at the back. This will be sandwiched in layers of the mask and tie the finished mask to the child. It can be put round the tin before any maché is put on, but there is a danger then of it coming away from the dry mask. Continue to add maché, pressing it solidly and firmly together, leaving holes for the eyes and mouth. Add lumps for ears, cheeks, lips and eyebrows, and wool for hair if desired. Young children will be satisfied by few features. Paint the mask after about a week's drying, allow to dry and remove from the tin. Remove the plasticine.

The mask could be held in front of the face on a piece of dowelling which is inserted up into the chin before the mask is dry. These masks are suitable for hanging on a jungle frieze, or mounting on a totem pole (use a cardboard carpet roll supported on a base).

2. Older children can use this method, which is more precise. The features are first modelled on the tin in plasticine. Small torn squares of newspaper are stuck over them with cellulose paste, leaving holes for mouth and eyes. With this method large ears or beards can be made on the mask. After the layer of

46

newspaper add a bandage strip for tying and then paste on tinted paper bits. (This is to differentiate the layers and make sure that an even thickness is built up.) Again, a layer of newspaper, and then a layer of white paper which is the final surface for painting. Allow to dry, colour by paint or torn coloured tissue paper and remove the mask from the tin. Scrape away the plasticine. The mask may be sprayed by clear gloss polyurethane which is particularly beautiful over layers of tissue.

Masks and faces for displays can be made from any junk materials, such as pieces of wood, plastic bottles, tin lids, trays etc., and features from wood, wood shavings, wool, plastic tops, bottle tops, fabric, and so on. Children will devise all manner of fantastic creations and often need very little technical help.

The masks may be used with life-size figures whose bodies are made of cardboard boxes, toilet tubes etc. (See below, left.)

Tubes in nylon stockings may be used.

Plastic bottle for face, with inserts of card or wood.

Arms and legs of interfolded strips of paper shown below, right.

Puppets

A lot of unnecessary mystique surrounds puppet-making with young children. Elaborate materials and long preparations are

not required. Puppets should be almost instantaneous, as their interest life is short, and their use spontaneous. Use any material that is at hand and forget naturalism. Introduce young children to puppets by using paper bag puppets to tell stories or poems, such as 'The Owl and the Pussycat'. While the children watch, blow up the paper bags, tape onto pencils, paint the faces, and use them at once. This is often sufficient to stimulate the children to make their own simple puppets.

Provide a variety of materials, such as stockings, socks, boxes, cartons. The children will be happy with faces only, to begin with, and will invent limbs if required. On a simple hand-held rod puppet, like one made from a paper bag, the limbs can hang loose or be fixed to wooden pieces also.

Paper bags taped to a pencil or rod.

Arms may be added by twisting a stuffed stocking round the rod (above, right).

Make properties for the puppets to act with if possible.

A sock makes a good glove puppet. Use badges for eyes or sew on buttons or beads. The age of the child will again determine how much time to spend on the preparations.

A simple sock puppet with beads sewn on.

Cardboard boxes can be used to make puppets with legs and arms. The children may need help to fix on the limbs.

Most of the best work using puppets occurs in small groups in the playground or class corner, and the adults may only perceive the interest and stimulation. Older children who have seen puppets used by adults may want to use them to give a performance to other children. This should arise naturally and not be imposed. It is at this stage with older children that more elaborate puppets could be made which take longer to produce, such are those with papier maché heads, or puppets controlled by strings, with properties and settings.

Again it all depends on how long the children will be interested, and why they are doing it.

A box puppet controlled by a rod.

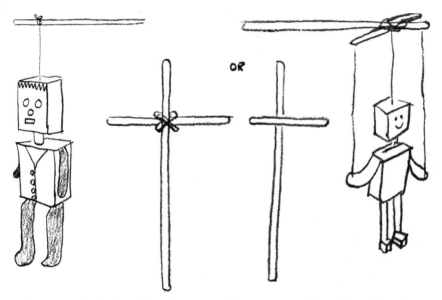

A control for head and arms. The arm rod is either fixed or left loose to enable the child to use both hands by lifting off the arm control and moving it in front of the puppet.

This kind of rod control can be used for animal puppets which have articulated bodies, such as caterpillar or snake. Use threaded cotton reels, egg cartons, or woolly balls to make the puppets and work with strings fixed to a rod. Children can make wonderful monsters this way, using whatever is at hand.

49

Egg carton tops.

A simple control with two strings.

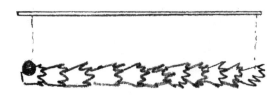

A monster made of junk materials. The control cross pieces may be fixed or loose.

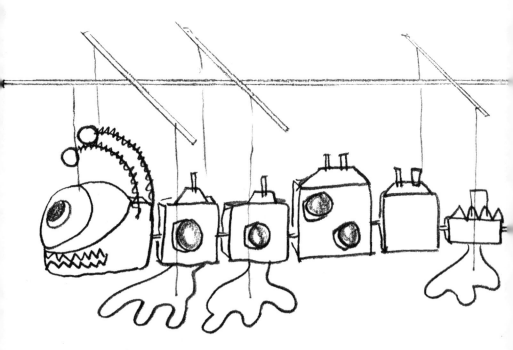

5 Models from paper squares

Houses

It is worthwhile to teach each child formally how to fold the basic shape, because it is the technique for beginning many models of houses and boxes. A square of newspaper can be used to practise with. Go slowly through the folding processes, emphasising the care required, how to lift the paper up and away from the body using both hands and matching the edges, and working with the paper flat on the table. Use crayons to mark in the cutting lines and check the marks before the child cuts.

The basic shape of a sloping roof.

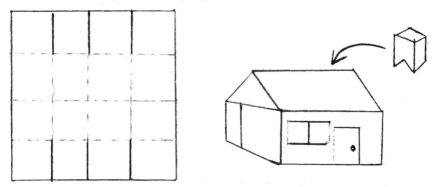

The chimney is a folded strip taped onto the roof.

The fixing of the ends is often the most difficult and stapling may be easier than glueing. The two centre tabs are overlapped and the end tabs half overlapped.

The basic shape of a flat roof. A polystyrene dome may be added and outer steps.

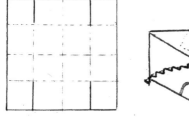

51

 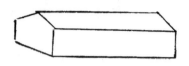

The folds in an oblong paper, suitable for a farmhouse, school or hospital.

An extension to a simple house. Cut away the shaded area. Tabs may be used to fix the extension.

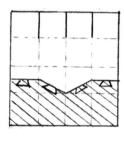 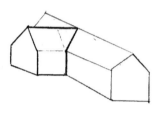

Young children can crayon the houses before fixing into shape. The completed models may be decorated with paint, matchsticks, lollipop sticks, straws, wallpaper, corrugated paper etc.

Other buildings

Two pieces to make a village church. The length of paper for the tower is 1½ times the length of the paper for the church. Tape the edges of the tower together.

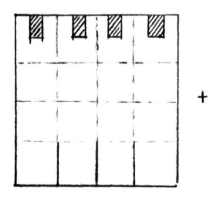 +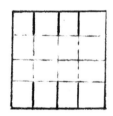

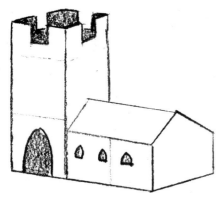

A *pointed tower*, with or without tabs. Join to a house shape.

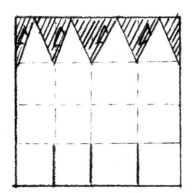
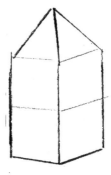

A *round tower:* cut two of the tower shapes and tape together.

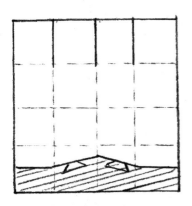
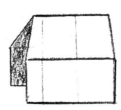

Glue to a house shape cut as shown.

The length of this paper is $1\frac{1}{4}$ times the length of the tower paper.

Noah's Ark is a more difficult model. Two squares are required. The smaller is for the simple house shape, and the larger (length 1½ times that of the smaller) is cut as shown. The dotted lines are folds. Staple one end, and make a ramp at the other. Fix to a baseboard and add animals and figures.

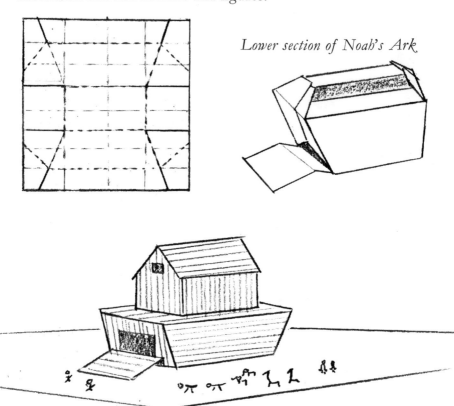

Lower section of Noah's Ark

Yachts and catamarans

The basic four-fold shape can be made into a simple yacht. Overlap one edge onto the other and glue or staple. Cut slits in the outer folds and insert the supporting strips. Cut a sail and slot onto a dowel or straw.

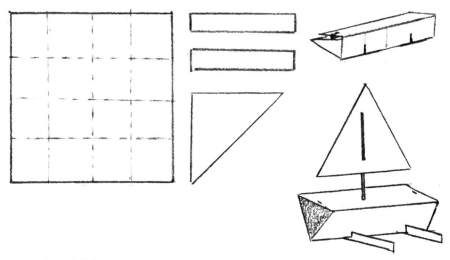

Older children can make a catamaran from the square.
Fold the two edges to meet in the centre. Turn the paper over.
Bring the sides over to meet in the centre.

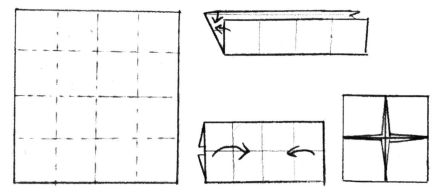

Push a finger into the top right-hand corner and push the
corner out sideways into a triangle. Do the same to the left
corner.

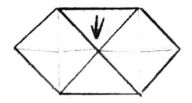 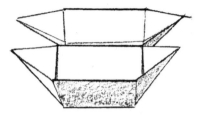

Turn the paper round to work the other corners the same way.
Fold over the top half to the bottom and glue.
Turn over and open out the twin hulls.
If the paper is wax-crayoned before folding, the boat will float.

Paper boxes

All these things are made from a square, the size of which depends on the size of the finished box. Multiply the required height of the box by four to give the length of the square.

Fold the square in half, and half again. Open out. Fold in half and half again the other way. The folding should be done on a flat surface. Open out to the sixteen small squares.

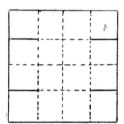 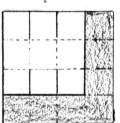 OR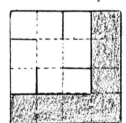

Different boxes have different numbers of squares cut away. This is indicated in the drawings.

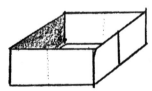

This is the simplest box. Glue or staple the ends. Make a lid with a square slightly bigger, about one cm.
Decorate with cut-outs, handle, shredded paper etc.

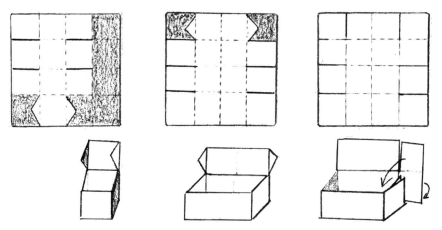

Tuck the flaps inside.
Bend the ends in over the others to neaten the sides.

Windmills

Each windmill needs a short length of dowelling, one nail or mapping pin, and a square of stiff paper at least 25 cm (10 in.) long.

The square is folded diagonally, coloured on both sides, and cut as shown. The pin goes through alternate corners and the centre, and anchors the windmill to the dowel.

The friction between the paper and the dowelling may be lowered, to enable the windmill to rotate quicker, by using a metal wire or stiff plastic instead of the mapping pin. Use also two metal or paper tubes as small sleeves over the wire, one on top of the windmill and one below. Beads may be used instead of tubes. Twist the end of the wire round the dowel to secure.

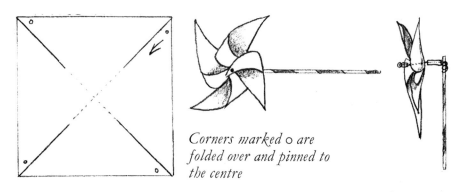

Corners marked o are folded over and pinned to the centre

6 Cards

Young children find it difficult to make a card which satisfies themselves and pleases others. Aim for simplicity and neatness and avoid complicated work.

A simple card is a cut-out from a magazine or catalogue stuck onto a folded paper.

A card using superimposed tissues is very attractive.

The tissue (or sticky paper) can be cut into a pattern before glueing.

These are cards using fabric, ribbon and wool. The snail is wool glued in a spiral on a piece of material glued to the card.

Any kind of fancy decoration, such as lace or doyley, buttons, stitching, fringing, bobbin work, plaited wool, etc. can be used on cards. The backgrounds can be paper, fabric or wallpaper.

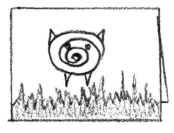

The pig is a spiral cut into a paper. The nose stands away from the face when the outer edge is glued to a card.

A large card, suitable for Mother's Day, can be made from a polystyrene tile. The oval is cut in the tile, and a similar oval in the right half of a paper or card large enough to fold over the

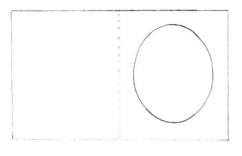

tile as shown. Glue the tile under the paper. Glue a piece of card on the back of the tile. Make paper flowers (tissue roses are easy, quick and attractive, see p. 97) or use pressed wild flowers, and mount them in the cut-out.

Cards shaped like letters and numbers are suitable for birthdays and festivals. The child may need a template to work from.

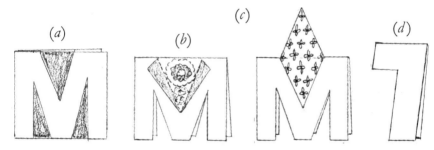

(a) The letter is painted or crayoned or cut in sticky paper.

(b) The letter is cut, and part of the top fold opened out to show decoration on the inside.

(c) The top of the fold is cut and folded back.

(d) The fold can be at either top or side.

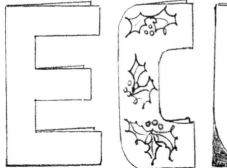

Further examples of cards

Pop-up cards

Fold the paper into a double card. Lift the inside centre fold and lay it across to the side to whatever angle is required. This can be used as the roof of a house, or turned over to be decorated as an Easter Card, or with a flower cut-out. (See pp. 144–5.)

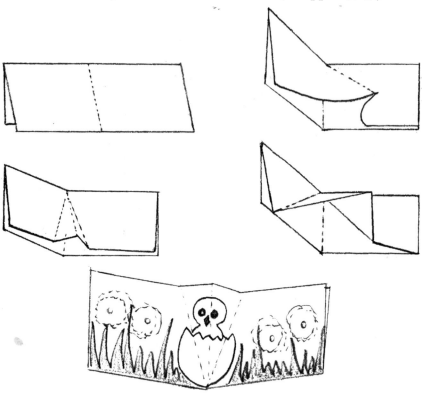

The lower edge of the flower is cut, the flower raised and the lower part of the card lies flat with the back of the card.

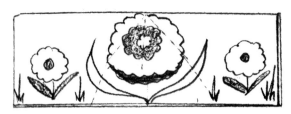

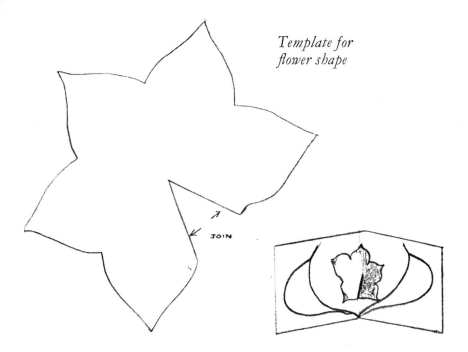

Template for flower shape

JOIN

Another way to raise the design is by using a template, and cutting the shape in sticky paper. The flower on this card is glued by the petal tips to the card and the flower folds forward when the card is closed.

A simple standing card is made in two pieces. The oblong paper is folded in half. Cut into the fold as shown. With a knife or scissor-point score from the cut to the edge, at both ends of the cut. Bend back along the scores. Cut two slots in the forward base and insert the decoration, such as a Christmas tree, a chick

 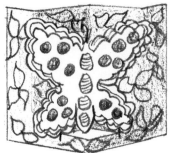 

in an egg, a figure etc. Decorate the background. The card travels flat if required. Further inserts may be slotted behind the front piece to add to the background.

A support which is suitable for mounting labels and display as well as greetings is made as follows.

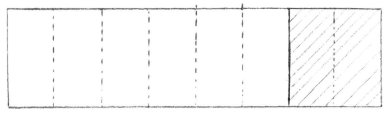

Cut a strip of paper whose length is four times the breadth. Fold in half three times, producing eight sections. Cut away two of them, and retain the piece.

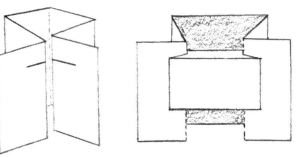

Open out into this shape. Cut two slits as shown. Insert the two sections to make a flat surface for mounting faces, figures, labels, trees etc.

This basic support can be cut in different sizes to make a tower of faces, like a totem pole, where each support rests on the larger one below. Rows in different sizes can make a pyramid, with Christmas cut-outs (such as the figures in the section on wall hangings (p. 123) for the twelve days of Christmas). This would be a very large display, and a paper trunk could be fixed at the base to suggest that the pyramid is a tree.

Cut slits in the top instead of the sides and insert the two section piece to make a roof, or sloping surface for a name, label or cut-out.

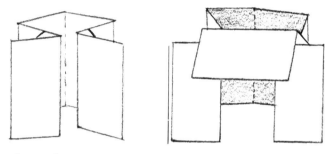

Seasonal cards

Using a seasonal shape for cards is easy for most children if a template is provided. For example, cut a snowman or tree for Christmas, flowers for Mother's Day, rabbits for Easter.

This is a simple card cut from a folded piece of paper using a template. The design can be crayoned, sticky paper, fabric or tissue blobs. Draw round a coin for the chicks and sun. The centre strip can be a piece of braid or lace.

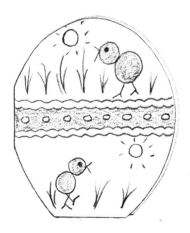

These are more difficult Spring cards requiring a delicacy of touch with the scissors. Provide templates for the flowers and the bowls, and cut in sticky paper. Encourage the children to arrange all their pieces before sticking.

Flower templates (see also p. 86).

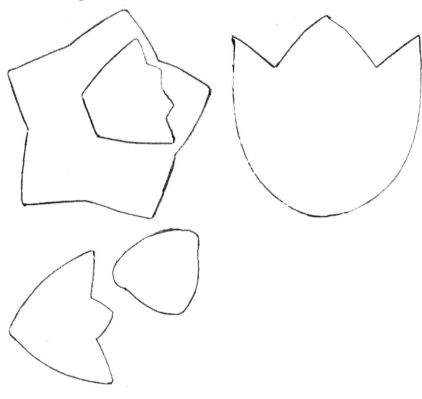

This is a template for a chick and egg to be glued to an egg-shaped card.

An Easter card shaped like a rabbit. Cut to a fold.

FOLD

This is an easy cut-out for younger children.

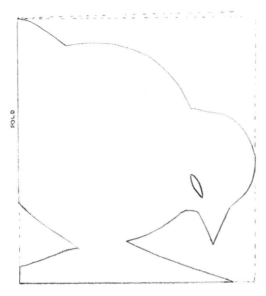

A more complicated card. The amount of cutting depends on the ability of the child.

There are more cards in the Christmas section (p. 139).

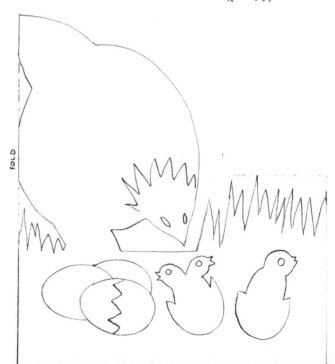

7 Friezes

A frieze needs some order and purpose. The composition of a frieze can be arranged regardless of what the frieze is made of (sand, fabric, paper, seeds, straw, twigs etc.).

First, decide on the reason for the frieze.

Is it to convey an idea, such as a snow scene, a rainy day, a windy day with kites?

Is it to convey information, about farming perhaps, or fishing, or wildlife?

Is it to convey pleasure as an entertainment to the eye, and a seasonal decoration?

How important is the background? One may not be required. This depends on the reason for the frieze, and the age of the children. Young children draw things as they are, and do not need perspective. Older children draw things as they see them, and young juniors may suggest that distances are necessary, as in the background of mountain and tarn. The rainy-day frieze drawn here could be the composition for a snow scene, shopping, traffic, and be a familiar and secure setting for younger children.

It may be necessary to mount the children's work deliberately along certain lines to influence the eye of the beholder.

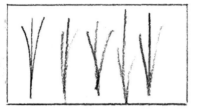 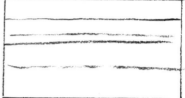

For example, vertical lines shorten a long frieze.
Horizontal lines are restful and reduce height.

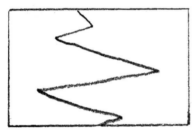 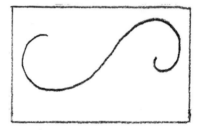

Movement is suggested by zigzags or spirals.

A good place to put a focal point in a mural which is not very long in relation to height is about a third in from the edge. Any of these positions is pleasing and balanced to the eye, and the guidelines and colours will suggest the mood. A good place also for a horizon is a third up or down.

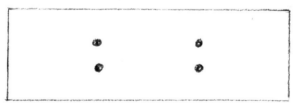

Simple backgrounds for different themes.
A suitable ground for holiday activity. The sea can be cor-

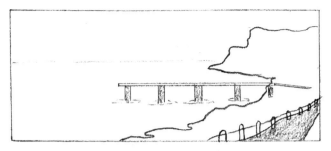

rugated paper, the beach can be sand shaken over wet glue. Figures can be both large and small.

A less controlled environment, suitable for older children who are familiar with fishing, or boats or climbing.

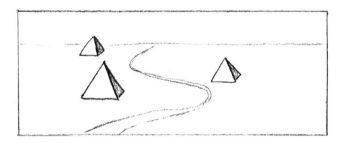

A desert setting. Oases could be shown, instead of pyramids. Distance is important here. Let the colour and texture of the ground suggest heat.

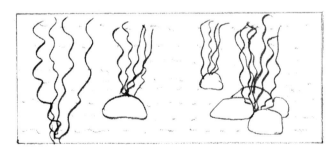

An underwater background: the lines of weed (in tissue, wool or crêpe) suggest movement in a harmonious setting.

A lunar landscape. The children can suggest colours for this ground.

An agricultural mural, conveying information with drawings or texts alongside a farm setting. Colour will suggest season.

These are four murals where the height is greater than the length.

A harbour scene.

A stylised setting for bees and hives (*right*). Other insects would be suitable. The paths along which the insects fly suggest their activity.

A foreign hillside, possibly a setting for cocoa harvesting, or coral island life (*left*).

A change from the usual Noah's Ark setting of a long procession of animals across the bottom of a frieze. Mount the animals in a zigzag path (*right*).

It was a favourite device of early stained-glass window designers to use white or pale coloured spots in rows down the sides of windows 'to stop the colour jumping out', and it is a device which can be used very effectively in friezes, such as the nativity setting below. Stars, spots, shapes, flowers are all suitable, depending on the frieze.

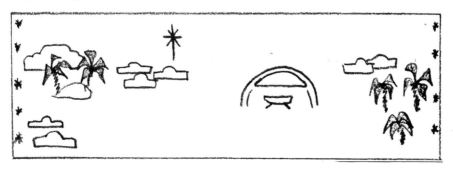

Long narrow friezes are well suited to repeat designs. The motifs should be identical, and mounted equally apart. Almost anything done as a class activity can be mounted very effectively this way.

Choice of colour can suggest mood and time. Orange and yellow ground imply heat, blue and purple ground suggest cold. White ground means snow, green spring, red and brown autumn, and so on. Choose black or dark blue for a dramatic setting to lighter colours where no background is drawn, such as flower friezes, heads, or insects. Choose a yellow ground for silhouettes of witches or angels.

The following designs are suggested in greater detail as class activities, for any age and ability.

The park

A good theme for any age of child. Draw the background and encourage the children to suggest the parts of it. Make it as large and as busy as possible. Perspective allows each child to choose the size of figure he wishes to place there. Add flowers, animals, toys—whatever the children's own environment stimulates.

Pin up a dark ground and sketch in the layout to the children's suggestions. The children can paint the details in black and white.

Any season of the year is suitable. In winter, skaters on the pond, winter buds on the trees, tracks in the snow, sledging, snowman and snowball fights. In spring, nest building, spring flowers, animals emerging from hibernation. In summer, butterflies, bees, fruit blossom, hedgerows. In autumn show a gardener building a bonfire, leaves on the path etc.

Let the paths wander and take the eye into the picture.

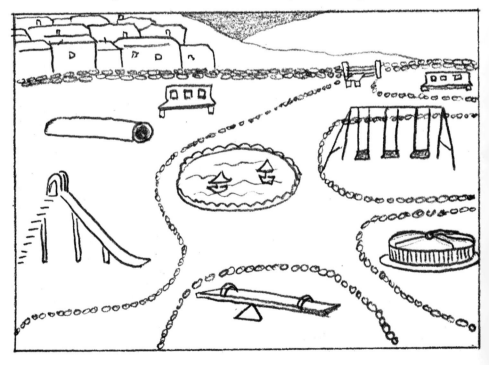

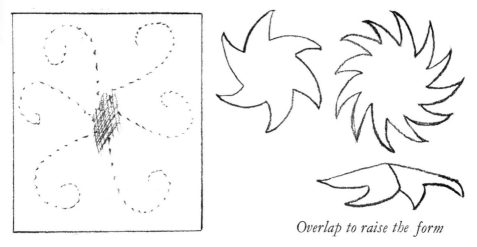

Overlap to raise the form

Bonfire night

Make as magnificently elaborate as the display space permits. On a shelf or recess construct a three-dimensional scene.

The basic design requires a Guy Fawkes, fireworks, sparks, flames and sticks, displayed against a black ground. To suggest movement of sparks mount them along dynamic lines. Put the largest sparks at the edge and the smallest in the centre round the Guy and the bonfire.

Sparks: a circle with its edges cut is the easiest. Colour before cutting out. The form can be raised by overlapping the radial slit. The sparks can be hung from threads, and in this case both sides must be coloured.

Guy Fawkes: for a flat figure, draw round a child on strong paper, let a group colour it, and mount on the background.

A simple figure of rolled paper can be made as shown. Cover the lower half of the tube. Make limbs of paper tubes, stuffed stockings, old clothes, and footwear. Use Catherine Wheels for eyes and nose, and cut out a beard. Make a hat brim. Put another roll of paper into the body for the hat. Pad the body if required with newspaper.

73

*Score and fold on
the dotted line*

Flames: colour and stand among a heap of straw or twigs. The flames may be scored, on top and below.

Fireworks: cut out the shapes, colour and attach to the Guy.

Hallowe'en frieze

This depends more than most on accurate cutting, and several templates are therefore suggested.

This is a frieze for young children, who cut witches in different sizes in black to mount on a yellow ground. The ground can be a wash of red, yellow and orange worked in horizontal layers.

These retreating witches are the easiest to cut.

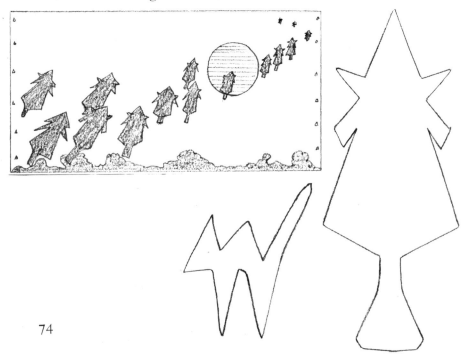

Both profile and retreating witches could fly this path.

Bat

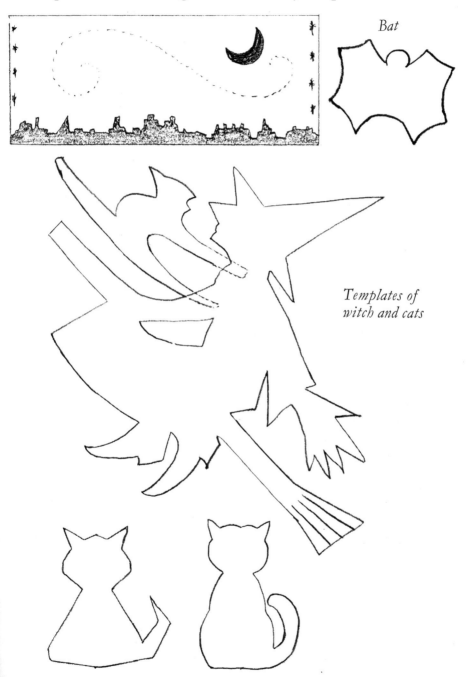

Templates of witch and cats

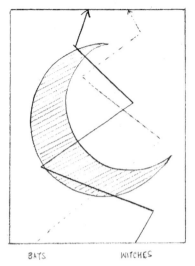

This diagram illustrates the flight paths of the bats and witches

BATS   WITCHES

This is a more sophisticated design. Mount red witches, white bats and a silver moon on black paper. The bats and witches must be of different sizes, and fly different paths.

Witches: children can use the templates to make fabric or paper collage of witches with woolly hair and straw brooms.

Autumn friezes

There are many ways of making attractive autumn friezes, depending on the interest of the children in their surroundings, and the materials available.

The leaves can be made to a template and coloured with crayon or paint or fabric. Interesting textures result from a wash over clean paper with paint blobs flicked over it. The colours spread, and leaf shapes are cut when it is dry.

Leaf rubbings can be made with crayon over collected leaves. The pattern can be varied by a thin colour wash over the leaf, when the crayon resists the paint.

Make leaf prints by coating a collected leaf with a thick paint (a mixture of powder paint and washing-up liquid has a good consistency) and press over it a clean paper.

Young children can make large leaves with blobs of tissue stuck on them. Mounting them on a black ground is attractive and simple.

76

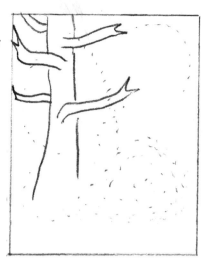

Outline of tree. Templates for leaf shapes are on pp. 78–9

The first mural is a simple background for a heap of leaves. A pair of bright red wellington would cheer up the picture. Young children will be able to suggest things which might be almost covered by the leaves (waving arms, feet, bicycles, etc.) and they can be added to the picture.

The other design conveys more information. Winter sillouettes of trees are sketched lightly and accurately in black or brown or white and the relevant leaf shapes are glued on. Suitable animals can be added, depending on the interest of the children.

Use a familiar background where possible, such as a park for town children, a forest or hillside for rural children.

The frieze can be combined with other subjects. For example, witches above the trees, fishermen, harvesting in the foreground, fruit picking in an orchard, garden bonfires, animal preparation for hibernation, dairy farming, forestry work in a clearing, and so on.

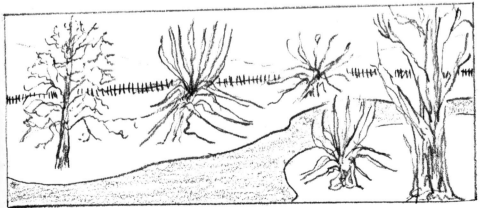

Leaf templates are drawn below:

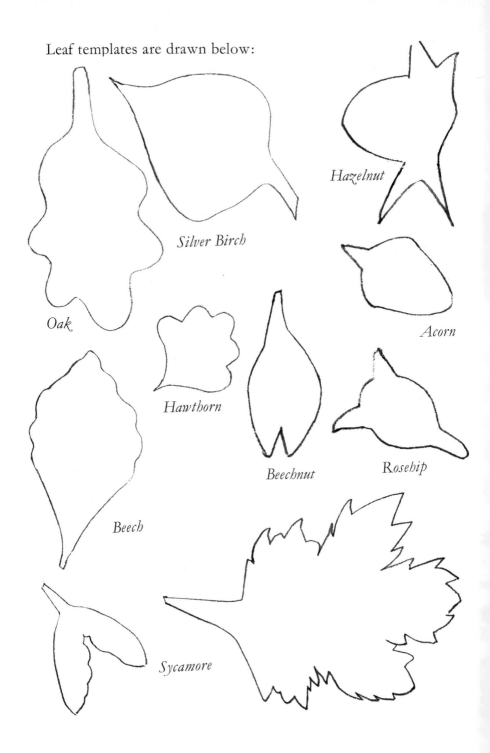

Hazelnut

Silver Birch

Oak

Acorn

Hawthorn

Beechnut

Rosehip

Beech

Sycamore

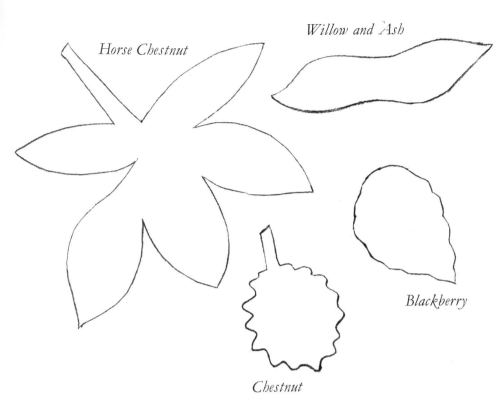

Horse Chestnut

Willow and Ash

Blackberry

Chestnut

A summer's day

This is a suitable frieze for any age of child.

The flowers and butterflies are simplified. Beyond comparing the way wings fold on butterflies and moths, do not insist on copying nature. The butterflies are cut to a fold and coloured on both sides. Punch holes to insert antennae of paper or wool or pipe cleaners. Staple to the frieze by the fold. Encourage

older children to design individual flowers. Young children can make paper or tissue ones of three circles of diminishing size, or may require templates which are easy to cut (some are suggested below).

Border the edges with tiny flowers. A dark blue or yellow ground is suitable for a colourful frieze.

Flower templates

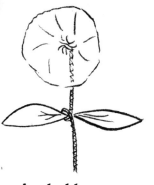
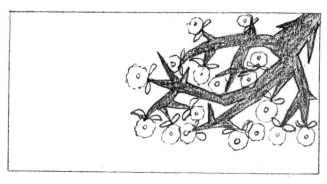

Apple blossom

This is a background for insects in flight. An alternative (a hedgerow) is described later on p. 87.

The blossom is made of a circle of white or pink tissue paper which is gathered at the centre, and twisted over a wire or pipe cleaner.

The leaf is a green semi-circle, twisted beneath the flower. Twist the wire over dead branches or driftwood. Anchor the wood firmly. Hang the insects, made to a fold as drawn below. The point of balance for hanging can be found by balancing the insect on a pencil.

If it is not possible to provide wood to hang the insects, paint branches on the background, fasten on the blossom, and to each insect fix a matchbox or folded strip of card which will mount it away from the backing.

Bee

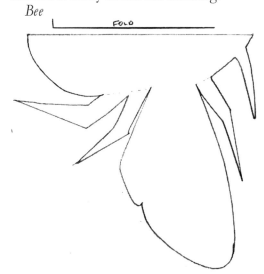

FOLD

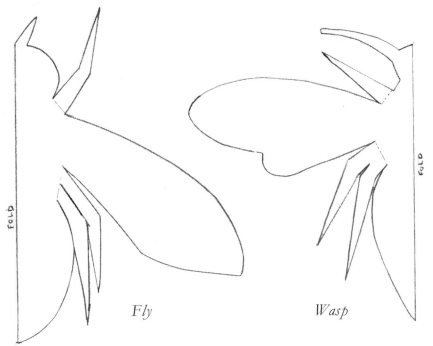

Fly   *Wasp*

These three insects are cut to a fold. Legs may be omitted. Fold up the wings. Fix on a wall by a wing, hang by a thread or use as a model with legs bent under.

A background for caterpillars, which should be as large and colourful as possible. Nature may camouflage a caterpillar, it is not necessary to do so here. Use large leaves of paper or fabric. The body of the caterpillar may be scored to raise the form. Butterflies, moths, ants, ladybirds etc. may be added.

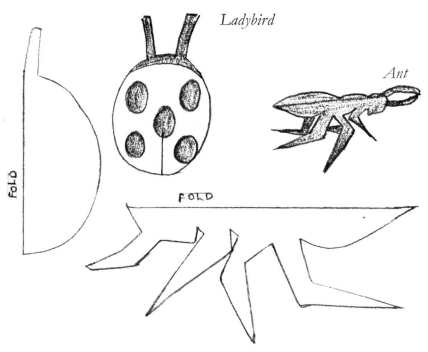

Ladybird

Ant

FOLD

FOLD

The form of the ladybird can be raised by overlapping the slit.

A butterfly template.

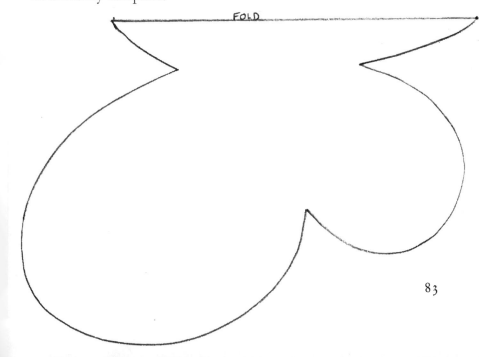

FOLD

Snails

An easy frieze for young children and a good exercise in colouring and cutting. Large snails are made by drawing round a tin lid, and adding the head. Or a strip can be extended, cut as shown, and after decoration the piece is bent backwards and fixed. The radial slit when overlapped raises the form of the snail.

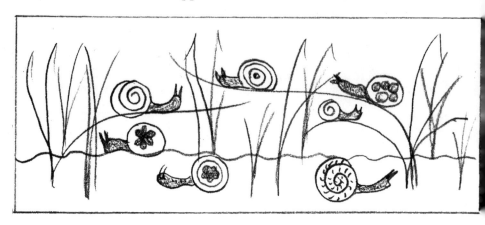

Snail made from a long strip. The cuts are made with a knife.

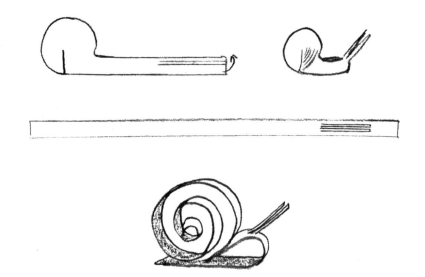

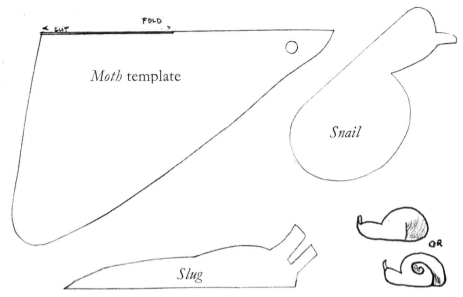

Moth template

Snail

Slug

OR

An easy snail cut from a template. The form can be raised in these two ways.

A Summer's night

An excellent companion to the day frieze. Dark or royal blue crêpe paper is a good ground colour. Make a silver moon, and border the frieze edges with silver. The form of the moth is raised by overlapping the central slit. Add antennae of pipe cleaners or feathered paper. Less flowers are required to make the effect than in a day frieze, and pale blue and pale pink ones preserve the moonlight atmosphere.

Other nocturnal animals may be added, depending on the experience of the children.

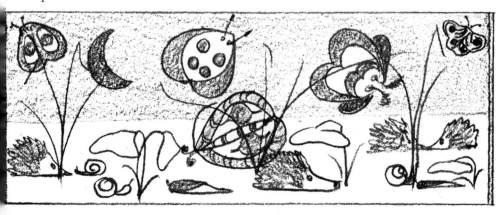

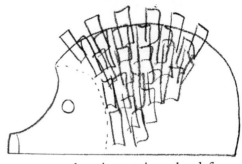

The spikes of the hedgehog are overlapping strips glued from the outer edge inwards.

Spring garden

The flowers may be mounted flat or raised. A ball of white tissue will suggest a snowdrop if the cutting is too difficult for young children. Any hibernating animal can be added, such as a hedgehog, butterfly or tortoise. The background could be used for a frieze of busy ants. (See also p. 64.)

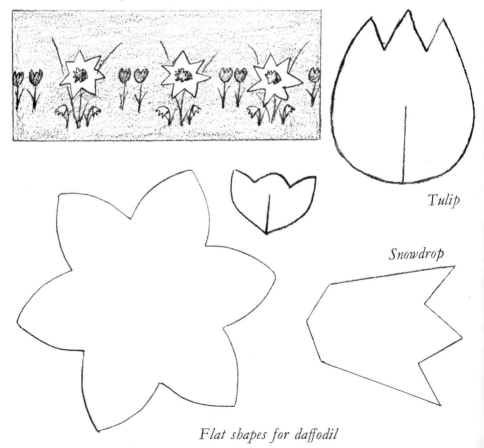

Tulip

Snowdrop

Flat shapes for daffodil

Raised form templates for daffodil

Part of an egg carton to make inner flower

Roll and insert into the petals

Hedgerow

This is a suitable background on its own, or to display insects, birds or spider's webs, depending on the amount of space

available. Use a dark tone ground. The stems of honeysuckle and bindweed are covered wire, green string or wool.

Bindweed: use a square or a circle of white tissue or crêpe. Fold in half three times. Draw the shape as shown and cut away the shaded part. Open out the shape, which has eight segments. Cut away two and a half of them as shown, overlap the rest and glue. Twist green tissue or crêpe round the base under wire or a pipe cleaner. Fix to the stem.

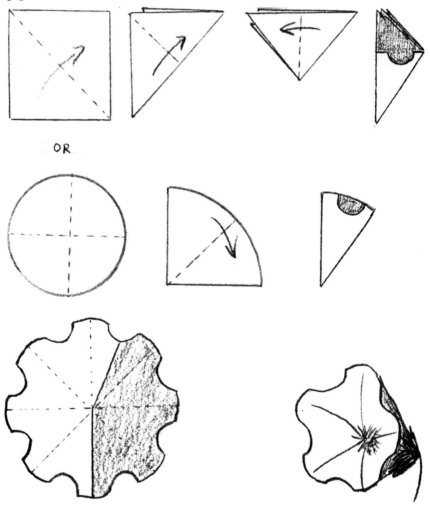

OR

Honeysuckle: use pink or white crêpe paper. Fold in half with the grain lengthways. Cut along the fold at centimetre intervals. Run a scissor point or fingernail down each double petal to curl it. Gather and fix to a wire. Cover the junction of wire and petals with a piece wound round.

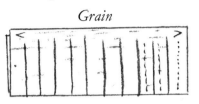

Grain

Cornfield frieze
This can be a project on its own, showing wheat, oats or barley. The corn can be balls of yellow tissue. Mice and their nests could be put in the foreground, and various wild flowers.

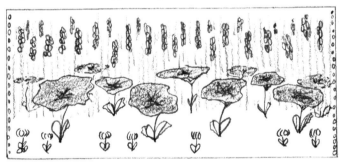

Poppy: fold red crêpe (or tissue) in half with the grain running fold to edge. Gather along the fold, round a tissue ball, and fasten with a pipe cleaner. Stretch the edges of the flower gently. Cut a leaf (double) in tissue or crêpe and twist the wire round it.

Clover: fold a strip of pink or purple crêpe or tissue. The grain runs lengthways. Snip at quick intervals along the open edges. Gather the fold and attach to wire. Tissue is better than crêpe for this flower.

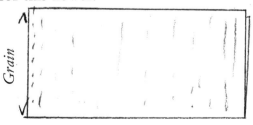

Grain

89

Friezes for very young children

Use fabric pasted on paper for the clothes.

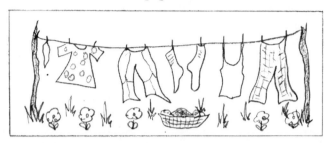

Fruit and vegetables are cut from templates in paper or fabric and mounted as a repeat pattern.

A simple background for snowflakes, made by cutting a folded paper (see Christmas section pp. 166–9). The houses are large and cut from wallpaper. Mount on a black ground with cotton-wool snow.

Three very easy cut-outs in sticky paper. The cuts are on straight lines, which are easier than curves. These three examples could be worked consecutively with a group of children. Each child should have its own pair of sharp-pointed metal scissors.

The first subject is the poem 'Three shining sailing boats'. Display on a dark ground.

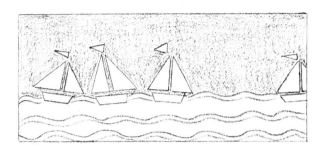

The second illustrates the poem 'Rain on the roof top'.

The windows and doors can be cut from small strips and allow for individual decoration on the houses. A dark ground will show the colours to advantage.

Straight cuts again to make funny faces. More individual decoration here.

8 Flowers

There are four methods of making the petals of a paper flower. Not all are suitable for young children, who find it easiest to cut the corolla in one piece.

1. From a template. For young children whose eye for proportion is not good enough for the second method.

2. Cutting a folded paper. Use a square or circle. Fold in half three times as shown. Cut away the shaded area.

Cutting from a square

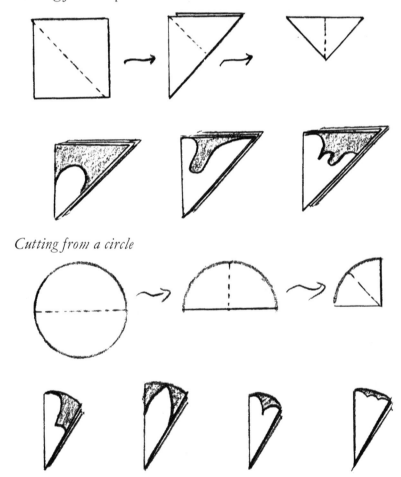

Cutting from a circle

Three folds give eight petals. (For 4-, 5-, 6- and 8-point shapes see the stars in the Christmas section.)

The circle is easiest to use. When tissue paper is cut this way it is often simpler to cut two or three pieces together.

 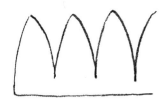

3. Cutting a folded strip. Make a long strip into a concertina fold, or a series of folds into halves. Cut the petal shape, leaving part of the folds. The petal strip is sometimes difficult to gather satisfactorily with wire or pipe cleaner. Tissue paper is the easiest to use. Fold as shown.

4. Cutting individual petals of various shapes and gathering or glueing together. Again, not recommended unless the petals are large and easy to handle.

Choice of paper is important. Tissue, crêpe and cartridge have their own individual properties.

Crêpe paper: this can be bought in a beautiful range of colours. The grain must be noted. In some flowers the way it runs is important. Crêpe stretches against the grain. This property can be ignored by young children who find it difficult to stretch without tearing. Some flowers can be stretched over a scissor point which makes the paper curl, for example hazel catkins and honeysuckle. Crêpe is difficult to draw on. The grain gives strength to long leaves when it runs lengthways.

Tissue paper: good choice of colour. Easiest to cut in layers of two or three pieces. Not easy to draw on.

Cartridge or any stiff paper: use where a raised form is required. Easy to draw on before cutting (on the wrong side in case of mistakes) and easy to score (with a scissor point or compass point). Flowers in this paper are more elegant than in tissue or crêpe.

93

Buttons and beads of any size or shape make good flower centres, and fuse wire or coloured pipe cleaners can be used to hold the flower shape.

A bouquet is easily made by mounting a bunch of flowers on a doyley, a paper plate or card.

Crêpe flowers

The easiest crêpe flowers are a circle, or more than one circle, with or without stamens or centre, fixed with a paper fastener or wire. Beginning with a circle is a useful introduction for infants to the gentle technique of stretching crêpe. Take a circle in both hands and pull the centre against the grain. Gather and twist with wire. These flowers make a quick and simple bouquet, and leaves can be inserted to hide the wires.

Crêpe circle

Circle and tissue stamens

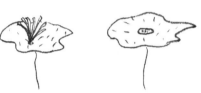

Circle and bead

Crêpe stamens made from a long strip are attractive and easy. As for tissue stamens, the strip is folded in half. The stretch is lengthways. Cut down from the fold as shown, and roll the strip. Use on petals of crêpe or cartridge. A bead on a wire makes a good flower centre, rolled stamens can be stapled over and the corolla threaded on the wire. Quick infants can easily make a bouquet of this type of flower for Mother's Day or Christmas.

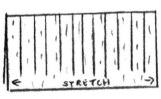

Cut and roll

94

Leaves may not be required with these flowers. If they are, add a simple twist of semi-circle tissue.

For an intricate petal design cartridge paper is best, cut with a template or from folded paper.

Use this method of making stamens to make honeysuckle (described in the section on friezes, p. 89) and hazel catkins (use a short piece of crêpe).

A rosebud can be made in crêpe like the tissue rosebud described later. The flower is the same size as the tissue rose for the same size paper but not quite as attractive. It has the advantage for younger children that the gathering on the ruler or knitting needle is omitted. The stretch in the paper is lengthways. Stretch in the middle between thumbs and fingers. The strip may be folded or single. Roll loosely and secure.

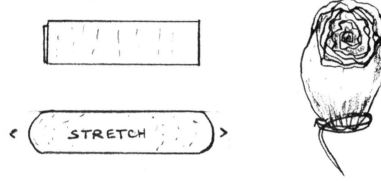

Another easy crêpe flower is made by rolling a long strip. Stretch the edge or edges (the paper may be folded) roll the unstretched edge or the fold, and fix with wire. It has the disadvantage of all crêpe flowers made by rolling a strip in that the base is bulky and may need hiding with a piece of green paper.

If the fold is stretched instead of the edges the bulky base may be thinned by cutting off at least a centimetre along one edge. Roll with the longer piece outside.

95

Make a sunflower with a card circle, cheese box or margarine tub lid. Make a hole in its centre. Cover the inside with yellow or orange crêpe to conceal any printing. Fringe a long folded strip of yellow crêpe whose length is twice the circumference of the box. The stretch is lengthways. Staple or glue this to the box. Fold two pieces of crêpe three times and cut the petals. Glue to the back of the box. Either cut will do.

Fix on a wire, dowel or paper straw.

This is a heavier flower than most and may be best fixed to a frieze.

Fold a long strip into concertina folds as shown. Staple the fold at the bottom and open out the top fanlike. Join the edges. A tissue ball can be put into the centre, or a bead, buttons, or a double fringe. This flower can be hung in a mobile.

Staple and open out.

Tissue flowers

A blob of tissue stuck onto a painted or crayoned stalk with drawn leaves is the simplest flower, and a good introduction to the delights of tissue paper for four year old children.

Berries: glue balls of tissue round wire for berries.

Glue and roll a long thin strip of tissue onto a knitting needle to make a tissue bead, which easily pulls off when dry and can be threaded on wire.

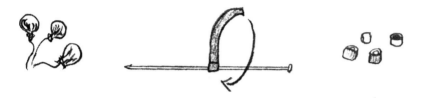

Rosebuds: one of the easiest and most delightful flowers. The technique is simple, and quick children can make a bouquet in one session. Each child needs a knitting needle or stick. Fold a long strip of tissue in half lengthways. Push the stick down the fold and gather the tissue into a tight bunch as shown. Remove the stick and pull the paper out gently. Roll loosely with the fold on top and twist wire round the base. Add a green semi-circle of tissue for a leaf.

Use at least nine flowers for a bouquet. Twist all the wires together and push down a central hole in a card circle which

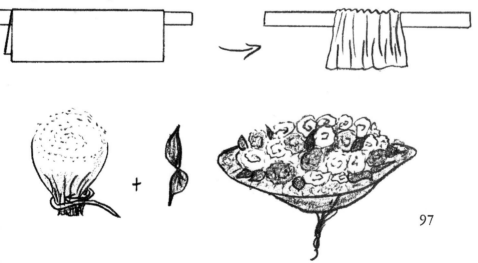

has been overlapped and covered in lace or a doyley. Cover the bare wires below with twisted paper to make a handle. Put in extra leaves in any gaps in the bouquet.

A box lid can be covered with rosebuds, the base filled with chocolates or sweets, and the whole tied with ribbon to make an attractive present.

Rosebuds of paper handkerchiefs can be made the same way. Omit the gathering on the stick. Fold in half, roll over a finger with the fold on top. Fix with wire. Young children can practise with paper handkerchiefs before using tissue paper. The pastel shades are quite pleasing en masse, and white rosebuds with green leaves on a dark red ground look very attractive.

Stamens in tissue can be wired beads or fringed strips. Fold a piece in half and cut either the fold or the edges. Roll and secure. Use on corollas of crêpe, tissue or cartridge.

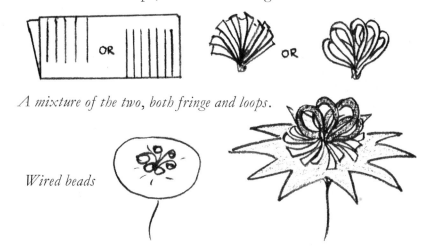

A mixture of the two, both fringe and loops.

Wired beads

Corolla: the simplest is a circle of tissue gathered over stamens or beads and fixed by wire. A poppy and apple blossom are made this way. A single circle can be used or several, and the sizes can be varied. The flower centre can be a paper fastener, a button, a bead, fringed tissue etc.

More interesting petal shapes are made by folding and cutting a square or circle of tissue. Three folds are made. Young children often cut the wrong part of the triangle and find a circle easier to begin with. Able children who can fold and cut accurately can try a fourth fold which gives sixteen petals.

Templates are not easy to use with tissue paper.

Very large flowers which are attractive and striking are made by glueing tissue over a wire support. All ages of children can make them easily. Young children will need help in bending the wire into shapes.

Wire frameworks

Bend the soft wire into a flower with stem and leaves if desired. Cover the wire ends with pasted strips of newspaper. Cover the spaces with the overlapping tissue. Texture may be added by blobs of tissue or cut-out patterns. Cover the newspaper.

Insects can be made the same way. Build the body of the insect with strips of newspaper, and cover with tissue. Older children can make exotic birds and fish. Spray the finished model with clear polyurethane to restore translucency where several layers of tissue overlap.

Display this type of flowers and insects against the light wherever possible, as for example, hanging in a tissue-covered hoop as shown.

Strong paper

White or coloured cartridge, sticky paper and metallic foil can be used for the following flowers. These papers can be exactly folded or scored. In addition, metal foil can be textured with a pencil. Rest the foil on soft paper and 'draw' the required pattern, such as veins in a leaf, shapes on a petal, and so on.

Encourage the children to draw on the wrong side of these papers in case of mistakes. Templates can be used by young children. Some are suggested on pp. 103–4. The form of the flower can be raised by overlapping and fixing. In some of the templates the overlap is indicated. If the flower is made by folding, as described before, raise the form by cutting out a segment. The bigger the piece removed, the sharper the flower cone.

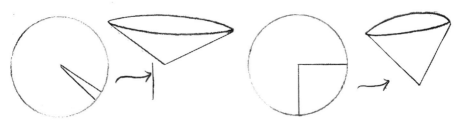

Small segment removed   *A quarter removed*

Older children can try additional shaping of the flower. A circle is scored on the wrong side with a sharp knife or scissors. The centre is raised into a small cone when the overlap is fixed.

(*a*) Cut from a template, scored and overlapped.
(*b*) Fringed, scored and cut to the centre.
Almost any shape is suitable for this extra frivolity.

(*b*)

(*a*)

Cartridge and foil can be gently curled over scissors, a property useful in bending stamens and petals. Gather a fringed piece of paper with wire and thread through the centre of a corolla to make a simple flower.

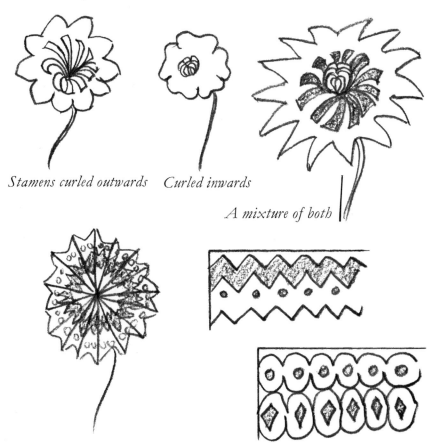

Stamens curled outwards *Curled inwards*

A mixture of both

A concertina flower is made like the one on p. 96, and keeps the shape better. Made in crayoned white paper it is a useful end product for infant handwriting patterns.

If the folding is first done the strips can be crayoned different colours. This type of flower is a good one for young infants who are learning to fold and to colour, though they may find the fastening difficult.

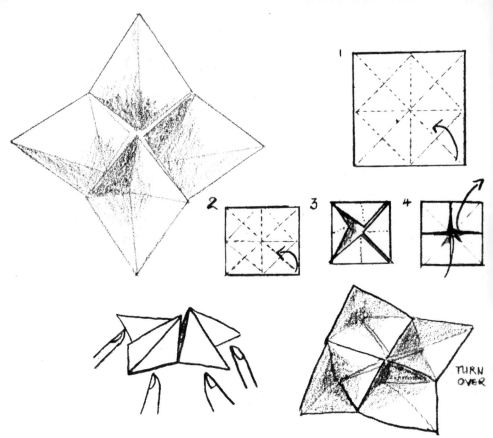

Older children can make this flower shape.

(*a*) Fold a square diagonally both ways and open out. Fold in half both ways, open out. Fold each corner to the middle. Turn the paper over.

(*b*) Fold each corner to the middle into 3. Turn over 4. Flatten all folds, and insert fingers and thumbs into the four flaps. Push up. The centre triangles on the inside come together. This part is the most difficult and children may need help. Turn the shape over, glue the four bottom corners together or fix with wire, and the result is a four-pointed flower.

Cartridge is the best paper to use for this flower and children find its precision pleasing. Cover any wire with green tissue. Several make an attractive bunch, which can be mounted on a frieze or displayed in a paper vase.

Moulded flowers

Fun flowers for rooms with large glassy expanses. The flowers are made of thin layers of tissue and mounted against the light. Glue tissue pieces to large moulds such as margarine containers, mousse moulds, saucers etc. The layers must be transparent when dry. Remove the mould when the tissue is dry and cut petal shapes if desired. Glue to the window. Use transparent plastic straws for stalks, and tissue circles for leaves.

Apple moulds in pressed paper can be cut out and painted for frieze flowers, and a tissue ball centre can be added.

Circles of Cellophane, each loosely folded into quarters, and stapled together by the centres make beautiful exotic flowers. The staple can be concealed with a piece of tissue. About six circles are needed for each flower. Petals may be cut by older children. For other flowers see Sections 6 and 7 on Cards and Friezes.

These templates are for young infants.

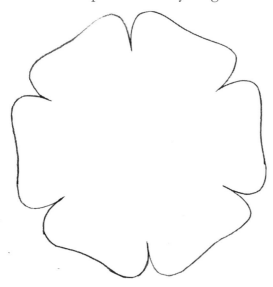

Leaves and stems

Coloured pipe cleaners (bought coloured or dyed in ink) are the easiest stems. Wire covered in plastic, or tissue is adequate, as are straws, and long stems can be made with rolled tissue or crêpe bound knitting needles.

Green wool or string is sufficient for stems on a frieze where no weight is to be supported.

Small leaves:

(*a*) A tissue semi-circle with a twist of wire.

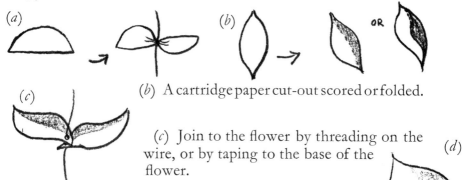

(*b*) A cartridge paper cut-out scored or folded.

(*c*) Join to the flower by threading on the wire, or by taping to the base of the flower.

(*d*) The leaf may be cut to the centre, overlapped and glued.

(*e*) Cut a crêpe leaf and stretch at the base. The grain runs lengthways. Staple or glue to the stem. The traditional way of making crêpe and tissue leaves (cut two and glue wire between) is too difficult for young children.

(*f*) To make a fringed leaf, snip the edges of an oval and twist centrally. (*g*) Another easy leaf like the semi-circle tissue, is made with a square of tissue folded diagonally. Nip the centre with wire.

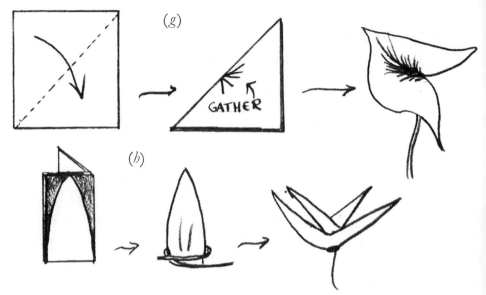

(g)

GATHER

(h)

(*h*) Spring foliage on painted or wire or real branches can be made in tissue. Twice fold a square, cut the shape as drawn. Twist wire round the base and spread the leaves.

Crêpe paper can be cut the same way. The grain runs down the leaf to give it stiffness. Cut a long strip for grass.

Daffodil and tulip leaves in cartridge can be scored for strength. Mount on a frieze or in a vase.

Where the grain is across the crêpe leaf the paper can be stretched and curled into this shape.

Young children can make quick and easy leaves from a strip of paper. The strip is folded as shown and the ends stapled to the centre. Holly leaves can be made in any kind of paper. Use tissue paper double (for colour strength) and cut several at once. The way of stretch in crêpe is not important, though the leaf can be curled if the stretch is across (pull gently with thumb and finger).

9 Starters

This is work in various materials and techniques which can be done by young children who enjoy the skills and disciplines involved in pattern and picture-making in the following ways.

Block printing

This is printing onto paper or fabric in paint, ink or fabric dye using a block. The block can be a found object, such as a cotton reel, a tube, a matchstick, a cork or a sliced vegetable such as a cabbage or onion, or the block can be prepared (a roll of paper, a roll of corrugated paper, a halved potato, a shaped piece of polystyrene, or string, sticks or cord glued to a piece of wood).

The medium (ink, paint or dye) is either applied to the block with a brush, or the block is pressed onto a piece of foam rubber which is soaked in the medium. Keep one block for each colour.

Young children need only one colour and small pieces of paper. It may be helpful for them to fold the paper to make small squares as guides to the printing. Large pieces of paper can be confusing at the beginning. Encourage the children to look for different blocks to use, and to make their own individual blocks.

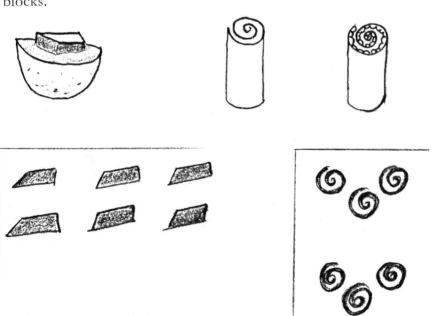

When printing on fabric with a fabric dye, rest the fabric on several sheets of newspaper to give a soft surface. Follow the manufacturer's directions for making the material wash-fast after printing.

Use the block-printed patterns as bookmarks, mats, shelf paper, aprons, T-shirts, and so on.

Printing patterns can be turned into illustrations by adding brush strokes, for example a row of fingerprints may suggest a caterpillar, oblong prints houses, tube patterns snails, and so on.

Similarly paint blob patterns, made by folding over half the paper onto a print or blob, may suggest an animal or object or pattern which can be improved by lines.

Rubbings

Rubbings are prints taken from a textured surface. This can be a found object, such as a coin, a medal, a leaf, a church brass or fabric. Or the surface may be prepared by glueing string, pieces of card or wallpaper or fabric onto a board.

A board prepared for a repeat resist pattern

A prepared board for a single illustration

Thin paper is placed above the textured surface and wax crayons rubbed smoothly over it to take the impression. Young children will find large crayons used sideways the easiest to work.

Wax resist pictures

Wax resists water. This is the principle used in wax resist pictures. A rubbing, illustration or pattern is done in crayon, leaving untouched areas of paper which will take up paint when a thin colour is applied. (If the paint is too thick the wax will be covered.) Any water-based medium will do. The colour should be applied evenly in a wash. The finished picture can be lightly sprayed with clear polyurethane to restore the gloss of the wax.

Collages

These are pictures made by assembling pieces of various textures and mounting on a strong base of card or hardboard.

Corrugated paper pieces are easy enough for young children to handle. Light falling across the corrugations creates interesting shadows. The pieces can be cut or torn and mounted flush with the backing, or mounted as strips or rolls on edge. The pieces can be painted before or after glueing.

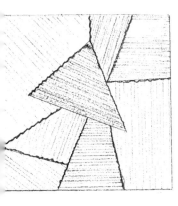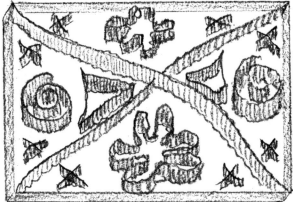

Tissue paper collage produces interesting colour combinations when pieces overlap. Mount with cellulose paste on a white ground. Use weights at the corner to stop the picture curling if cardboard is the ground and not hardboard. If using offcuts of hardboard paint them first with white undercoat. Spray the finished collage with clear polyurethane for an attractive finish.

Wallpaper pieces with interesting textures make pleasing

collages. Young children can make mosaics in pre-cut or torn sticky paper or wallpaper. Older children can form the paper into tubes or spirals before fixing.

Seed and pasta collage

Use a strong card or hardboard base for a seed or pasta collage. Thin card will tend to curl.

As many sizes and colours of seed should be provided as possible. Encourage the children to collect seeds during the Summer and Autumn. Use an adhesive which is not water based. Do not attempt too large a picture at first, and spray the finished picture with clear polyurethane.

Older children can make interesting pendants using seeds.

Punch a hole into a metal or card base, such as a lid. This is for the ribbon or thong to go through. Place a lump of papier maché on the lid, making sure it is firmly fixed. Allow to dry. Glue on seeds and spray with clear polyurethane. Make stage jewellery this way for school plays using painted papier maché with beads and clear gums for jewels.

Larger models to display on the wall can be in the shape of a face, like a mask.

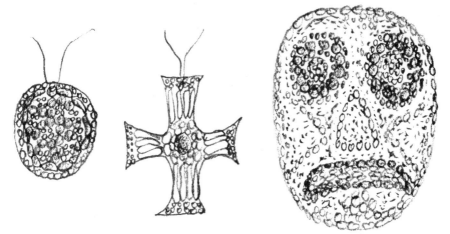

Papier maché is moulded onto a strong base of card or hardboard. The features must be fairly shallow and large, for the attached seeds follow the contours of the eyes, nose and mouth.

Pasta in its various shapes makes interesting collages. The colour can be applied as spray paint. A mixture of seed and pasta in a collage is better for young children to work with.

A better base than ordinary papier maché, which dries light grey, is Polyfilla, or plaster, or papier maché made with clean white paper. (For papier maché see p. 127.)

Polystyrene: polystyrene shapes used in packing can be obtained from shops. The pieces are various shapes and sizes. The finished collage can be colour spray painted.

(Humbrol make spray paints which can be used on polystyrene as well as wool, paper, seed, pasta etc.)

Metal: bottle tops, milk tops, buttons, washers, cogwheels etc. can be used very effectively to make abstract or pictorial collages.

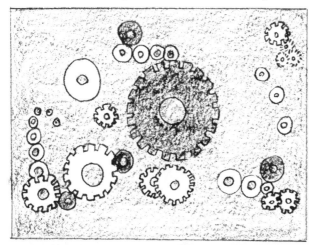

Use a strong base and a good adhesive. Colour the base before fixing the pieces.

Fabric: young children can glue the pieces onto a card or fabric base, and older children can stitch them. A group of children can make a large wall hanging using fabric and thread.

String or wool can be fixed to a base for an interesting collage. The thread can be used to outline fabric areas, or be spirally fixed to create the pattern.

Curved stitching

The stitching is done in straight lines. Lines are numbered (practise by drawing on paper first) and consecutive numbers joined as shown. It may be easier for young children to join 1 to 1, 2 to 2, etc. In this case number from 1 at the end of the first line to the angle, and number from 1 at the angle to the end of the second line. The pattern of stitching is then up 1 down 1, up 2 down 2 etc. Stitching may be replaced by glueing tapes, ribbon, wool, rods, or by fixing nails at the points on a board and making the pattern with rubber bands, thread or wire. The wall hanging suggested later could be made by a group of children.

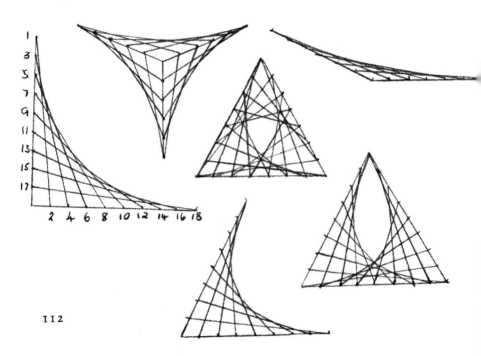

Tie and dye

All ages of children can use this process, with assistance, to dye shoe bags, costumes, clothes, handkies, music bags etc. Use any white cotton which is clean and fairly small. Follow the manufacturer's directions for the dye process.

Provide the children with string or raffia. (Thin wool or twine may be difficult to use.) Explain that where the string is wound tightly the dye will not penetrate. Young children may need the beginning and final knots tying for them.

The simplest patterns made by the tie and dye process are a circle and a stripe in a long border. Objects tied in the centre of the tying produce a centre circle of colour, with the pattern round where the string has been. Use pebbles or cotton reels or beads. Pick up the centre of the fabric, tie tightly. This is the circular pattern.

Pleat the fabric and tie tightly to produce the striped effect.

Older children who have experimented with one- or two-colour dying may like to try the more prolonged procedures involved in batik work. (This is usually more suitable for older juniors however, and involves hot wax and cold dyes.)

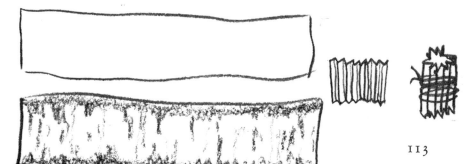

Wall Hangings

These are fabric hangings supported on rods, which are fun to make and suitable for any number of children. Use whatever is available, and whatever the children can suggest. The finished result should be colourful and decorative and interesting to see or touch. Display in corridors and halls low enough for the children to feel the texture, and use beads, sequins, buttons, etc. Make as large as possible. Sew, weave, or glue the pieces onto the fabric backing.

These suggestions are suitable for any age and any number of children.

A large piece of tie and dye is fixed to two rods as a backing for plaited wool or fabric, finger knitting (a long chain worked without needles) or bobbin work (worked on the four nails in a bobbin top, p. 126). The circle segments can display other wool or fabric circles or loops, depending on the skills of the children.

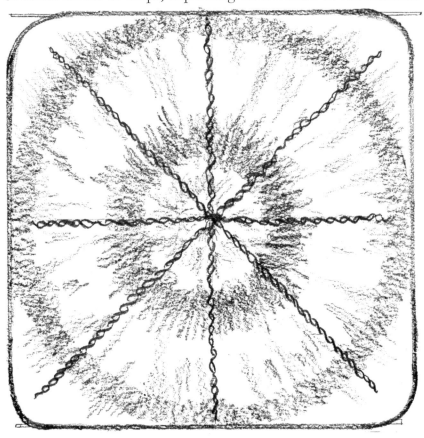

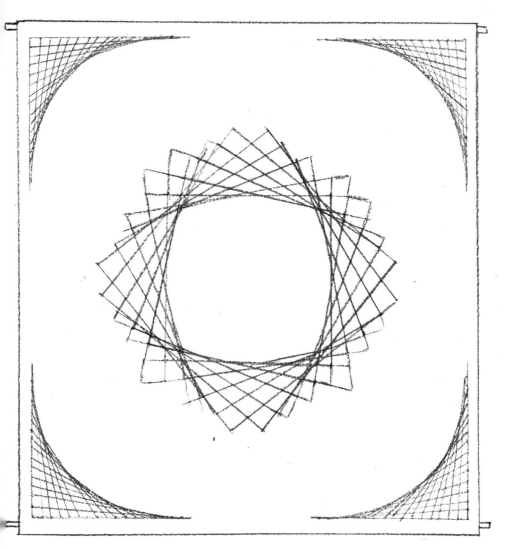

This is a large decoration using curved stitching, which on a large scale can be sewn or glued. Use rug wool, ribbon, dowelling, fabric etc. The background can be tie-dyed, or be a textured fabric such as hessian. A clean potato sack from a farm makes a good backing. Other decoration can be added, and in this design it is best to use geometric rather than irregular shapes.

The fabric backing can be painted in ink or paint, and the circle can be in one piece (glued on or sewn) or segments in different colours fixed under the centre circle. The flowers can be printed, cut-outs or loops of wool. Add buttons or beads, and if the children can tie bows decorate a fringe. This design is only a starting point for a sunny, cheerful decoration.

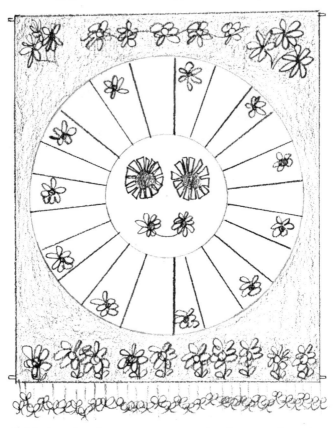

Bits of fabric glued onto a strong background make a bird, fish or figure. Rough out the outline in chalk first. If a figure is to be done, such as a warrior, a knight, a queen, chalk round a child lying on the fabric on the floor. Birds or fish are easier for younger children because bits of fabric already resemble feathers or scales, and cutting fabric is not easy to do accurately.

116

A large collage of letters and shapes. (Numbers instead of letters would be easier for younger children to cut out.) Glue or sew the pieces onto a dark background. Each letter can be decorated with beads, stitching, sequins or buttons.

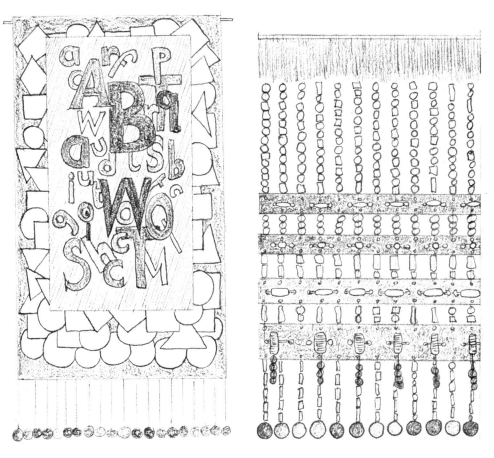

This is a wall hanging using anything that is threadable, such as beads, pasta, ring-pull can tops, serviette rings, punched cards. Tissue beads can be made by rolling strips of pasted tissue over a knitting needle. Allow to dry before use.

The two outer threads are fixed first, and threaded with pasta, bead etc. and the cards. Fix the middle thread, and groups of children can fix the rest. The horizontal weaving of ribbons, wool or string is done last, and beads or pasta or wool covered rings can be woven in. The cards may need strengthening with wood battens at the back.

This is a woven hanging, made on a large picture frame with a rug wool warp. The warp is not wound continuously, as in small looms, but is in pieces, each tied at the back, so that it can be fixed to a rod when the weaving is finished. Put a drawing pin at the top and bottom of each thread at the back to secure. The weft is pieces of fabric, slightly longer than the width of the picture frames. This weaving on a large scale is easier for young children than individual box or card looms, because no needle is used, and the spaces between the warp are large enough for hands to be inserted.

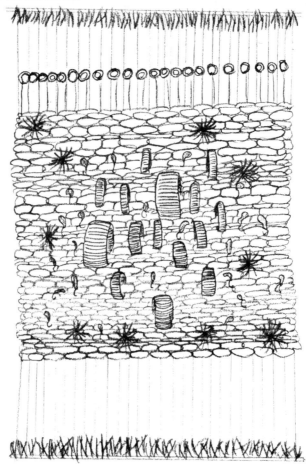

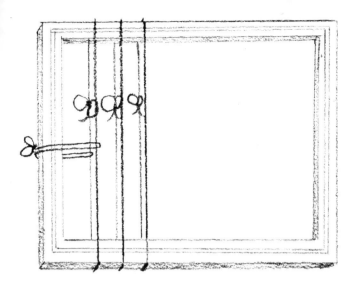

*Preparing
the picture
frame loom*

Slide a piece of newspaper or black paper under the top warp to cover the bottom threads and remove when the weaving is finished. Tie a spare thread or piece of wire to each of the outer warp threads and move it down as work proceeds. This prevents the sides of the weaving from being pulled inwards. This is more of a problem with a continuous thread weft than with single pieces, as in this wall hanging.

The ends of the fabrics can be glued onto the underside.

Ring-pull can tops, tufts of wool and wool covered rings can be woven in with the fabric pieces. As the work proceeds the children will be able to suggest what to put in. When the weaving is finished, untie the bows on the back two at a time and tie them together to prevent unravelling. Pin or glue with the knots to rods for hanging.

The fixing can be concealed with threads or fringes.

Hang beads or rings below, or spiderwebs worked with wool (pp. 126–7), or make a simple fringe of wool or threads.

Older children may wish to make an individual woven piece, and a wooden box or smaller picture frame is suitable. If the box is very small a needle will have to be used to make the weft, and the weaving may be tedious and fiddly. A piece of weaving which grows quickly is much more enjoyable. Strips of paper can be woven quite satisfactorily into a paper or rug wool warp.

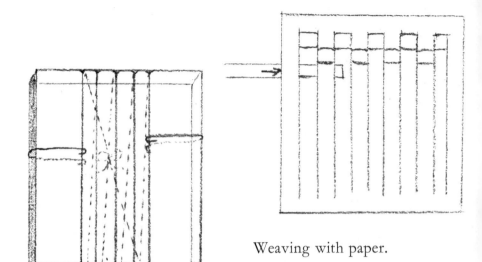

Weaving with paper.

Weaving in a wooden box with a continuous warp retained by notches cut in the box edges. A piece of wire keeps the outer threads from pulling inwards.

Christmas tree wall hanging

Three suggestions for Christmas wall hangings

The tree with presents and symbols of Christmas is a regular arrangement using any suitable material. Older children can decorate each item, or it can be left as a simple cut-out in felt or fabric. Very young children could cut triangles in different sizes instead of shapes to glue inside the tree and add buttons and sequins. The Christmas effect will still be there.

A Christmas hanging for older children. It can be made of cut-out fabric, or wool or ribbon, glued on paper bases to make the shapes. The pieces could be stitched or glued.

This is a more ambitious wall hanging, using the shapes for the twelve days of Christmas. Cut the shapes in felt. The milk maids may have churns or yoke and buckets. This is a large hanging.

To use the same theme in a smaller hanging cut one of each shape and fix in a smaller triangle.

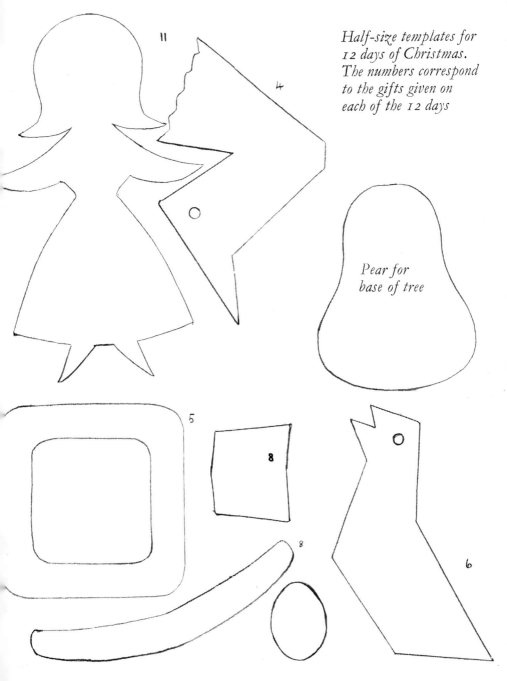

11

4

*Half-size templates for
12 days of Christmas.
The numbers correspond
to the gifts given on
each of the 12 days*

*Pear for
base of tree*

5

8

8

6

3

10

8

8

Bobbin work is the production of a continuous tube using a wooden bobbin with four nails in the top. The wool is wound round the nails and hooked over each nail one at a time with a needle or long nail.

Tie the wool round one nail, twist once round the second, the third and the fourth. Pass the wool round the first nail and lift over it the lower wool. Pass the wool round the second nail and lift over the twist. Repeat this process of lifting lower over upper wool on each nail always taking the wool in the same direction.

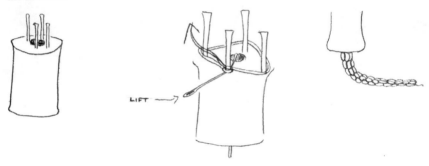

Spider webs of wool are a twisting of wool under and over two sticks or plastic straws. The thicker the wool the faster the square pattern grows. The wool must be wound loosely so that the shape is not distorted. Hang the finished pattern from a wall hanging, or use as a Christmas decoration. Make a large one for hanging stars at Christmas time. Use raffia, or silver or gold thread.

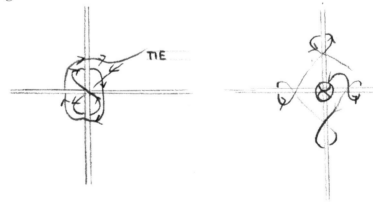

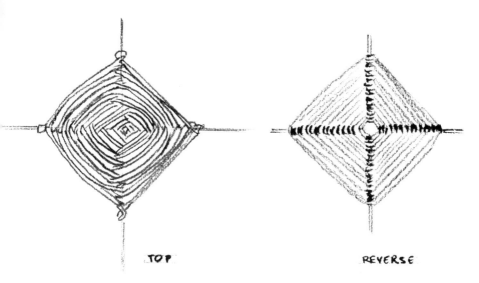

TOP REVERSE

Fix the straws by tying in the middle. Working always in the same direction take the wool over a cross piece, round it and up and across to the next. Many different colours and thicknesses of wool can be used on the same design.

Modelling

There are several modelling materials, such as clay and plasticine, and the commercial materials which can be baked or painted. The two cheapest homemade materials which are as useful are papier maché and a salt and flour mixture.

Papier Maché: tear newspaper into small pieces—the smaller the better—and fill a bucket. This is sufficient for a large handful of papier maché for six children. Soak the bits in water and pour off the excess. Mix a small packet of cellulose paste, and add to the soaked newspaper. Knead and mix well. This is a heavy medium to work and the modelled forms may need wire or cardboard supports. Very large models can be made over a chickenwire frame, bottles, or a wire frame wound with bandages. Allow the finished models to dry in a cool oven or in a draught and turn frequently. Then paint, and spray with clear polyurethane.

Salt and Flour Mixture: mix salt and flour in a bowl or bucket in the proportions of 4 units flour to 1 unit of salt. Add water slowly while stirring until a dough-like consistency results. The finished models may be dried in a moderate oven. Paint and spray with clear polyurethane. This is a good material for small models, as it keeps the modelling detail better than papier maché.

Carving

Older children who can control a tool such as a knife, saw, chisel and so on can use a variety of materials to carve. Block kitchen soap is a cheap and useful material, easy to work, and clean to handle. Plaster blocks are softer than wood, but messy. Builders' merchants will often give the small bits which have crumbled off building blocks which are soft enough to work with a knife or file. These are also dusty to work. Use both blocks and plaster outside on a sunny day. Balsa wood is easy to work but expensive. Driftwood pieces may be too hard to carve, but are attractive when sanded and polished.

Paper textures

Texturing a surface makes it more interesting by creating light and shade, or by exposing the ground beneath to display coloured papers, tissues and Cellophane. Children enjoy texturing paper and can invent interesting variations.

These are the simplest textures:

Holes made by a paper punch, usually only possible along an edge.

Slits opened up or removed to expose the ground. Pinch the paper in the fingers and cut a slit. A sharp knife may be needed for triangles close together.

Slots which can be curled backwards. Cut with a knife.
Crosses cut with a knife.

Curves cut with a knife. Only older children will manage the control required for these.

Slits on a curved surface where the pieces are pushed back gently into a reverse curve.
A combination of curved score and straight slit, also on a curved surface.

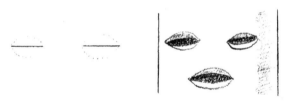

Scoring is a neat way of preparing a fold. For straight scores use a ruler and scissor or knife point, and the point alone for curved scores.

Curling is more difficult. Close the scissors, hold in one hand with the thumb over the blades, put the paper to be curled under the thumb and pull it gently along with the other hand. The paper is stretched on one surface and curls. Young children often lack the delicacy of touch required and may tear the strips.

Insertion is an easier activity. A piece of paper is inserted into another to support it, as in the half slots on the boat, aero-

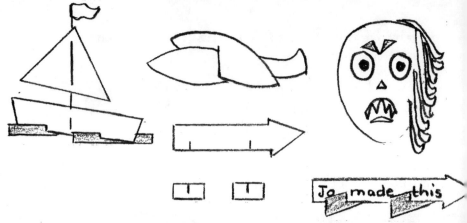

plane and label, or for decoration, on butterflies, witches, fishes etc. Ribbons, wool, straws, metal pieces may be used instead of paper, and children enjoy inventing individual decorations.

Books

These are made with concertina folds or separate pages.

The simplest book is made from a strip of paper in a concertina fold. This gives seven pages and a cover, which is usually sufficient for individual books for younger children. The same fold can make a work book for a project by a group of children. This can be pinned on a wall to display.

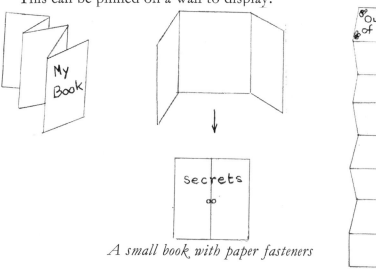

A small book with paper fasteners

Wall book.

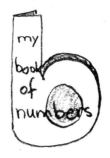

Books can be all sorts of shapes. A thin book which is quickly filled is an incentive, especially if it has an attractive cover.

Children's work (printing, patterns etc.) make good book covers. A book made with a concertina fold will require two pieces stuck onto stiffening pieces of card. Making the end covers is not difficult for older children, and the procedure is a good introduction to book binding techniques.

Cut 2 pieces of card slightly larger in length and width than the book. Cut the patterned end covers at least 2 cm (1 in.) larger than the cards. Paste the wrong side of the patterned paper and place the cardboard on it centrally.

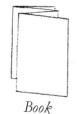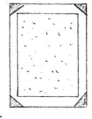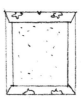

Book   *Cardboard*   *Patterned paper*

Cut off the corners of the paper, but not too close to the card. Leave at least 3 mm ($\frac{1}{8}$ in.).

Turn down the top edge of the paper over the cardboard. Do the same with the bottom edge. Press a thumbnail down the side edges of the card, at each corner, pressing in the folded paper. This makes the corner bend in slightly and when the side is stuck over, a neat corner results. Fold over the sides.

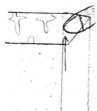

Because the cardboard will shrink on the pasted side and curl up, the cover must either be stuck immediately onto the end of the book fold or backed with a piece of paper slightly smaller than the cardboard. This will make a mat which can be used as such or stuck later onto a book.

When both covers are stuck onto the book allow it to dry pressed between clean papers under weights.

Large class books and small individual books with several pages are better sewn than stapled. Sewing is not difficult for older children. The centre can be sewn in four or eight sections. Gather the cover and sheets together and fold in half. Take a strip of paper the same height as the book and fold it in half twice. Open it out and place it along the central fold of the sheets.

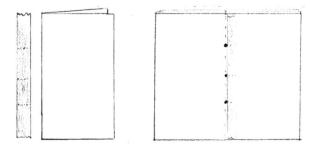

Mark on the sheets where the three folds on the strip occur. Using a needle threaded with strong cotton or wool, go down the centre mark. Bring the needle up through the top mark, across the centre to the bottom mark. Go down that and bring the needle up the centre mark. Tie the ends across the central thread.

A very large book may need an eight-section sewing, and possibly a reinforced spine of card, or sticky tape, or fabric. The sewing is similar to the four section, with the ends tied across the central thread. Mark the positions with a strip of paper folded three times.

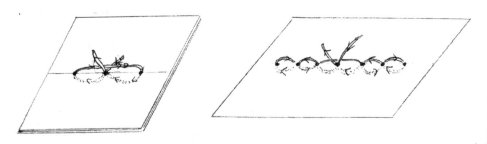

Painting

All too often the quality of a child's painting is directly proportional to the amount of space he has and his distance from other groups of children. Crowded classrooms and tables mean small sizes of paper and a shorter period of concentration. A child should be learning while he paints or he will leave the infant school producing the same house and grass and sky he painted at four years old, with the same lack of brush control.

Aim for a good working atmosphere where care can be taken and the painting enjoyed. Know what to suggest (techniques) and when not to interfere (in colour or subject matter). Don't ask a young child what he has painted; say 'That looks interesting, tell me about it'. Show young children how to paint by practising brush strokes, and encourage their attempts to control the brush.

Young children do not need a wide range of colours. A box of watercolours is too confusing. Older juniors may appreciate this, but give young children powder or block colours. Red, clear yellow and blue (ultramarine) will be required, also black and white. In powder these colours can be easily mixed to give orange and green, and any more subtle colours required. Since any three colours mixed will give brown or grey, keep the colours widely separated before mixing. Whenever possible let the children see the colours mixed if they don't do it themselves. Keep block paints apart also.

The advantage to young children of having ready-mixed paints is that the paints do not become dilute with rinsing water. Make the colours strong. Stand the jars or pots of paint in a wooden tray to prevent spillages. Provide three brushes of different sizes in each pot of colour. Stress how important it is to return each brush to its own colour. As the brush leaves the pot loaded with paint, it must be wiped on the rim to take off the drips. This action should be automatic.

Block paints can be more wasteful than powder paints. Younger children may scrub instead of stroking the paint onto the brush. Older children who rinse the brush between colours should run the fingers down the brush to squeeze out the water and avoid diluting the colour. Use this technique to mop up too much colour or spillages on a painting.

Older children may like to have an individual palette or saucer in addition to the paint pots in order to mix their own powder colours and experiment with using unusual colours.

Easels may look quite professional and can be used to display finished work, but are not easy to work on. What adult would choose a sloping surface for painting in a watery medium? It is most frustrating for a child to see rivers of paint ruining his picture. Provide a table covered in newspaper with lots of elbow room. The children can then sit or stand. Working on a newspaper on the floor is the next best place.

Provide as good a selection of brushes as possible. One long-handled brush is too restricting, at any age. At least three sizes should be available, a fat bristle, a thin bristle, and a fine brush for detail. Large murals will require decorator's brushes. Children quickly learn that large areas need large brushes, and thin lines need finer brushes. Brushes should be washed gently, in running water, and stored upside down.

Young children can practise brush strokes each time they paint before working on their own painting. They enjoy a brief learning period and it is a good chance to provide small papers in various shapes, sizes and colours which may be in short supply. Printers and paper mills will often give off-cuts to schools and play-groups. The practice the children do often stimulates them to a larger painting. This is useful for the child who wants to use colour and brush but isn't sure what to paint.

The brush should be held like a pencil. It should be held upright, or the end of the brush should point in the direction of the proposed line. The elbow should be free to take the hand along. Point the end of the brush at the chest for a downward line. Filling a large area should be done in a series of smooth strokes, and not by scrubbing the brush backwards and forwards.

These practice suggestions may be used over several painting sessions.

Practise straight lines across and down in the same colour of paint. Use newspaper pieces, then small pieces of different papers. Try wavy lines also. The continuity of the line is important.

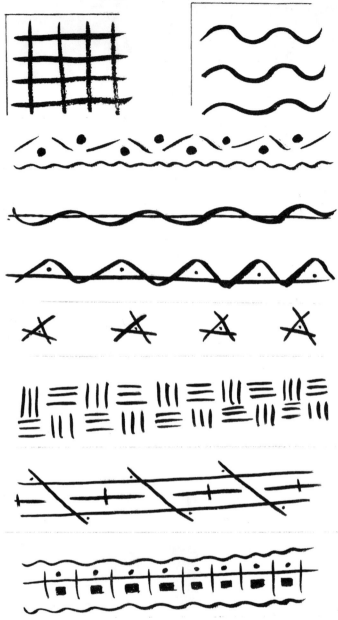

Encourage one long sweep to form each line, and not a series of short tense strokes. Practise a variety of line and shape.

Provide long strips of paper to paint a fence pattern.

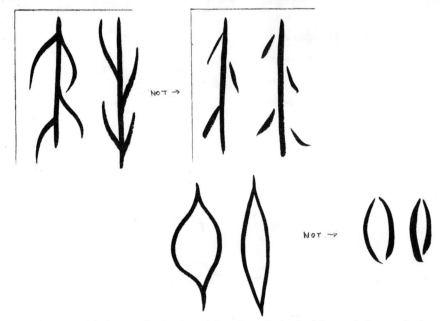

Practise blobs and circles. The brush is held upright and the wrist curves the brush. Practise fish and balloon patterns.

When the child has good control of the different sizes of brush using these straight and wavy lines, he can practise joining one line to another, where the second brush stroke needs to merge someway into the first. Use seaweed or leaves as examples to practise. The technique is not easy.

Practise putting one colour onto another wet colour (wiping the brush before returning it to its pot) and putting one colour onto a dry colour. Encourage patterning of large areas, as in a 'scribble picture'. A dark crayon traces a pattern over a large paper and the areas are painted in. The areas may be overpainted in patterns and colours.

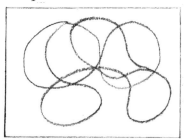

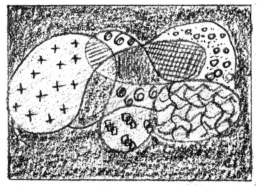

Show older children how to do a wash, using gentle strokes with large brushes. Wet the paper on both sides under a tap. Place it on sheets of newspaper and smooth the corners gently to make a flat surface. While the paper is still wet brush in the colour in light, even strokes all in the same direction. The paint must not be too thick. If the wetting, flattening and wash are too difficult for young children pin the paper to a board by each corner and wet with a sponge. Use a large brush for the colour wash.

The wash can be used over crayon drawing, or to make pictures with a wash of different colours. Care must be taken when the colours merge. Use as few strokes as possible.

Interesting patterns result when paint or dry powder is spattered onto a wet ground. The colours merge and spread and the attractive pattern when dry can be used to make book backs, or water, autumn leaves and hillsides etc. on friezes.

Attractive patterns can be produced by using a tool, usually a piece of card cut into a comb, to spread thick paint and expose the paper beneath. The paint is mixed to a thick consistency with cold water paste. Paint the paper. Trail the cut edge of the comb through the paper. Fingers, crayons etc. can be used instead of the cardboard.

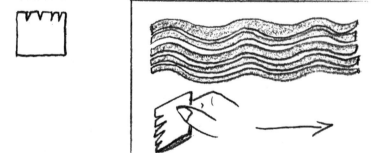

Easy repeat patterns can be prepared for painting by using charcoal. The design is drawn in charcoal on the paper. This is folded over and the back rubbed firmly. The design transfers to the lower part. Fold again for further transfers. When the design is painted in thick colours the charcoal is covered.

Provide paper as large as possible, and not always the usual oblong in shape. If the children are having a free choice of subject, let them choose from a variety of paper and shapes and colours. If they are to illustrate a specific theme, provide a suitable shape of paper. Sometimes it is stimulating to older children to restrict the choice of colours, particularly for patterns.

Mount children's painting where possible on dark toned paper, leaving a little more room at the bottom than elsewhere.

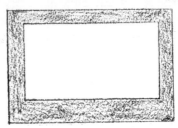

Themes for illustration should be specific rather than general. Too wide a choice can be confusing. For instance, suggest 'Eating our icecreams' rather than 'What I did on holiday'. There are many poems which can be splendidly illustrated, such as 'Don Durk of Dowdee', 'The Gingerbread Man', 'Three Poor Witches', and many more.

Older children enjoy making designs based on geographical or historical cultures, such as American Indian patterns, South American designs, Celtic or Egyptian motifs. The patterns can be used to border murals, decorate books etc.

Use children's painting (and any other works, for that matter) wherever possible, and if it isn't possible to display at once, store the paintings in individual folders. Sheets of newspaper stapled make an adequate folder, which will last a term. The children should trim any torn edges before storing. If they see that care is taken of their paintings after they are finished they will take care in their creation.

10 Christmas

Christmas cards

Since the cards are for special occasions encourage neat work and plenty of practice. Allow access to precision tools (stapler, spotstick glues, paper punch, pinking scissors, rulers, compasses, geometric shapes, alphabet stencils, templates and sharp scissors). Provide a variety of decoration, such as ribbon, tinsel, pre-cut stars, pre-cut paper strips for edges, doylies, bits of lace, glitter, cottonwool, baubles and buttons. Let the children choose their materials, colours and textures where possible, and encourage older children to design their own card, and make envelopes for them.

Young children may find it helpful to work to a prepared design and may also need templates.

Do not let the attempted design be too ambitious. Better simple and neat than clever and messy. Sticky paper is more attractive than crayoning on a card. Young children are often eager to stick the pieces as they go along. Encourage them to cut all the pieces and arrange them before fixing. This will give them a better eye for proportion, and they can see what they want to add or discard before it is too late.

Provide mounts, one or more, which are smaller than the finished card. Some cards will look better with different coloured backgrounds, and some look well with strips to edge the motif.

Cartridge, white or coloured or wallpaper (plain backed) will be suitable for the card, which should be folded before the child begins the front design.

The following suggestions are in increasing order of difficulty:
(*a*) A foil star, made by folding and cutting, mounted on bright sticky paper.

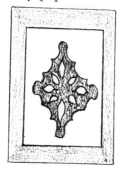

(b) A cut-out tree, cut to a fold using a template, with an edging strip in a contrast colour.

(c) This is the discard piece from card (b), mounted on a contrasting colour, with dots made by the paper punch.

(d) Made using four templates. The pudding in dark brown sticky paper is textured with snippets of red, orange, yellow and green. The pink or white sauce piece is stuck over the pudding.

(e) The candle is mounted on one piece, and then onto the card. Strips may be added as well.

(f) Templates may be needed for the bells. Holly or flowers or ribbon would do instead.

(g) This is a simple tree, made to a fold, with extra cuts as drawn. The flaps are turned down to reveal the backing colour.

(h) A tree made to a fold, with a triangle cut from it. The triangle may be omitted, or made smaller and glued inside the larger, as shown here.

(i) The star is made by folding (see pp. 166–9 on folded stars) and a piece is cut out, made smaller and glued inside.

(f)　　　　　　　(g)　　(h)　　　　　(i)

(*j*)

(*k*)

(*l*)

(*j*) A silhouette of a toy. The children can suggest their own subject.

. (*k*) A snow scene. Vital here that the pieces are arranged before sticking if perspective is noted as in this drawing. Younger children can cut houses of equal size.

(*l*) A crib scene, using left-over bits for stable and hay.

(*m*)   (*n*)   (*o*)   (*p*)

(*m*) A Christmas rose (template on p. 170.)

(*n*) Traditionally, Mary is dressed in blue. Templates will be needed by young children for this design. Older children can draw the outline and cut pieces to fit. (See p. 145.)

(*o*) Doylies or foil can be used for the wings.

(*p*) The scarf can be a piece of ribbon inserted from the back of the mounting paper.

(*q*) Father Christmas. His clothes could be red fabric.

(*r*) A suggested design for one of the three kings. Older children will be able to make their own. Provide foil, beads and sequins for the gowns.

(*q*)

(*r*)

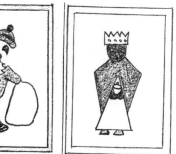

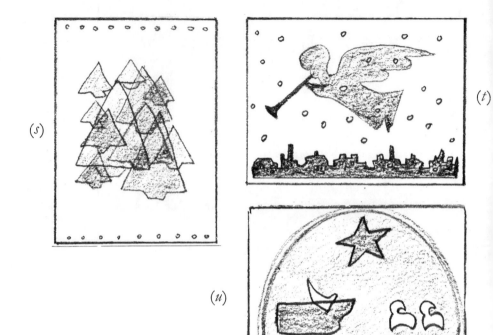

(s) Overlapping tissue cut-outs, mounted on a white ground.
(t) An angel in gold on a dark ground.
(u) A design using semi-circles of tissue, pasted on top of each other. The animals and stars are simple cut-outs.
(v) Using the same shapes as used for card (q).

These smaller cards are made by twice folding the card paper.

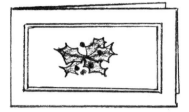 

A simple holly design, with two mounting papers.

Lettering sprayed through a stencil, drawn or cut-out, and robins, or pre-cut stars.

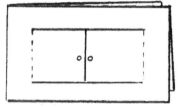

Doors with paper fastener handles which open to reveal a scene or lettering on a bright ground.

These are simple enough for young children to do well.

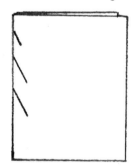 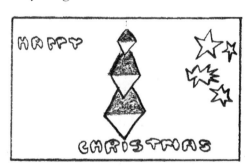

Interiors of cards can be cut decoratively, as suggested here. Bend the flaps down and push in.

Cut trees, and glue the largest to the flap. The tree pops up when the card opens. The flap may be hidden by a smaller triangle.

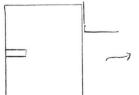 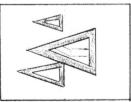

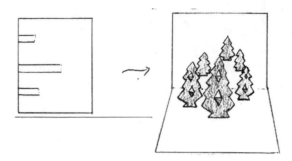

Three pop-up trees for this one.

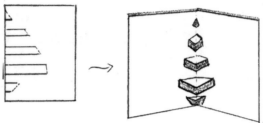

Bend in each flap. Crayon, paint or cover them on the inside with sticky paper. The card can be mounted onto another of the same size.

Another kind of pop-up using an inserted strip.
When the card is closed the flap should not show.
The flap may be concealed.
A third kind, made after twice folding the card paper. The inside fold is laid along the edge. (See p. 60.)

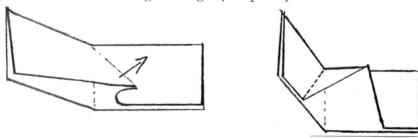

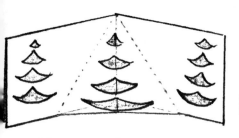 

Shapes can be cut into the fold, and coloured paper inserted behind.

The fold becomes a stable roof with cut-outs and tissue behind.

Encourage the older children to experiment with scrap paper and plan and cut their own designs.

Children like to make something which is acceptable to others, and some need the security of a given design. It is useful to demonstrate how some of the cards are made in order to stimulate ideas. Provide templates only if they really are needed, since part of the attraction of sticky paper pictures often lies in the vivid chaos of proportion.

These are the templates used in the cards.

There are other seasonal and festive cards in Section 6: Cards.

Mary (n)

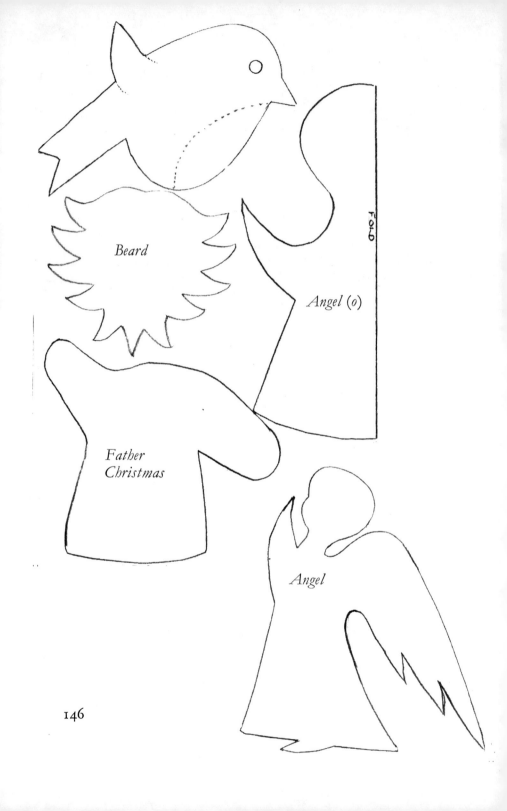

Beard

Angel (*o*)

FOLD

Father
Christmas

Angel

146

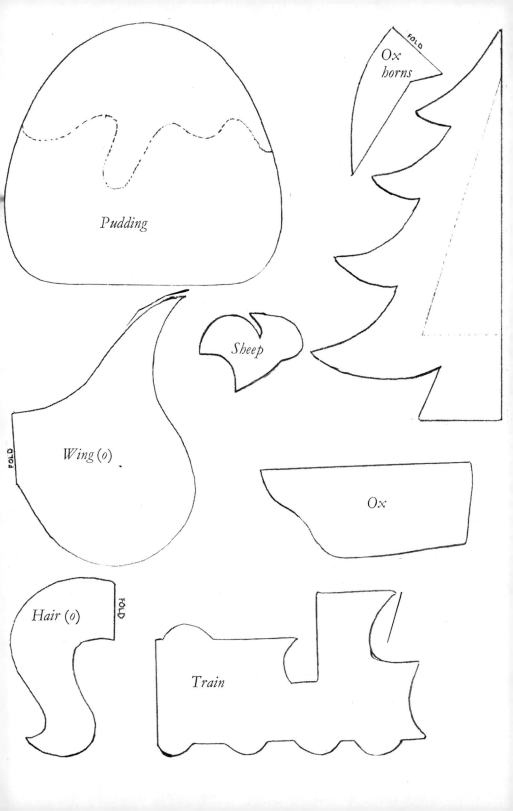

Pudding

Ox horns

FOLD

Sheep

Wing (o)

FOLD

Ox

Hair (o)

FOLD

Train

Stained-glass windows

Three methods are suitable for infants:

(a) With a group of young children the design is better crayoned.
Use the thinnest paper available, such as tracing paper. The
crayoning must be done thickly and evenly. Thick lines of
black crayon represent the leads. Crayon these last, because
the black may smudge with lighter-toned crayons. Polish the
surface to a gloss finish with a duster.

If the crayoning is not well done, rub the back of the paper
with a light oil. This makes the paper translucent.

Young children can choose a simple design, such as stars,
and older children can design windows with figures.

Mount against the light.

(b) Begin with a large sheet of black paper. Fold in half as shown
and cut out the pattern. Glue Cellophane behind the paper.
Small individual ones can be mounted on a hoop, or displayed in groups against a window.

(c) A third method consists of pasting black strips onto pieces
of Cellophane or tissue. This is a method more suitable for
older children.

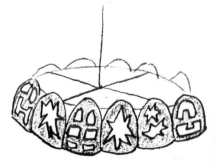

A Snowman scene

A very easily made model, for any age. Each snowman is made from a ball and a jam jar covered in cotton wool. Small cotton wool rolls can be added for arms. The junction of ball and jar can be hidden with a ribbon.

The subject and decoration of the snowmen can be suggested by the children. The hats and features and props are made from whatever is available.

White crêpe paper can make the ground. Take a piece larger than the area of window sill or shelf to be covered, and roll it into a loose tube which can be pushed over a ruler or knitting needle. The grain of the paper must run the length of the roll. Crush the paper together. Remove from the ruler and unroll. The crushed paper will keep its creases well.

grain

Angels

These suggestions for free standing or mobile angels are based on circles and in order of difficulty. The first two are slotted together, the next two are stapled by the skirt at the back.

Very young children can cut this simple angel in cartridge, plain or coloured, or foil. Templates will be needed.

Hands and arms may be added, using a curved piece folded in half at the hands. Most of the fold is then cut away. The arms are glued or stapled to the skirt at the back.

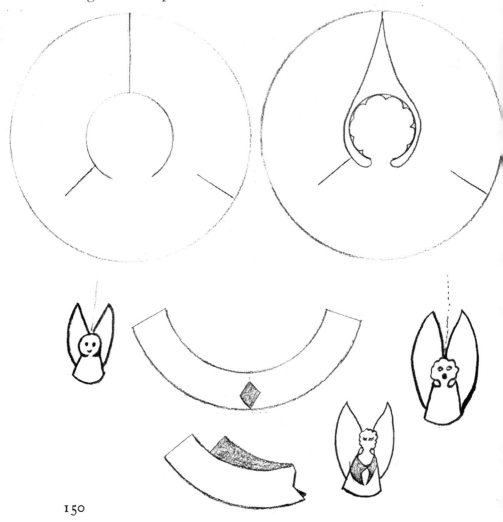

These two angels, where half the shape is shown, can be done by older children with or without templates. The arms bend forwards.

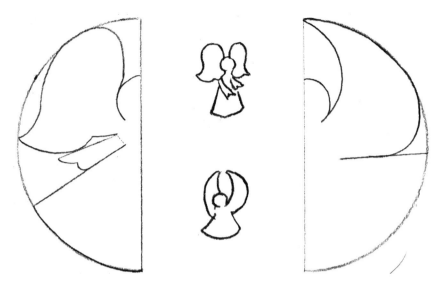

These two angels have longer wings, and require stiff paper. The bodies slot together. (Half the shape is shown.) The slot on the other half is from the arm downwards. These may be free standing or hung on a mobile.

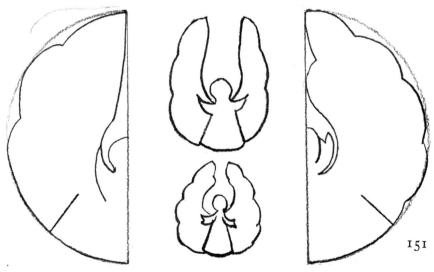

This angel is made in four parts. A group of children could make a set. Give the skirt template to the least able child. Cartridge or foil are suitable papers. The skirt is stapled at the back, and the other pieces drop in it. Older children, making the wings in foil, could pattern the paper by resting it on a soft surface and drawing on it with a knitting needle or blunt pencil.

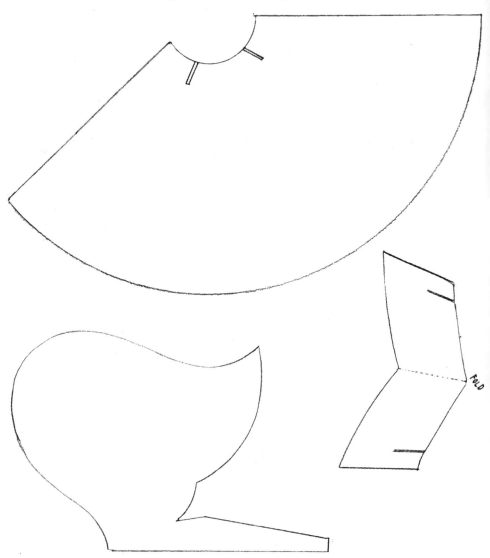

These two angels swing. The first is easier to cut. The body template goes to a fold, in cartridge or wallpaper. The head, which may be made to a fold for extra strength, is inserted in the central slit in the body. Two long strips of paper or ribbon folded in half, are inserted in the slots in the hands. If this is too difficult for young children the slots may be omitted and the strips glued to the hands. The skirt can be formed into a cone by overlapping the sides and stapling.

The larger these angels are made the better. Young children can decorate them with paint, crayon, wool, fabric, etc. Provide a variety of materials and strong paper for the body.

FOLD

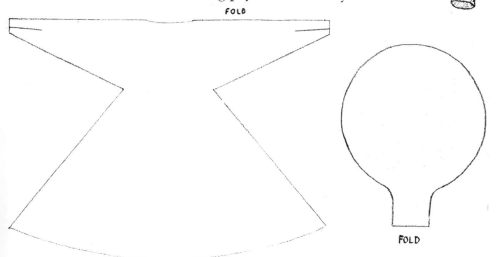

FOLD

The second swinging angel is more difficult to cut, and several are needed to make an attractive mobile.

Two pieces of cartridge are cut to a fold. Omit the pony tail for a boy. The angel slots top and bottom onto the swing. The two head pieces are glued together. A sheet of music may be added on the arms

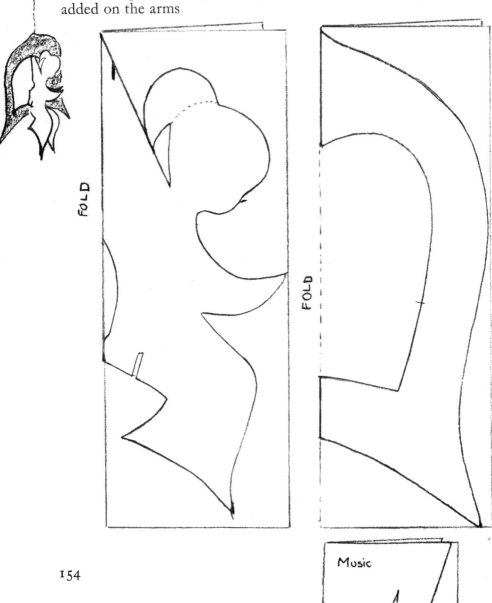

FOLD

FOLD

Music

Angels may be mounted on a frieze, stood on a shelf or window sill, or hung in mobiles. Three suitable supports are suggested below.

The first is made from two polystyrene tiles or one lump of papier mâché shaped like a cloud. If tiles are used one is cut in half and glued above and below the other.

The second is made from curved wire. Points of balance must be found practically when the angels are tied on to each piece.

The third is made from straws or dowels made into a star shape.

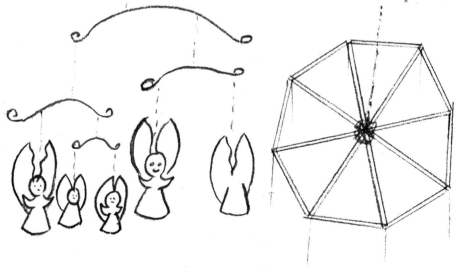

Trees

Young children will need a template for trees. The template goes to a fold. Use a single tree for a card. Glue two trees together to make a tree for a frieze, and glue four trees together for a free standing tree. Older children can cut out shapes into the fold. The template with the triangle cut away makes a tree where the two pieces, slit as shown, slot into each other. Sticky paper is not suitable for this tree unless it is self backed.

To give additional support for large tree stand the bases in rings cut from cardboard tubes. Slit the ring to insert the base.

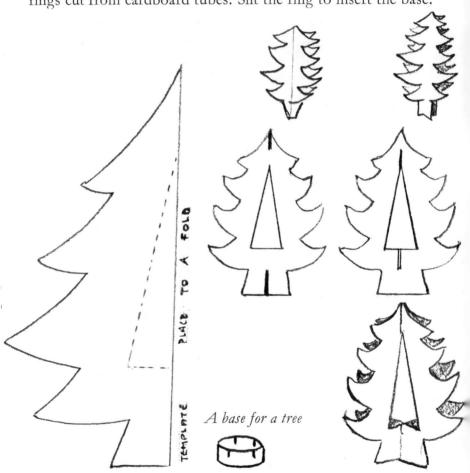

A base for a tree

These are simple trees which can be decorative or used to display sweets, flowers, small gifts, name tags etc.

The basic shape is a third of a circle made into a cone. Any stiff paper can be used, and any size.

Top the cone with a glass ball, a cut-out star, or whatever is suitable.

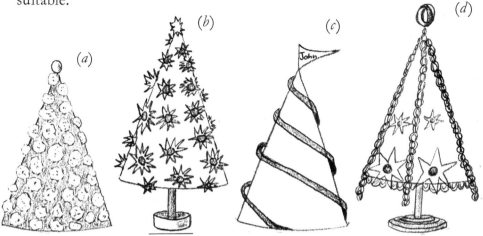

(a) A dark-toned paper cone, displaying cotton wool balls which have been dabbed in glitter or sequins.

(b) A display of sweets. Each sweet is mounted on foil cut-outs, and the weight of the cone supported on a stick and a base.

(c) A quick and easy place name, a way of concealing a present, or a cover for food at a children's party. The cone is wound with a foil strip which has been curled over scissors, and secured top and bottom.

(d) Young children can hang paper chains over a huge cone to make a large Christmas tree. The cone is attached to a broom stick held in a tub of sand or, better still, to a standard lamp support, and the chains are fastened to the top. Conceal the fastening with a bauble or paperball. The whole of the cone could be made of paper chains. It depends on the industry of the children and how much space is available. Angels and stars can be hung alongside the chains. The cone may need supporting underneath with wire. (See p. 164.)

Trees like these can be cut as shown, the pieces separated and then mounted flat. This is suitable for young children. The tree is cut to a fold, each piece opened out and mounted. If two trees are cut together, older children can make them into a hanging decoration. This is rather fiddly to fix. The pieces of one tree must be separated, and thread glued centrally. The pieces of the other tree are glued over the matching bits.

Older children also can invent variations on the straight edge cuts, like the wavy lines shown.

Another way of making a hanging tree by older children is shown here. A quarter circle of cartridge, foil or sticky paper is folded into less than half to leave an overlap. Fold in half again. Snip the fold at intervals. Open out, staple or glue the overlap. Push in and crease alternate pieces. Thread cotton through the top to hang.

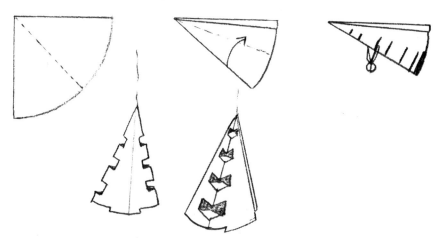

Hanging decorations

This is a simple shape which can be decorated with whatever is available by any age of child. A square or slightly oblong shape is the starting point. Foil is excellent but any stiff paper will do. A square gives a long thin mobile and an oblong gives a fatter one.

Roll the paper into a tube. Secure the overlap all along the edge. Flatten one end of the tube and glue or staple. Insert any fancy fringes before stapling. Flatten the other end at right angles to the first. Glue or staple as before.

The younger the child the larger should be this shape to make it easier to handle. Provide cotton wool, sticky paper, sequins, ribbon, tinsel, and templates if required. Allow the children free choice of materials and pattern.

Hang the mobiles where they can turn.

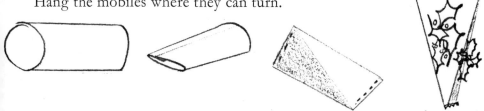

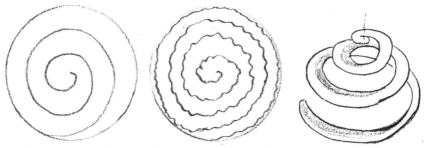

This is a simple mobile for any kind of paper.

Begin with a circle or square, no bigger than 15 cm (6 in.) across. Draw and then cut a continuous line from the edge to the centre as shown. Suspend centrally with thread.

The bells are made to a fold. Cut two, either slit as shown and slot together, or staple at the folds. Hang in a tinsel-covered cardboard ring, as a garland, or in a cluster in a mobile.

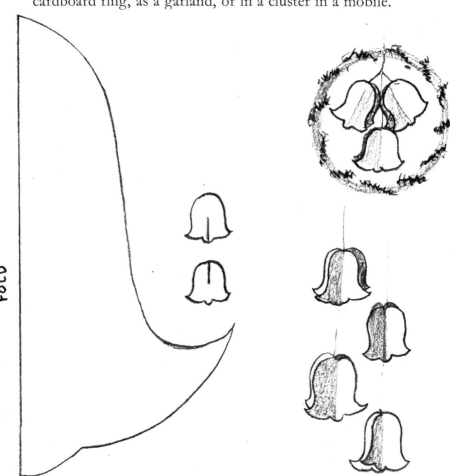

FOLD

This is a simple decoration, fun for young children, who can also enjoy using a stapler in an easy construction. Provide three strips of coloured cartridge. Make one into a circle. Join the other two end to end and staple. Put the circle flat on a desk or table and coil the long strip inside it. Staple where it touches the circle's circumference. Other patterns can be devised. Older children can make fish, butterflies, birds or faces.

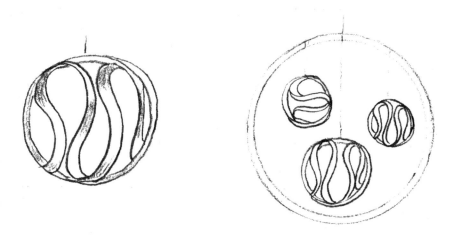

This is a more difficult decoration. Fold a strip as shown, leaving a piece to overlap. Form into a square and secure. The two smaller pieces slot together and are glued inside the shape. Staple one corner to distort the square. Older children can invent other variations quite easily. (See pp. 166–9.)

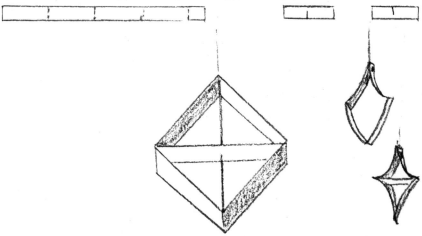

A ball of tissue circles is easy to make. At least eight circles are needed, and a threaded needle. Cellophane or crêpe circles can also be used but the finished ball is not as delicate and varied in tones. Lightly fold each circle into quarters without creasing the folds. Thread the eight together by the centres, gather the thread and tie. Fluff each circle out gently to make the ball spherical and hang by the thread.

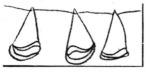
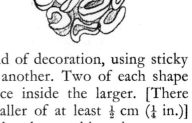

Older children can make this kind of decoration, using sticky paper. One cut-out swings inside another. Two of each shape must be cut. Lay the smaller piece inside the larger. [There should be a gap all round the smaller of at least $\frac{1}{2}$ cm ($\frac{1}{4}$ in.)] Lay the thread on top of both and glue the matching pieces over. There are several ways of cutting the shapes.

1. Fold two pieces of paper into the desired pattern, cut the smaller, remove $\frac{1}{2}$ cm ($\frac{1}{4}$ in.) and sandwich the cotton.
2. Cut with templates.
3. Glue the two pieces with the cotton before cutting. It is difficult to cut the paper without cutting the cotton.
4. Glue the two pieces before cutting, leaving one corner unglued where the cotton will go. Cut the shape, remove some of it, insert the cotton and glue.

Older children can invent many variations on this basic style, such as several smaller shapes inside a larger, irregular as well as regular shapes, faces, fish etc.

Supports for hanging decorations

These are some suggestions in various material. Others are suggested throughout the text.

A simple support can be made using four pieces of dowelling for heavy mobiles, or straws for light ones. The thread to tie is wound as indicated once and woven twice again.

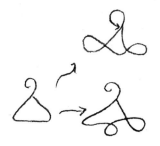

A wire coat hanger can be twisted into these shapes before disguising the hook either by covering with crêpe or twisting down to echo the shapes of the other corners. The hanger can be hung from its hook, in the usual vertical position, or turned to hang horizontally, supported by threads at each corner.

A wire spiral makes an interesting variation. The wire must be strong, and can be sprayed or paper covered, and the mobiles must be lightweight.

These three dowel supports are simple to construct. Vary the design to fit the space available.

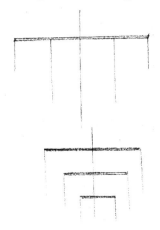

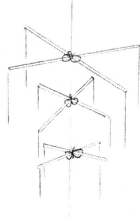

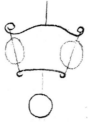

This is a simple wire support of two arms. The threads supporting the lower wire also support the decorations. The central decoration may need weighting to give stability.

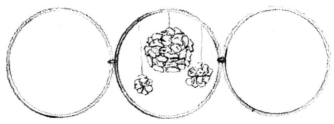

Hoops hung vertically, singly or joined, make attractive frames for spherical decorations, birds, fish, butterflies, moths and flowers.

A useful, cheap and easily dismantled support for Christmas decorations or birds is a tree made of a broomstick with dowelling. Drill a series of holes in a spiral path along the stick. The dowels can be different lengths or two or three of each length. Insert the end of the stick into a tub of stones and sand. Disguise the top of the stick with a cone or decoration. This dowel tree could serve as a support for the cone to display paper chains as described on p. 157.

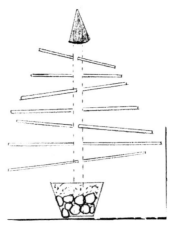

Lanterns

Lanterns can be as complicated as the child wishes. Cartridge papers, wallpaper or foil are suitable. The outside can be crayoned, or painted. An inner lining of tissue or crêpe can be added by younger children who find crayoning or painting difficult.

In the following diagrams the dotted lines are folds, and the straight lines are cuts.

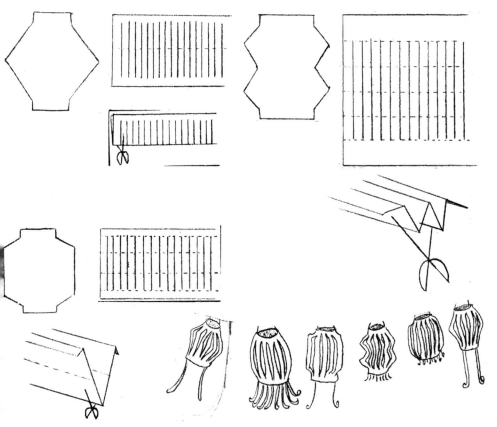

Suspend the lanterns by thread, or cut a strip across the width before making the lantern and staple or glue it as a handle. Extra pieces may be glued or stapled on.

Young children may find it useful to practise first with plain paper in case they end up with a heap of strips.

These more difficult lanterns can be made from circles or squares in any kind of paper. Fold the paper in half two or three times. Circles are easier, and three folds makes a more interesting decoration. Make alternate cuts from fold to fold inwards as shown. The closer the cuts the better, but practice may be needed. Open out and pull gently. The decoration may be mounted as a tree. A bell can be suggested by hanging a milk bottle top cone from the centre.

Two decorations the same size can be fixed together to make a long oval. Pull the bottom four points on each together and tie or staple. This is satisfactory with paper coloured on one side only, such as foil or sticky paper.

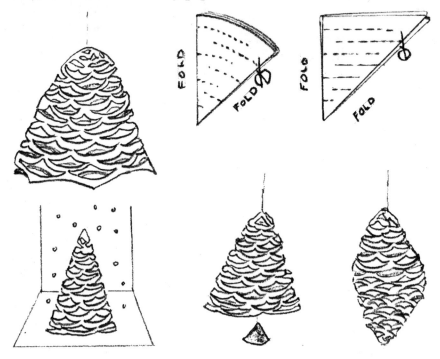

Stars

The diagrams show the methods of making stars, but once the basic folds are made the cutting can be a star, an abstract, a snowflake, flower etc.

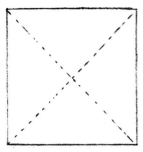
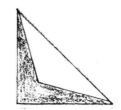

I. *A four-pointed star.* Two folds. Fold in half diagonally and fold again.

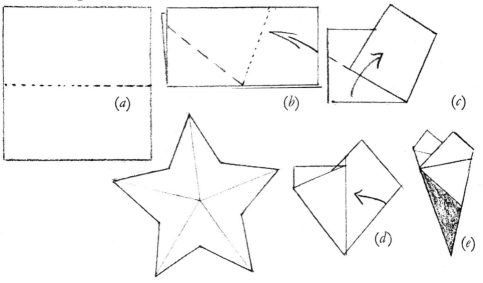

(a) (b) (c) (d) (e)

2. *A five-pointed star.* Four folds.
(a) Fold in half.
(b) Take the right hand edge over to the left up to the dotted line. (Over two-thirds).
(c) Fold left hand corner up and over right along the same line.
(d) Fold right over left.
(e) Draw the pattern from one corner to the centre.
(f) This is the pattern for a ten-point star.

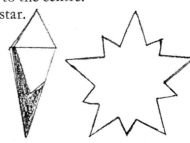

(f)

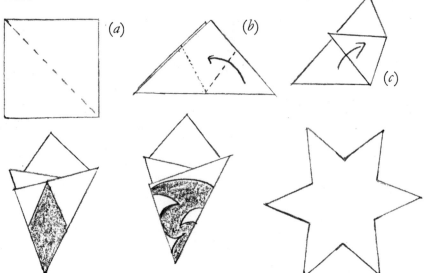

3. *A six-pointed star*. Three folds.
   (*a*) Fold diagonally.
   (*b*) Fold up right corner on dotted line.
   (*c*) Fold over left corner.

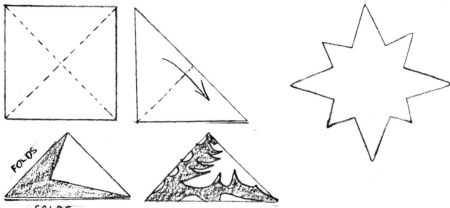

4. *An eight-pointed star*. Three folds.
   (*a*) Fold diagonally once and once again. Fold again. Draw
   the pattern.

 (*a*)

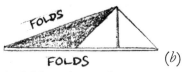 (*b*)

(*b*) For points of equal length fold again as shown.

The form can be raised. Open out the star and crease all the long folds one way. Turn it over and crease the shorter folds the other way. Additional folds may have to be made between the arms. Large stars may need to be scored. Encourage the children to invent their own patterns once they know the basic folds.

Two identical stars can be fixed back to back together for a hanging star.

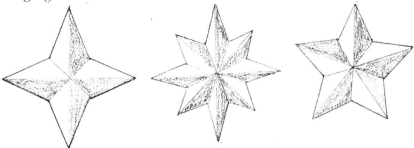

This is a simple cut-out star suitable for young children to cut to a fold with a template. The star can be mounted or hung. Cartridge or sticky paper is suitable. The dimensions of the star are as shown.

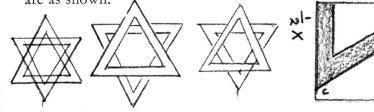

Another easy star for young children is a folded strip with a piece allowed for the overlap. Fold in half, in half and half again. Open and refold concertina fashion. An eight-pointed star results with twice the number of folds.

Christmas rose

Cut in cartridge or sticky paper. Tissue paper can be used if it is cut double or treble. Most children will need a template. Cut to the centre and overlap. The petals can be curled over scissors.

The natural Christmas rose has white petals and orange stamens. These colours can of course be used, but for brighter effect use red petals, with centres of silver bead, coils of white tissue, glass balls, gold cigarette paper etc. Use on presents, on friezes, in glass or paper vases. Add leaves of paper or foil, or real holly with glass or tissue berries.

Candle decorations

If real candles are used wrap the bases in aluminium foil. Straws or cardboard rolls can be covered in patterned paper and used instead of actual candles. Box lids, aerosol spray tops, papier mâché or polystyrene moulds can form the bases. Some spray paints dissolve polystyrene. Choose one which does not, such as those made by Humbrol. Add fircones, glass balls etc.

Garland

A garland for a wall or door can be made by young children. Cover a cardboard ring with crêpe and tinsel, make a paper candle and holly leaves and fix into the ring as shown. Smaller rings may be fastened behind the candle flame.

Tissue balls

These are suitable for older children to make. A spotstick dispenser is the best way of glueing the pieces. The basic shapes of the tissues are indicated. The ball partially completed can be mounted on a background, such as a cut-out bird or animal, or

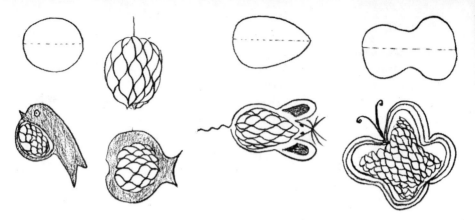

hang in a mobile or inside a cut-out (such as the robin) as a complete sphere.

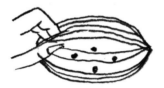 

Take a pile of tissues (at least a dozen for a sphere). Fold them all together in half. Cut to the basic shape. Hold the folded tissues in one hand and beginning with the bottom tissue dab glue on the edges in the pattern indicated by dots. One dab on one piece, two on the next, one then two and so on, or on bigger pieces make a two/three pattern. Open out the finished shape when the glue is dry.

The tree opens out with the card. Six sheets folded make a satisfactory tree which is not too bulky, though more would be better.

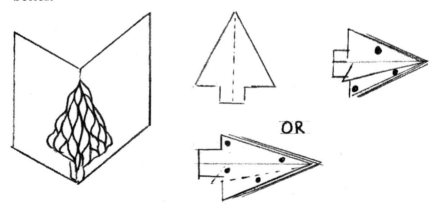

Streamers

Young children love to make paper chains. Instant satisfaction is guaranteed. But rapidity and ease of production is not often equalled by swiftness of anchorage in a busy room. The following suggestions may be welcome alternatives.

1. Make a paper-chain tree as described on p. 157. Lots of floor space required for this.
2. Use the chains as a frame round a frieze or Christmas scene.
3. Place a table, semi-circular if available, against a wall. Anchor equal lengths of chains from a high central point, such as a nail or hook, and tape along the circumference of the table. Spaces can be left for displaying gifts on the table. A cut-out tree may be displayed on the wall behind the chains.
4. Slow down the production line by letting older children glue or staple each strip into a figure of eight which is then joined into a chain. Variations of this may be devised if the children experiment with the strips.

Older children can make this two-part streamer which runs along a thread. One piece supports the other, and that can be single or continuous. Either cut to a fold or staple. Any combination of seasonal motifs will work if both are cut to a fold. The hole in the supported piece must not be too big or it will slide down too far on the other.

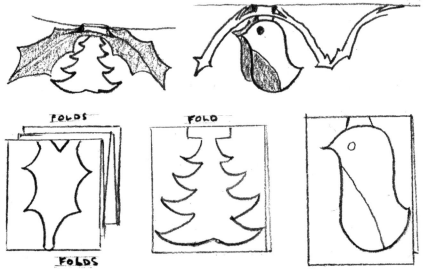

Father Christmas

This is an easy Father Christmas, made in four pieces with a reindeer and sledge, both cut to a fold. The dotted shape is half the template for the body. Cut all the shapes. Overlap the body at the back and staple. Fold the face piece at the fold and insert into the body. Glue on the nose and hat. (See p. 41 for other Father Christmas figures.)

Cut the sledge to the fold, curve the sides and glue at the end. Cut reindeers to a fold, using a template. Older children could curve the sledge and reindeer sides. Straight lines are used here because they are easier for young children to cut.

Provide colourful papers for these models. Display in a group with additions such as trees, birds, houses, presents etc.

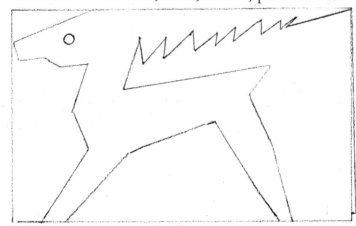

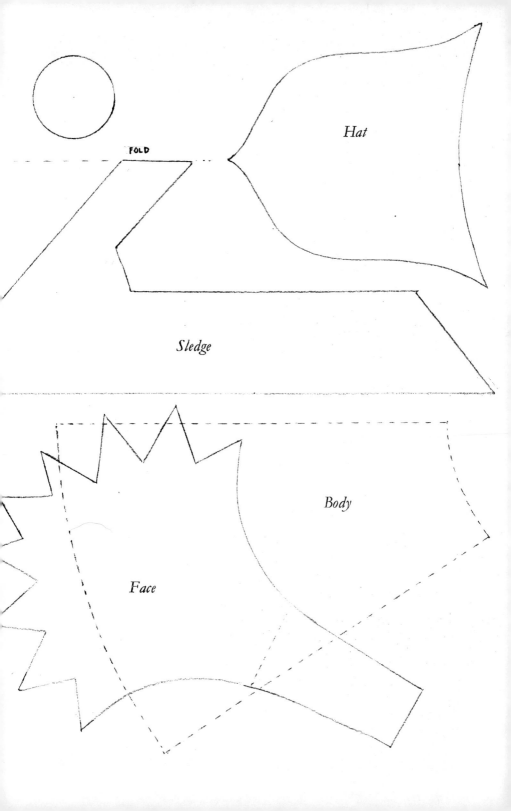

Hat

FOLD

Sledge

Body

Face

These are two variations suitable for older children. The Father Christmas is a mobile. Each piece is cut twice and cotton is sandwiched between the pieces. Younger children could use the design as a collage. (See p. 121 in the section on Wall hangings.)

The candle is made as a mobile or a table decoration. Each piece is cut twice (the flame can be separate from the candle), slit to the middle from top or bottom and the pieces slotted together. The base is a circle with the cross cut to insert the candles. Berries can be made as crossed pieces also.

CHILD-CENTRED
ATTACHMENT THERAPY

Other titles in the UKCP Series:

CHILD-CENTRED ATTACHMENT THERAPY

The CCAT Programme

Alexandra Maeja Raicar
with contributions by Pauline Sear
and Maggie Gall

On behalf of the United Kingdom Council
for Psychotherapy

KARNAC

First published in 2009 by
Karnac Books Ltd
118 Finchley Road, London NW3 5HT

British Library Cataloguing in Publication Data

A C.I.P. for this book is available from the British Library

ISBN-13: 978 1 85575 505 5

Edited, designed and produced by The Studio Publishing Services Ltd,
www.publishingservicesuk.co.uk
e-mail: studio@publishingservicesuk.co.uk

Printed in Great Britain

www.karnacbooks.com

CONTENTS

ACKNOWLEDGEMENTS

Child-centred Attachment Therapy (CAT) was developed and piloted in Essex during 1995–1996 as a brief therapy programme. Its aim was to foster mutual attachment in adoptive families where placements of children were in jeopardy because of the child's failure to attach to her new carers, despite their apparent willingness to meet her needs. Over the past ten years CAT has been used independently with birth, extended, foster, adoptive and step-families.

The programme is based on attachment theory, derived from the work of the late Sir John Bowlby and his successors. I am indebted for the following concepts to: Vera Fahlberg: "Positive/negative interaction cycles" and fostering attachments; Selma Fraiberg: "Ghosts in the nursery" and attachment/child protection work; Charles Whitfield: "Inner child healing".

My grateful thanks to Clair Pyper, Children and Families Service, Essex County Council, for permission to reproduce here materials from earlier publications written during 1995–1997 for the CAT pilot project; and also to

- my three enthusiastic colleagues who helped to co-develop and pilot CAT at Southend Family Finders during 1995–1997, and for their significant contributions to this book: Pauline Sear, Dr Maggie Gall and Margaret Saxby;

- our team leaders, Carol Collis and Di Hart, who allowed us time to test CAT;
- Tony Sharp, County Adoption Manager, Essex, for facilitating the pilot project and leading a County Focus Group of adoption practitioners to reflect on our learning;
- Lesley Smith, senior researcher, Essex Social Services, who evaluated the project;
- Mike Leadbetter, then Director of Social Services, Essex, for his encouragement.

I am grateful to Dr Hisako Watanabe and Dr Stella Acquarone for modelling family attachment work, and all the teachers and therapists and writers I have learned from over the years, unconsciously as well as consciously.

My thanks to the many, many children and families whose stories are shared anonymously here to help illustrate our learning from CAT work, and to all who have contributed to this book for sharing their thinking and experience and stories so openly and generously, especially "Rose", "Gemma" and "Emily"; see also list of "Permissions", below.

I thank Dr Stella Acquarone and Bernie Laschinger for their insightful supervision throughout, and colleagues who, despite their very busy schedules, took time to read and comment so helpfully on an earlier draft or parts of it: Angela Reynolds, Anne Wardrop, Bernie Laschinger, Colette Salkeld, Eve Menezes Cunningham, Franca Brenninkmeyer, Inger Gordon, Jasmine Shekleton, Maggie Rogers, Monica Duck, Richard Bowlby, Rosie Ingham, Sue Dromey, and Vivien Nice. Any errors or omissions remain my responsibility.

Grateful thanks to Eve Menezes Cunningham, for her invaluable support and ever helpful advice and comments; and finally, thank you to Christelle Yeyet-Jacquot and Pippa Weitz at Karnac for their editorial help, patience, and encouragement throughout this writing project, and to the copy-editor and the production team.

Permissions

My special thanks for permission to include their own perspectives on CAT to: Angela Reynolds: "A clinician's perspective" (in

Chapter Eight); Colette Salkeld: "A music therapist's perspective" (in Chapter Eight); Linda Fowler: "A fostering agency's perspective" (in Chapter Seven); Sir Richard Bowlby: "An attachment researcher's perspective" (in Chapter Eight).

*To Tim, Eve, and Alan, who have taught me about
building healthy attachments;
to Angela, Tony, Melita, Frank, Flora, and our parents
for helping me to start this journey all those years ago;
and to "Rose" and "Emily" whose family stories were the
inspiration for The CAT Programme.*

Alexandra Maeja Raicar is a UKCP registered psychoanalytic psychotherapist, parent/infant psychotherapist, life coach, NLP Master Practitioner, EFT and Emotrance practitioner, and a crystal therapist. Maeja has a BA (Hons) degree in English, an MSc in the Sociology of Health and Illness, and a CQSW. Her dissertation on her social work experience of adoption work with young birth mothers was published under the title of *Teenage Pregnancy: The Social Making and Unmaking of Mothers* (1984, Birmingham: Pepar Publications). Maeja has an Essex-based therapy and supervision practice and works part-time at the Post-Adoption Centre, London.

Maggie Gall worked in various social services settings for thirty-five years; these included mental health, disability, the elderly, child protection, fostering and adoption, and hospital social work. Maggie has a CQSW and an MSc in Social Administration and Social Policy from the London School of Economics, where she gained her first degree, a BSc in Social Anthropology with Psychology. Maggie obtained a PhD in the "Psychiatric, psychological and sociological aspects of plastic surgery" through Bedford College, University of London. She carried out research on mental health issues for Essex Social Services, and also for London Roehampton Hospital on the long-term effects on the family of psychiatric illness.

Pauline Sear worked in Social Services for twelve years, supporting struggling families, before co-developing The CAT Programme with Maeja Raicar, Maggie Gall and Margaret Saxby in the mid-1990s. Pauline trained in counselling and play therapy, and her contributions to CAT through play and family work have been invaluable in shaping the Programme.

ABOUT CHILD-CENTRED ATTACHMENT THERAPY

Child-centred Attachment Therapy (CAT) is a brief, focused, family programme for children with attachment and related behavioural difficulties. These include children who, without therapeutic intervention, remain at risk of significant harm or family breakdown with multiple moves. In our experience over the past twelve years, we have found family attachment work to be very effective in helping troubled children.

CAT is a social work initiative that was developed during 1995–1997 and successfully piloted at a family-finding unit with a small number of struggling adoptive families. Our experience since then has shown that the programme can be effectively adapted to meet the needs of birth, extended, foster, and step-families, too, *where parents are committed enough to engage in such collaborative work with them and the identified child client.*

CAT was initially developed as post-placement support for very hurt children in adoptive or long-term foster families where disruption and further moves otherwise seemed likely. CAT has also been used very successfully in carrying out exploratory work, preparation, and support for children and birth families where reunification is being considered, as well as in "therapeutic assessments" for

Social Services and/or the Courts of placements at risk of break-down, sibling and family attachments, and complex contact arrangements.

CCAT is a compassionate and cost-effective service in that it combines *assessment, treatment and support from the start, through working in partnership with the family.* We seek to empower troubled families by encouraging them to draw on their own creative resources in finding solutions to what they perceive to be the child's problems.

The success of The CCAT Programme, therefore, depends on the carers' commitment to the child, and their willingness to explore not only the context and triggers for the child's problematic behaviours, but what may be very difficult issues for themselves. These include family relationships, parenting styles, and their own childhood legacies of hurt and loss, which might be inhibiting their attachment to the child in the present, and, consequently, their ability to care for and protect him effectively.

CCAT is based on the premise that *a child who* feels *securely attached to her family is likely to be rewarding to care for and, therefore, well parented.* Sadly, the opposite is also true and the primary focus of the programme is, therefore, to foster mutual attachment between child and carer through identifying and correcting dysfunctional patterns of interaction.

Our experience shows that issues of *attachment, protection, separation, and loss* for both child and parent are crucial to such work. CCAT seeks to address these through discussion, play-work, family and inner child healing in a programme specially adapted to each family's needs. CCAT Programme therapists aim to model open communication and honest feedback in the sessions.

The initial contract is usually for eight two-hour sessions, weekly or fortnightly, of parent–child, family, individual, and couples work. This is then reviewed with the family to assess any future needs. Follow-up support is offered at three, seven, and twelve months afterwards.

Most importantly, *CCAT combines assessment and therapy in the one programme and so offers a secure base to families in crisis who need continuity and support in exploring, grieving, and changing their reality.*

Maeja and her colleagues have written about the development of the GAT model of working with children with attachment difficulties. They describe, in a vivid and accessible manner, the complexities involved in supporting parents in their struggles to respond positively to the needs of children who have been traumatized by their early experiences.

After many years of working with a number of families with children who "act out" their hurt through difficult behaviours, the authors offer their insights to help both parents and professionals to understand and deal more effectively with such behaviours. The GAT therapists give an impressive account of their belief in a therapeutic approach that focuses on attachment and protection as prerequisites for promoting healthy relationships.

Through the descriptions of their work with a number of clients, the reader is encouraged to gain an insight into the complex challenges encountered by individuals, families, and professionals. Major strengths of the book are the authors' clarity in describing the theoretical perspectives that underpin their model and their huge knowledge base of the issues directly related to children fostered or adopted through the "care" system.

In sharing their experiences, the authors' descriptions of their interventions convey a warm and empathic approach, demonstrating their ability to join together with families in order to bring about positive change.

I believe that this book will provide excellent learning material for parents and professionals alike. It highlights the need for both parents and children to be able to recognize, verbalize, process, and understand the unconscious feelings that are acted out in challenging behaviours. Only then can positive changes be achieved through the building of reciprocal and trusting relationships.

Monica Duck
Director, Post-Adoption Centre
London
October 2007

Calling Home

The telephone rings.
Our daughter on the line.
I lift the receiver
From its cradle,
Check that she is fine,
Pass her to her mother
As before. No need to feed,
No nappies to be changed,
But she touches it
Tenderly as skin.
The cord stretches
Umbilically.
She listens, breaks
Into that primal smile,
Translates excited,
Articulate words
Into a gurgle
Or a cry.

[Cunningham, 2006]

CHAPTER ONE

The long-term impact of attachment difficulties on families

Introduction: learning from family stories

All carers and therapists—like the children, families and adults we work with—will have had to deal with key attachment, separation, and loss issues at some time or other in their lives. Many might have joined the caring professions in an unconscious attempt to rework their family scripts, heal from deep wounds of the past, or, as wounded healers, to try to understand or make reparation to others representing hurt children and other family figures from their childhood, as in "Emily's story", below.

It is likely that John Bowlby's prodigious work, *Attachment, Separation and Loss*, was fuelled by his early life experiences. His sensitivity to the plight of young children separated from their parents, and his intuitive awareness of the importance of mourning, may have been deepened by his own unacknowledged loss at the age of four of his beloved nursemaid, Minnie, who had helped to care for him since birth.

Louis Cozolino (2006, p. 19) argues that therapeutic work *requires* the inclusion of our personal experience, which is just as

1

important as scientific evidence. As therapists, we learn all the time from our clients, and we are likely to be more affected by certain stories that echo our own family narratives. Such stories tend to inform our therapy practice, consciously or not, and add to a rich and inexhaustible source of learning about the human condition and our varying reactions to it.

And so it was that, through my gradual learning about "Rose's story", below, I, too, came to realize the importance of openly acknowledging and mourning family losses, and the corrosive life-long impact of family secrets on each and every member of that family. The power of this tragic story fuelled my own unconscious search for ways to help rebuild mother–child attachments.

*   *   *

Rose's story

Once upon a time, long, long ago, in a far-off land in Africa, there lived a young Indian, Tom, with his wife and their four small children. Tom's mother had died in childbirth, and his father died when Tom was only twelve. An aunt in India grudgingly offered Tom a home until he was sixteen and thought to be old enough to make his own way in the world. Tom loved music and heard he could get a job as a pianist in Singapore, playing accompaniments to silent movies. So he worked in Singapore until "talking pictures" made him redundant there. Tom then travelled to be near relatives in a British colony in Africa, where he got a day job as a clerk and played music in the evenings.

Tom was now able to get married and start a family of his own at last. After living for several years in Africa, his young wife, Marie, longed to return to India and visit her family again. She was still grieving for their first-born daughter, Tina, who had been tragically killed in an accident. As an expatriate worker, Tom was allowed a paid passage back to India by ship once every five years, and eventually he and Marie thought they could afford to arrange a six-month holiday back home. The couple were so excited and busy preparing for weeks ahead that their two older children, Jenny and Peter, realized that this holiday would be different from the short trips the family sometimes took by railway to the coast.

After travelling by land and sea for almost two weeks, the family at last arrived at Marie's parents' home where they were all welcomed and the children made much of by relatives and friends. However, almost at once disaster struck. Marie suddenly became so dangerously ill that the doctors predicted she would soon die, and the children were gathered round her bed to say goodbye to her.

Jenny and Peter, only eight and five years old, were immediately sent away to live with different aunts, one in the north and one in the south, and so they could not meet. Three-year old Emily sensed that she, too, might be sent far away to live with strangers; she soon stopped walking and would only crawl, so that a worried Tom began to carry her around with him. The baby, Rose, was only seven months old and had fast become a great favourite with her grandparents, whom she learnt to call "Papa" and "Mama". Emily and Rose were no longer allowed to see their mother, since her illness was contagious and it was feared that they might contract it.

Miraculously, Marie did not die, but she remained too ill and weak for the remainder of their holiday even to play with her children, especially Rose. The baby no longer seemed to know who her Mama was and so avoided going to Marie, who felt very hurt by this rejection. However, Emily had learnt to stay by Marie's side, while Jenny and Peter were very glad to be brought back from their aunts to join their parents and little sisters again. The older children were now eager to return to their home in Africa.

The grandparents remained concerned that their daughter would not survive the long journey back, and they persuaded a reluctant Marie to leave Rose with them until she was strong enough again to carry her baby, already a year old. They reasoned that Tom could soon return to collect Rose, forgetting that he would not qualify for a paid passage to India for another five years.

No one knows how the parents explained this life-changing decision to the children, who never afterwards spoke about it, not even among themselves when grown up, until long after both Tom and Marie had died. Jenny loved her baby sister and did not understand why Rose was not returning with them to Africa. But she was shushed angrily by the adults whenever she tried to ask, and Jenny became afraid that she, too, might be left behind. She had not liked living with her aunt, who was very strict, while her cousins teased her for not speaking their language and for crying for her mother at night.

Peter remained silent about their leaving baby Rose behind. Being an only son, he was Marie's favourite and he had greatly missed being with his mother for so many months. However, Peter was a placid child and he had got on well with his caretaker aunt and cousins.

Little Emily may not have understood what was happening, except that she was back with her beloved mother, who could only carry one child at a time, and that would now be her. So Emily clung tightly to Marie and to Tom, afraid that she too might get left behind like Rose, who always got all the grandparents' and relatives' attention for being so cute.

And how could baby Rose understand that, in her need to survive the sudden separation from her mother at seven months old by forming strong attachments to her grandparents, and in later turning away from a convalescing Marie, she was co-creating a tragic new history for herself and her family: one of lifetime abandonment and disrupted relationships.

Theirs was a long and tragic story, with lasting impact on each family member, who remained indelibly scarred, not only by their sudden separation from, and loss of, baby Rose, but even more by the parents' inability ever to talk to the children truthfully about what had happened and why.

Five years later, when Tom obtained another paid passage by ship to travel back to India and reclaim his youngest daughter, the damage had already been done. He took with him Peter, now aged ten, as a companion for little Rose, but she was not used to sharing adult attention or treats. Jealous that their grandmother had begun to favour Peter, who was still a very placid child, Rose would tantrum and scratch and bite him. Her reputation as "a naughty child" preceded her return to Africa with Peter and Tom.

Marie soon began to dread Rose's rejoining their family. The little girl gradually became a scapegoat for the parents' early abandonment of her. Marie convinced herself that their "bad" little daughter was the reason that Tom became increasingly ill. He died when Rose was only twelve; this was another major and unacknowledged loss for her.

Neither Rose nor Marie trusted each other by then, or had any help to rebuild their long-disrupted attachment. Rose, at six years old, was expected simply to slot back into her birth family, who were by now complete strangers to her. Overnight, she lost her beloved grandparents, relatives, and friends, a country that had become home to her, its culture and even its language, since Tom forbade her to speak it at all. He had become anxious that this little daughter was already behind in her schooling and would not learn to speak English correctly, which he knew to be essential from his experience of being a foreigner in a British colony.

Years later, on returning to live and work in India as a young adult, Rose must have unconsciously remembered her father's injunction to her as a child, for she never relearnt the mother tongue in which she had once been so fluent. Her now hesitant use of it and anglicized accent were a constant source of amusement to native speakers.

Growing up as a stranger to her own family, pretty little Rose sought comfort and attention from neighbours and family friends, who kept bringing round new clothes and gifts for her to her surprised and increasingly mortified parents. Naturally warm and nurturing, Marie felt branded as "a rejecting and abandoning mother". In turn, she projected all her bad feelings about herself and anger at what had happened on to this youngest daughter, who, not surprisingly, became more and more difficult for Marie to manage or love. Rose's constant lying was particularly hard for her mother to tolerate, given her own valuing of honesty. Their "negative interaction spiral" was never interrupted. Rose remained the bad, unwanted child and emotionally outside her family, even when living with them.

Marie became increasingly preoccupied with caring for Tom, whose health had greatly deteriorated. He died a few years later, leaving Peter, at sixteen, to provide for the family. Jenny had never forgiven her parents for their abandonment of baby Rose in India, and her unconscious blaming of Marie for this got in the way of their relationship from then on. After Tom died, Jenny left home to get married and she soon became pregnant and busy with her new family, determined never to abandon her own children.

Emily, at nine, had resented her little sister's return to the family and displacement of herself as the favoured youngest child, since Rose was cleverer and prettier, and much admired by relatives and family friends in Africa, too. Emily retreated into a world of books and only gradually became aware that Rose and their mother did not get on at all. Marie still favoured Emily, to whom she confided her distrust of the little girl, so sowing the seeds of lifelong conflict between the two sisters. Emily, like Peter, was too loyal to their beloved mother to realize that not all Marie told them about Rose was true.

Instead, the family secret of these ongoing losses and how they came about was maintained by the parents. An unspoken injunction was placed on the children never ever to question what had happened. Peter's deep love for, and loyalty to, his mother prevented him from ever admitting the truth, even to himself; he died relatively young from a corrosive bone disease.

So, poor Rose remained outside the family and unconsciously sought to emphasize her difference when growing up by speaking English with an affected American accent and using slang from the cowboy comics they read. She became more eccentric in her ways as she grew older, justifying Marie's description of her as "odd" and "not quite right in her head". By her early twenties, Rose had acquired a psychiatric label that stuck to her, making it even more difficult for her family to embrace her difference.

Rose returned to India on her own at nineteen, but now felt just as alien in her former homeland because of her independent thinking, western ways, and strange accent. She lived in various institutions thereafter, forever abandoned by her family.

* * *

I have chosen this particular family story to illustrate how easily attachments can be disrupted, and with such tragic results, even in a relatively normal family with kind and well-intentioned parents. This has been powerfully demonstrated in James and Joyce Robertson's deeply poignant films, made in the 1950s, about the immediate *and* long-term impact of sudden separation and loss on two previously "securely attached" toddlers, "John" and "Laura" in *A Two-Year-Old Goes to Hospital* (1952).

It must be remembered that, in "Rose's story", Marie remained a loving and caring mother to Peter and Emily in particular, and that Rose must have been securely enough attached to Marie for those crucial first seven months of life to be able then to develop strong bonds with her grandparents, who became her substitute carers. However, Rose's inability at a year old to reclaim a convalescing Marie as her *primary attachment figure*, and her mother's felt rejection by Rose, sealed their fate. Neither had help thereafter to acknowledge and mourn their losses and rebuild their early attachment.

The unheard story of this "lost sister" divided the family forever; however, their scripted version was of being a loving and united family. As John Byng-Hall points out, *"the family myth is the family's consensus about which home truths cannot be told"* (1995, p. 139, my emphasis). Anyone who challenges the truth of this myth is likely to be scapegoated, as Rose continued to be even as an adult.

Rose was neither neglected nor abused in infancy, but the impact of sudden separation from her very ill mother at seven months and the loss of her birth family at only a year old, followed by that of her grandparents at six years old, must have been more than her developing psyche could deal with, especially as she then became the unwitting scapegoat for all the family's problems after her return to them in Africa.

Fifty years on, an early diagnosis of "attachment difficulties" might well have been made about a child such as Rose, given her behavioural problems as a result of the traumatic maternal and family losses she suffered in her first few years of life. Any therapeutic help for Rose and her family would have needed to address the painful truth of the ongoing losses for her as a child, and to work on rebuilding positive relationships with her parents and siblings to help them all to heal and move on as a family.

*   *   *

There is an intriguing counterpart to Rose's story in that of her sister, Emily.

Emily's story

Emily must have learnt very early on from the family's abandonment of baby Rose not to be openly rebellious. She readily accepted her father's oft-repeated dictum: "A laughing child is a portrait of happiness." Emily kept any sad, bad, mad feelings to herself and looked down on little Rose for not being able to do the same. Their rivalry when growing up soon petered out for Emily as she left school and began working, achieving some independence from family mores and beliefs.

As "the chosen daughter", however, Emily felt increasingly uneasy about Marie's continued scapegoating of Rose for all the family's problems, especially after this youngest daughter was sent back to India on her own at nineteen in what became a lifelong exile. Their mother's divide-and-rule tactics made friendship between the two sisters impossible until much later in their lives, long after Marie died in her late eighties. Emily gradually came to realize that the story of the "lost sister" she had grown up with—Marie's continual recounting to her of a much earlier and greatly mourned family loss of her first-born daughter, Tina—masked that of Rose, whose loss was never openly acknowledged or mourned by anyone in the family.

Emily drifted into social work, and was soon drawn to working with foster and adoptive families in an unconscious wish to help children outside their birth families to find a new and loving home. Was it simply chance that Emily then married a man with early parental losses of his own? Decades later, he suddenly discovered that he, too, had an unacknowledged lost sister, given up for adoption at birth, who had grown up unknown to him on the outside of his family.

Rose's story became Emily's unconscious motivation for learning more about how disrupted attachments can be rebuilt. Even after training some years later in adult psychotherapy, her focus remained that of helping to heal mother–child relationships. The answer came to Emily very simply one day after her own openly rebellious teenage daughter, Zoe, left home to go to college. Their conflicted attachment had always surprised Emily, who believed she had a good role model in Marie of a warm and nurturing mother. However, Zoe's open rejection of her mother in her teens left Emily feeling increasingly bad and inadequate, perhaps just as Marie had felt when, at six years old, Rose was brought back unwillingly to her care.

Zoe decided to go to a distant college, as far away from home as possible, and only reluctantly involved Emily in moving her there. However, Zoe soon became homesick and began to write very affectionate letters to her mother, letting her know openly at last how important Emily was to her. It was an "aha" moment for Emily, both as a mother and a therapist. Now that she was at last being given positive cues by Zoe, Emily could respond affectionately, too. It was the start of their rebuilding in the second generation a disrupted mother–daughter attachment. This took years of mutual commitment and honest communication, but it provided a new model for Emily's family work.

* * *

My growing awareness of the relevance of Rose's and Emily's stories helped me to understand at *heart* level about disrupted attachments and how, as with Emily and her daughter, they can be rebuilt. The "needs" or "arousal–relaxation" cycle, of which I had been intellectually aware for at least a decade from Fahlberg's (1981, p. 16) and other attachment therapists' work, now made complete sense to me. I had the building blocks at last for an attachment therapy, and so The CAT Programme was conceived (Figure 1).

A working model of attachment theory

John Bowlby, the father of attachment theory, wrote over fifty years ago:

> what is believed to be essential for mental health is that the infant and young child should experience a warm, intimate, and continuous relationship with his mother (or permanent mother-substitute—one person who steadily "mothers" him) *in which both find satisfaction and enjoyment.* [1953, p. 11, my emphasis]

Bowlby already knew from his and other studies of young children in hospitals and other institutions in wartime Britain that, despite adequate physical care, they often failed to thrive, showing signs of

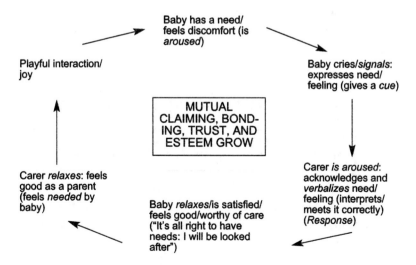

Figure 1.   Basic bonding cycle.

marasmus (a wasting away of the body) as if they were starved. Child evacuees, suddenly removed for their *protection* from their families in blitzed cities, provided further evidence of the crippling effects of separation and loss on their emotional, social, and mental development when substitute carers could not meet their basic emotional needs.

Based on their wartime work with emotionally deprived children placed in hostels, Donald Winnicott and Clare Britton (1947) suggest:

> Without someone specifically oriented to his needs, the infant cannot find a working relation to external reality. Without someone to give satisfactory instinctual gratifications the infant cannot find his body, nor can he develop an integrated personality. Without one person to love and to hate he cannot come to know that it is the same person that he loves and hates, and so cannot find his sense of guilt, and his desire to repair and restore. Without a limited human and physical environment that he can know he cannot find out the extent to which his aggressive ideas actually fail to destroy, and so cannot sort out the difference between fantasy and fact. Without a father and a mother who are together, and who take joint responsibility for him, he cannot find and express his urge to separate them, nor experience relief at failing to do so.

This does not mean that only a woman can fulfil the "mothering" role, or that there *has* to be a "parenting couple" or, indeed, a heterosexual one, for optimal care of a child. What is more important is "mothering of the mother" (Winnicott): the primary carer should be adequately supported by another caring adult in the ongoing and very demanding task of providing loving attunement and consistent care to a child.

In the late 1940s, an American researcher, Rene Spitz (1947), filmed Hispanic babies before and after separation from their mothers in penal institutions. These babies soon lost their early developmental gains, unless they were restored to their mothers' care within a few weeks. Beyond this "sensitive" period, the babies increasingly showed signs of mental retardation and autism, which soon became irreversible.

Spitz's film proved to be politically unacceptable and was banned from public showing in America. This reaction was similar to that in some English medical circles to the early showing of the "horror" films produced in the 1950s by Bowlby's research collaborators, James and Joyce Robertson, on the traumatic impact of sudden maternal loss for *even a few days* on previously secure "family children".

In the two films, *John*, about a "family child" who goes to a residential nursery for *eight* days while his mother is in hospital for the birth of her second child, and *Laura: A Two-Year-Old Goes to Hospital* (1953), both toddlers are initially friendly, co-operative, and hopeful, able to hold on to their memory of a good and loving mother. With each day of separation, however, as their successive institutional carers come and go, their distress becomes unbearable. Their protest, anger, and searching give way to despair and apathy, and then to withdrawal from, and distrust of, their mothers on eventual reunion.

Bowlby also learnt from the research of ethologists like Lorenz (1952), who got newly-hatched goslings to "imprint" on him as their care-giver; and Harlow (1958), who tested baby monkeys reared in isolation for their preferences for food or "love" (represented by soft, fabric-covered wire monkeys). These primates' early separation from their mothers led to long-term impairment of their ability to relate to peers and, eventually, to care for their own young.

Bowlby was convinced that human beings, too, have an innate biological need for *proximity to preferred attachment figures*. In times of perceived danger, this "drive" overrides those for food, sex, or exploration (our other main instinctual needs). Moreover, in all phases of the life cycle we show *normal* attachment behaviours: dependence on, and protest at, sudden separation from our attachment figures, anger at their leaving us, and pining for them if the loss is prolonged. When tired or unwell, our dependence on our attachment figure increases, and, for a mutually satisfactory adult attachment, partners normally have to take turns in *care-giving* and *care-seeking*.

Early attachment researchers like Ainsworth (1982), who continued Bowlby's work in America, showed that babies and toddlers need *a secure base*, often, literally, their mother's lap. From this springboard, they can safely explore the immediate environment and return to her for emotional "refuelling" and sharing of their new discoveries, as described in Mahler's *rapprochement* phase (Mahler, Pine, & Bergman, 1975). To feel secure, the infant needs to be within easy physical and emotional reach of its mother, as if attached to her by an invisible umbilical cord.

Ainsworth and her colleagues (Ainsworth, Blehar, Waters, & Wall, 1978) and, later, Main and Solomon (1986), studied one-year-old babies' reactions to sudden separation from their mothers in "a strange situation" (a room with some toys and an observer who joined them), and to reunion after three minutes. The twenty-minute observation included comings and goings by the mother and observer, without any preparation of the child for these.

Their findings led the researchers to categorize as *securely attached* those children who protested strongly at their mother's leaving, clung briefly to her on reunion, and were able to accept comfort from her before resuming play on their own in her presence, although perhaps with increased watchfulness. It must be remembered that even previously securely attached children (like John and Laura in the Robertsons' films) can be traumatized by prolonged separations if they have no consistent substitute carer.

Insecure attachments in "the strange situation" test were categorized by Ainsworth and her team as being *anxious–avoidant* or *anxious–resistant*. Later, Main and Solomon (1986, pp. 95–124) added a third category: *chaotic–disorganized*. (See descriptions of these categories below.)

* * *

There has been such a wealth of research and thinking about attachment, separation, and loss issues since Bowlby and his British collaborators, James and Joyce Robertson, began publishing their seminal findings in the mid-twentieth century that any Google search on the Internet on these subjects will yield a treasury of resources. What follows, therefore, is a brief working model of attachment and loss theory, and it includes terms in common usage in those contexts.

Attachment is a strong emotional bond to another person, independent of place and time; this may not always be reciprocal, as when we experience unrequited love.

The insecurely attached children in the strange situation studies carried out by Ainsworth and, later, Main and colleagues, showed three very different constellations of attachment behaviours from those of children who were considered to be securely attached:

1. *Anxious–resistant (ambivalent)* children were both clingy and angry with the mother on reunion, unable to accept comfort from her or to resume play even in her presence.

    It is now known that anxious-resistant children show ambivalent or "mixed" attachment behaviours: When faced with separation from their *attachment figure*, they tend to be clingy/angry, dependent/hostile, and find it difficult to trust, settle, explore, concentrate, or take risks. They are constantly preoccupied with a fear of rejection or, worse still, abandonment by him.

2. *Anxious–avoidant (dismissive)* children in the strange situation test seemed preoccupied with a toy and withdrawn from the mother, avoiding her gaze, perhaps fearing retaliation if they showed their anger at her leaving them. Their play was inhibited and, although they seemed not to react to the mother's leaving them or to her return, it was noted in subsequent physiological tests that their pulse rate was high, indicating great anxiety.

    Anxious–avoidant children tend to act as if they do not wish to be close to their attachment figure, since they fear rejection and/or abandonment if they show any neediness. They might, therefore, display a pseudo independence, even rejecting their attachment figure before they can be rejected.

3. Chaotic–disorganized clusters of behaviour were noted in a third group of insecurely attached children. These included frozen watchfulness, terror, confusion, helplessness, and a fear of seeking or accepting comfort from either the mother or the observer in the room.

    Chaotic–disorganized attachment behaviours are shown by children who have learnt *no strategy* for keeping themselves safe *and* close to their attachment figure, since this person might also be their source of danger. These children often seem both to want to move towards and avoid the same danger; they may be "frozen", wary children, unable to help themselves or to seek help.

Attachment cues: *anger, crying, cooing, calling, clinging, smiling at,* or *following/keeping close to* an attachment figure are all spontaneous biologically inherited attachment behaviours. They are necessary for our survival, especially when we are young and vulnerable and need protection from predators, just as in the animal world.

These *attachment behaviours* can be attractive to carers and, thus, encouraged and so reinforced, establishing learnt patterns of inter-action for the child. However, if the child's positive attention-seek-ing cues are ignored by a preoccupied, dismissive, or neglectful or abusive carer, she may then seek attention through negative behav-iours that are *aversive*; so the carer will act to stop her repeating these (Cairns, 2002, pp. 48–49).

Beth's story

Beth was only nine weeks old when I met her and her mother, Carla, who had rejected her soon after birth because the baby was diagnosed with a genetic disorder that leads to mental and physical retardation. Carla was an intellectual, and believed that the family's future was blighted because of Beth's diagnosis. She felt she dare not attach to this baby since she could not possibly mother her, so she was considering giving up Beth for adoption. Carla added that, if she had known about Beth's medical condition during pregnancy, she would have termi-nated it at once. All she could do now was care for Beth physically, but not look at or engage with her at all. Carla knew that this was not good for the baby, and she feared that she was already harming Beth through her emotional neglect.

While Carla was telling me this sad story, I became aware of Beth on the floor between us cooing at her mother. I pointed this out to Carla, who at once disagreed, saying that Beth was simply looking at her chair while making noises. We continued to talk, but I was now fascinated by the baby, who kept gazing at her mother while making soft cooing sounds. I pointed this out again, and Carla continued to ignore Beth and what I had said.

I then noticed that the baby, placed casually on her mother's folded coat on the floor, was somehow sliding towards Carla, who had also become aware of this and had moved her feet away. When this happened a second and third time, I pointed out to a resistant Carla that Beth was undoubtedly claiming her through this constant calling and movements towards her.

Carla seemed angry and upset at this, and later telephoned to cancel a follow-up appointment. However, I then learnt that she had decided to keep Beth and was researching local support services for them both. It was an amazing example of a baby continuing to claim her hurt and rejecting mother, and so succeeding in getting more positive responses through her persistence in reaching out to Carla through voice and gaze and movement.

* * *

Cues and responses

Cozolino (2006) explains almost lyrically how the "right hemispheres" of child's and carer's brains are linked "through eye contact, facial expressions, soothing vocalizations, caresses, and exciting exchanges". Interestingly, Cozolino also notes the plasticity of the mother's brain after birth, so that she, too, grows "emotional synapses" to help her to be more attuned to her child's needs.

Our development of our core or "true self" depends from babyhood onwards on positive affirmation by our carers: that it is all right for us to be who we are; to have feelings and needs; to know that these will be met *safely, consistently, and appropriately*; that our carers will be there for us when we need them for empathy, support, and understanding; that they will respond positively to us, enjoy being with us, and feel proud of us and our achievements.

All this caring makes us feel safe, protected, warm, loved, respected, and worthwhile as individuals. Our carers thus provide a secure base from which we feel able to explore the world, find out who we really are and what we can do, and enjoy this learning and take on new challenges. We grow in self-esteem and respect for ourselves and others.

In turn, because we trust them to meet our needs and acknowledge our feelings as valid, we are able to express these (*cues*) openly and directly to our carers, who can then *respond* appropriately. We learn to be predictable and make them feel good and proud that they can care for us so well. We give them love and appreciation and they enjoy being with us, being likely to spend more time in play or fun-time with us.

So, in summary, when we feel securely attached (Figure 2):

- we trust our attachment figure to be there for us;
- we feel good about ourselves, as we are special to someone;
- we believe we deserve love, care and acceptance as we are;
- we feel worthy of protection and, therefore, learn self-preservation;
- we come to believe that the world is an innately good place, and trust others;
- we feel it is safe to explore and learn about new things, and take on challenges;
- we seek out our attachment figure when we are anxious, tired, or unwell.

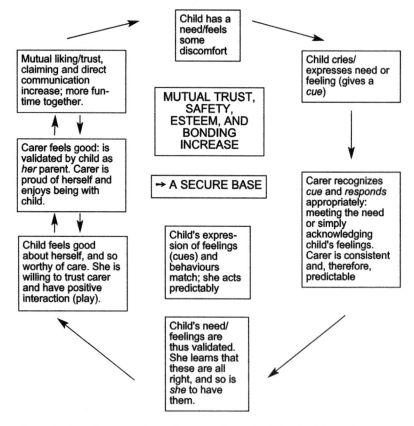

Figure 2. Development of attachment and predictability in child and carer.

Good enough caring

The importance of the endless repetition of the basic bonding cycle (see Figure 1) for a baby's healthy physical, mental, emotional, social, and spiritual development cannot be over-emphasized. There needs to be enough consistency of care for a "good-enough mother" (Winnicott, 1985, pp. 11–12) to develop with her infant a mutually predictable and rewarding relationship in which cues and responses are appropriately matched.

Cozolino explains how the infant develops emotional self-regulation:

> Sensitive caretakers learn to regulate their interactions with their child, respond to the child's responses, and allow for synchronized engagement and disengagement. As children and caretakers move in and out of attunement, the cycle of joining, separating, and reuniting becomes the central aspects of developing psychobiological regulation. Caretakers intuitively slacken their scaffolding as their children's self-regulatory capacities increase. Through these separations and reunions, their children learn that they can survive on their own, that caretakers return, and that they (the children) have some ability to regulate their bodily and emotional states on their own. [2006, p. 72]

This is similar to the concept of "the good enough mother" (Winnicott, 1985, pp. 11–12), who has to adapt to her baby's changing needs as he grows. Her total preoccupation with her newborn infant, meeting his every need at once, will not be so beneficial for him at six or twelve months old. Her attunement to his developmental needs will necessarily change over the months as the conflicting demands of the outside world intrude. However, the baby gradually learns from having *enough* good experiences with his mother or primary carer to wait for gratification and to trust that his needs will continue to be met appropriately.

Feelings of trust, self-worth, and a belief in a generally benign world outside are thus fostered. These shape the baby's self-image and expectations of herself and her carer and others with whom she comes into contact. If all goes well for the child, her early experiences and relationships will *mirror* (Winnicott, 1985, pp. 131–132) her developing sense of herself as a lovable and unique little person, with gifts and needs that are respected (Figure 3).

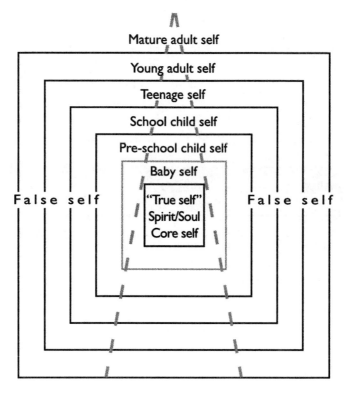

Figure 3.   Developing a "true sense of self" through positive mirroring.
Our capacity to function in "true self" requires positive mirroring when growing up. The "mirrors" held up by our parents, family, culture, community, school, peers, environment, religion, media, workplace, society, etc., generally determine whether we function more or less in "true self" or "false self" mode. Internalized oppression can make us feel that we are living in a "hall of distorting mirrors", unable to recognize who we really are and our full potential.

Sills goes further in describing this quite naturally occurring developmental process from a spiritual perspective. Sills draws on the work of Frank Lake, a perinatal psychologist, to describe the concept of "a good enough *womb of spirit*" in which the infant's innate needs of *being and well being* are adequately met by an attuned carer. Sustained "empathic failure" through neglect or abuse to meet these basic developmental needs will result in an obscuring for the child of her innate sense of *being* and inherent connection to *source* (Sills, 2008, pp. 132–136).

Disconnection from true self

Winnicott explains the profound implications of the "mirror-role" of the baby's mother and family:

> What does the baby see when he or she looks at the mother's face? I am suggesting that, ordinarily, what the baby sees is himself or herself. In other words, the mother is looking at the baby and what she looks like is related to what she sees there. . . . I can make my point by going straight over to the case of the baby whose mother reflects her own mood or, worse still, the rigidity of her own defences. . . .
>
> The baby quickly learns to make a forecast: "Just now it is safe to forget the mother's mood and to be spontaneous, but any minute the mother's face will become fixed or her mood will dominate, and my own personal needs must then be withdrawn, otherwise my central self may suffer insult". [Winnicott, 1985, pp. 131–132]

If our attachment figure is emotionally unavailable (through depression or self-preoccupation) or is unreliable or inconsistent, and we cannot predict their responses to our cues, or we fear their anger, avoidance, or punishment for our neediness, we learn very young— even as babies—to suppress our real needs and feelings from them and, increasingly, from ourselves. Growing up, we may then not know when we are cold, hungry, angry, sad, in pain, etc., or, indeed, who we really are, since we have become so disconnected from our core or true self, or what Sills refers to as Being (Sills, 2008).

Abuse and/or neglect by the carer is a distorted response to the child's expression of need, and hence affects his capacity to communicate it effectively (*cue*). One infant observer was horrified to note that a six-week-old baby was smiling with the mother as she pricked him with a safety pin each time she changed his nappy. He had already learnt that it was not safe to cry, a natural response of displeasure to the pain she was deliberately inflicting on him.

In this way, a child's ability to give the right cues and responses can become so skewed that neither he nor the carer knows how he really feels or what his unmet need is. Similarly, babies' and small children's mixed responses of laughter/displeasure or excitement/ fear to over-tickling, or rough-and-tumble play by adults, can be misconstrued as simple enjoyment, instead of being interpreted as a cue to the adult to stop such over-stimulation when it has reached a point of discomfort for the child.

Where infants and children are not so fortunate as to have had their needs met safely, consistently, and appropriately by a parent or carer, they may develop insecure attachments which shape their view of themselves and the world. If they learn very young that their baby needs and dependence on their carer are pushing him away, they will try to be independent prematurely in an anxious–avoidant style of attachment. If they are constantly neglected or threatened with abandonment by their carer for being too needy, they are likely to feel highly ambivalent, seeking to cling to him but getting no comfort from doing so; they might become passive–aggressive, afraid to express their frustration openly.

*   *   *

It is believed that repeated failure, for whatever reason, to complete the arousal–relaxation cycle (see Figure 1) inhibits the healthy development of neural connections to the "emotional brain" with its mood regulating functions. Fahlberg (1991) notes that there are several points where completion of the arousal–relaxation cycle can be interrupted:

- a neglectful or abusive parent might ignore or meet the baby's needs inconsistently or inappropriately;
- an overprotective carer might consistently meet a child's needs *before* she feels discomfort;
- he might not even allow her to have any stimulus that could be disturbing.

Thus, the child is deprived of her part in recognizing a sensation/need and communicating it (giving a cue) and therefore of any *sense of agency* in having it met.

The child's ability to communicate need may also be impaired because of illness or retardation (Acquarone, 2005, pp. 25–26) or non-attuned care-giving, as described above.

Separation and loss

Since attachment and loss are opposite sides of the same coin, any previous separation, or even the fear of losing a significant attachment figure, can greatly inhibit our willingness, even as adults, to risk a new relationship. We can reflect on our own experiences to help us empathize with how a child might similarly react to separation and loss, but without having our verbal resources to articulate how s/he feels.

We are likely to feel very angry, upset and rejected if our attachment figure leaves us. If separated for too long, we may start to feel hopeless, guilty, depressed, despairing, withdrawn, detached, and lose trust in our attachment figure. We may become forgetful, preoccupied, unable to concentrate, or become "busy" in order *not* to feel or think about our loss. Grieving children may become hyperactive for the same reason.

We might feel "not good enough", or really bad in some way, and blame ourselves for being left. We might feel punished for being who we are and/or for our neediness. We might then become afraid to show dependence on anyone, or our true feelings and needs, in case we are rejected and abandoned again. Instead, we put on a "false self" with a tough exterior to pretend we do not care.

Reactive attachment disorder

A baby's first attachment is to his mother, literally through the umbilical cord. If this is damaged or severed prematurely—before he can breathe or feed or excrete on his own, or artificially—the baby's future development or life itself could be threatened.

Similarly, if a baby's first emotional bonds with his mother, father, or other primary carer are damaged or suddenly severed before a new attachment can be sensitively developed between him and a new carer, his emotional growth might be inhibited for a while or even permanently stunted. He might have problems around trust and the making and sustaining of satisfying relationships. This is likely to result in the child feeling increasing anger, frustration, and low self-esteem, and lead to "acting out" accordingly.

By the mid-1950s, researchers like Bowlby, Spitz, and James and Joyce Robertson had documented very powerfully the traumatic impact of maternal loss on babies and toddlers. More recently, American therapists in the field of adoption, such as Lifton (1994) and Verrier (1994), have described the *primal wounding* that occurs when a child is separated early on from his mother. Verrier believes that early parental loss has an impact on the infant similar to the stress experienced by people living in a war zone, although the child's trauma is generally not recognized as such by the adults around, or its damaging effects on the development of his "social and emotional brain".

The popularized American description of "reactive attachment disorder" is sadly familiar to many foster and adoptive families who have found themselves increasingly baffled, deskilled, and helpless after struggling for months or even years with very hurt children placed with them. The analogy has been made that "parents and families of attachment-disordered children often develop post-traumatic stress disorder symptoms, in a similar way to those living in close proximity to the battlefront" (Parent to Parent Information on Adoption Services [PPIAS] [now Adoption UK], 1993, p. 15).

In the experience of such children, "Attachment is associated with loss and let-down . . . love is a Trojan Horse—a gift full of hidden dangers" (Delaney, 1991).

Internal working models

Attachment-disordered children have internalized *negative* models of parental care and availability; these are very different from the healthy "internal working model" of reciprocal attachments proposed by Bowlby (1969). The concept of an internal working model was derived from another scientific explorer, Kenneth Craik, who suggested that:

> Thought models, or parallels reality . . . the organism carries a small-scale model of external reality and its own possible actions within its head, it is able to try out various alternatives, conclude which is the best of them, react to situations before they arise, utilize the knowledge of past events in dealing with the present or future, and in every way to react in a fuller, safer, and more competent way to the emergencies which face it. [Craik, 1943, p. 61]

Having internalized a negative working model of a malignant carer and/or environment , "children and adults, who experience neglect, physical and or sexual abuse, frequently have paratactic distortions". Van Gulden (2002) explains these are *disconnected* (from the word *parataxis)* but instinctive survival responses in which "Sensory stimuli are (mis)perceived as toxic to our health. We react before processing the stimuli completely. This is an automatic, conditioned response".

Van Gulden makes an important distinction:

> Paratactic distortions are not PTSD (Post-Traumatic Stress Disorder). The process by which the individual experiences the environment as threatening is similar to the process in PTSD, but the child experiencing a paratactic distortion will experience the current parent as threatening, not as the parent of the past. Children can experience both paratactic distortions and PTSD. Both are strong inhibitors to attachment.

Van Gulden recommends patient observation of sensory triggers to such "paratactic distortions" and changing them, e.g., lowering the voice when speaking to the child, slow movements towards her, etc. She warns that this process of change-work is a very gradual but necessary one, since paratactic distortions are extremely distressing to both child and parent:

> these children react with anger, rage, aggression and/or flight responses to seemingly innocuous stimuli. A tone of voice, a sound, a body movement or position, a facial expression, a smell. Tragically, the child cannot feel safe, warm and secure in the care of an adult who unknowingly is triggering these defensive responses.

PPIAS (1994) lists the causes of reactive attachment disorder as follows:

> Any of the following conditions, especially if they have happened to a child under 18 months old, put a child at high risk of developing an attachment disorder:
>
> – pre birth and birth traumas
> – sudden separation from primary caretaker (e.g. illness or death of mother or sudden illness or hospitalization of child)
> – frequent moves and/or placements (foster care, moves in and out of the care system)

- undiagnosed and/or painful illness, such as colic or ear infections
- chronic maternal depression
- teenage mothers with poorly developed parenting skills
- inconsistent or inadequate day care
- neglect
- abuse (physical, emotional, sexual)

In endless studies, the following issues have been examined as causative issues in early developmental problems:

- intra-uterine factors (before the child is born)
- genetic factors
- hereditary issues
- the child's effect on the mothering figure
- the mothering figure's effect on the child

and "Common Symptoms of Reactive Attachment Disorder":

- superficially engaging, charming (phoniness)
- lack of eye contact
- indiscriminately affectionate with strangers
- lacking ability to give and receive affection (not cuddly)
- extreme control problems: often manifest in covert or "sneaky" ways.
- destructive to self and others
- cruelty to animals
- chronic, crazy lying
- no impulse controls
- learning lags and disorders
- lacking cause and effect thinking
- lack of conscience
- abnormal eating patterns
- poor peer relationships
- preoccupied with fire, blood, gore
- persistent nonsense questions and incessant chatter
- inappropriately demanding and clingy
- abnormal speech patterns
- passive–aggression; provoking anger in others
- unusually angry parents

Few children with Reactive Attachment Disorder will exhibit *all* of these symptoms!

Attachment disorder

Brenninkmeyer (2000) notes that the terms "reactive attachment disorder" (RAD) and "attachment disorder" (AD) are often used interchangeably, although they describe different syndromes:

> *The Diagnostic and Statistical Manual (DSM)*, published by the American Psychiatric Association, provides only limited help for the assessment of AD. Among a number of categories for childhood disorders and their diagnostic criteria the *DSM* included the category "Reactive Attachment Disorder" for the first time in its third edition (1980). The description of this diagnosis referred to infants younger than eight months who fail to manifest attachment behaviours; the cause for this was assumed to be a lack of parental care during those first eight months.
>
> In the revised third edition of the *DSM* (*DSM III-R*, 1987), the category "Reactive Attachment Disorder" was altered to include older children, whose main trait is a "markedly disturbed social relatedness in most contexts that begins before the age of five and is not due to Mental Retardation or a Pervasive Developmental Disorder such as Autistic Disorder". The cause for this disorder is defined as "grossly pathogenic care preceding the onset of the disturbance". It is further explained that the evidence for the disturbance has two forms: the child either persistently fails to "initiate or respond in an age-expected manner to most social interactions" or the child manifests "indiscriminate sociability; e.g. excessive familiarity with relative strangers, as shown by making requests and displaying affection".
>
> In the fourth edition of the *DSM* (1994) the two forms of "RAD", as it is sometimes abbreviated, are named "inhibited" and "disinhibited type" respectively. The definition of "RAD" remained unchanged otherwise. . . . The *DSM* definition of RAD does not mention any of the exceedingly difficult, destructive behaviours the AD children present, and neither does it specify that the disruption in attachment took place during the first two years of life.
>
> Randolph (1999) therefore argues that AD and RAD can be considered different psychiatric disorders; at best AD consists of the combination of the RAD category described by the DSM, plus at least one of two other DSM categories for childhood disorders: "Conduct Disorder" or "Oppositional Defiant Disorder". In addition, most clinical cases of AD present with at least one further

psychiatric disorder, such as Post-Traumatic Stress Disorder, Bipolar Disorder, Attention Deficit/Hyperactivity Disorder, Dysthymia, etc. [Brenninkmeyer, 2000, pp. 13–14]

Attachment disordered children may have had a number of moves within the "care" system, each move resulting in multiple separations and losses. It seems likely that the carers of these children get very mixed messages about their need for closeness and comfort when distressed or hurt. These children might have been discouraged or even punished by previous carers for grieving their losses or seeking proximity, e.g., showing attachment behaviours (cues), so they now reject new carers in a distorted response to caregiving (Figure 4).

* * *

Attachment therapies have proliferated over recent decades, offering despairing children and families a range of treatments from traditional play and talking therapies through grief therapy to the more controversial "Holding" and "Intrusive" therapies, used by Keck and Cline (1992), among others.

For families and professionals who consider such therapies too extreme or invasive, there are gentler techniques advocated by therapists such as Fahlberg (1991) for building attachments between bereft children and new carers. Theraplay™ (Theraplay Institute) is currently widely regarded as an effective treatment for children and parents who need help in thus connecting. Most parents in societies throughout the world know these ways intuitively as they learn to bond with their newborn babies through a spontaneous meeting of needs and increasing positive interaction, including loving, safe, and playful touch.

However, if either baby or carer is unable to play her part in signalling need (*cues*) or following cues (*responses*), their mutual attachment, confidence in each other, and self-esteem are likely to be impaired. The carer's growing feelings of rage, impotence, and worthlessness may offer a clue to the baby's. If the relationship then ends, and the child is not helped to express his feelings of sadness, anger, self-blaming, and loss, and to believe that his needs are valid and can be met, his next placement is already in jeopardy, thus

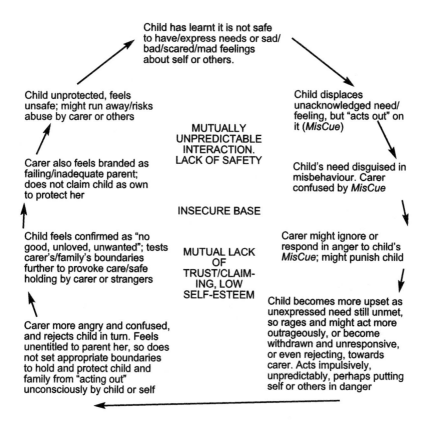

Figure 4.   Maintaining cycle of abuse.

perpetuating a negative spiral of deprivation. Both the child and the new carer may need help in synchronising signalling (*cues*), responding, and claiming behaviours in order to create a mutually rewarding relationship, and help the child to trust again.

The contributions of neuro-science: attachment and the development of the brain

Clinician–scientists such as Schore (1994) in the USA and Sunderland (www.naturallynurturing.co.uk) in the UK have helped professionals on both sides of the Atlantic to understand how nature and nurture interact to influence the crucial early development of pathways (synapses) between the limbic brain and the frontal cortex, so necessary for self-regulation of mood and healthy emotional and social functioning. In this way, our brain is both shaped by, and shapes, our relationships and environment.

Intriguingly, Acquarone (2004) concludes from reviewing research on "paternal" and "maternal" brain cells,

> cells in the brainstem appear to be the work equally of maternal and paternal genes. The maternal brain, or neo-cortex, would be a neural buffer for instinctual drives and demands arising in the limbic, paternal brain. [p. 22]

Schore's work pioneered the integration of neuroscience findings with attachment theory. His and other studies (Holmes, 1993, pp. 192–196, 2004) suggest that early "borderline attachment" or *disorganized attachment* histories, which include abuse and neglect, are likely to inhibit the healthy growth of regulatory circuits in the child's developing right brain. This hypothesis seems to be borne out by neurobiological research that show right brain and orbitofrontal deficits in people diagnosed as having borderline personality disorder. It seems that their brain is likely to be overstimulated in interpersonal situations, putting it on "high alert for danger while simultaneously decreasing inhibition, reality testing, and emotional control" (Cozolino, 2006, pp. 260–264).

Cozolino notes that "damage to the right hemisphere compromises our ability to interpret the (emotional) significance of facial expressions, hand gestures, and tone of voice". In effect, severe attachment disorders in young children, if left untreated, can lead to them as adults having ongoing difficulty in "reading" other people's cues and/or controlling their own mood and angry impulses, and, thus, in making and sustaining healthy relationships. Studies of those prone to domestic violence and uncontrollable "road rage" incidents might also point to links between early attachment failure and the impact on their developing brain's capacity to regulate emotions. (See Cozolino, 2006, pp. 269–279.)

Cairns (2002) points out that

> Traumatised people are unable to have intentions of their own beyond the will to survive; this supersedes all other intentionality.

They are also unable to judge the subtle intentions of others, for their whole being is focused on the possible threat others may present. [p. 107]

There is, however, hope for attachment-disordered children, as indeed for adults. Cozolino (2006) advances the theory of interpersonal neurobiology to demonstrate that the brain is "a social organ". It is therefore dependent on interactions with others to develop "social synapses" for interrelating and, indeed, for survival. Cozolino believes that healing relationships, both personal and professional, can facilitate the healthy development of the "emotional brain", despite previous impairment caused by early trauma.

Identity, multiple selves, and the body–mind paradigm

A leading American biophysicist and neuroscientist, Candace Pert, expounds the new "body–mind" paradigm about the quantal exchange of information, not just in our brain, but at cellular level throughout the body, through emotions that both shape and are informed by our experiences. Our "reality" and social interactions can, thus, be differently interpreted, and reacted to by us depending on what mood or altered state we are in.

Pert and Marriott (2006) consider that it is "normal for us to have subpersonalities, or altered states of consciousness, with whole bodymind changes from one to the other being triggered by our varying emotions". They go on to define emotions as "the flow of information perceived to be essential for the survival of any particular state of consciousness being observed" (ibid., p. 136).

In the 1990s, Southgate, co-founder of the Institute for Self Analysis (now renamed The Bowlby Centre) in London, had proposed that "the associating multiple person is the healthy norm" (1989). Multi-tasking demonstrates an everyday faculty we take for granted when we divide our conscious attention between completely different activities. Similarly, steering a car "on autopilot" is a common trance-like experience for most drivers on familiar routes while part of their consciousness is engaged elsewhere.

We regularly journey in our minds to other times and places in much the same way as when we carry out everyday tasks that do not require all our attention. We can thus be preoccupied with thoughts of something totally at variance with what we are doing. This distracted state is more evident when we are worried about something, and negative thoughts intrude at inopportune times despite every effort by our conscious mind to keep them at bay.

In Pert and Marriott's view, we have multiple selves, each with its own "thoughts, emotions, physical reality, and even the soul or spirit" (2006, p. 135). They suggest that, through meditation and other centring practices, we can become more aware of and "anchor" our "inner helper" or "higher self" as our "central organizing consciousness". They believe that this can assist us to understand, accept, and forgive our hurt or dysfunctional aspects in order to develop healthy selves-esteem.

The idea of having different selves or parts or levels of consciousness between which we switch constantly and without awareness, and from which we act, react, and interact, is not new. Freud had suggested an id, ego, and superego hierarchy; Perls coined the terms "top dog" and "under dog" to describe dominant and submissive aspects of our personality, while transactional analysis (Berne, 1961) postulates an elaborate structure of adult, parent and child selves to explain how we tend to operate, functionally or not, when we heed our critical "inner voices" that judge and condemn us without pity.

Hitlin (2002) refers to "Edge-figures—subpersonalities, shadows, demons, gremlins, introjects, Inner Children, archetypes—who are invested, for better or for worse, in keeping you from going past your edges" (p. 29). Hitlin defines "edges" as psychological barriers or self-limiting beliefs learnt from parental figures and previous negative experiences.

Hitlin recommends making affirmative statements that acknowledge both the difficulty and our innate potential for overcoming it while tapping on certain acupressure points, as in emotional freedom technique (EFT) or Tapas acupressure technique (TAT). Both therapies draw on western cognitive therapy and the eastern (Chinese) meridian system of energy. They aim to rebalance blocked energies in the body and connect right (emotional) and left (thinking) hemispheres of the brain.

Ford (1998) believes that it is vital to acknowledge our "shadow" aspects:

To get past your ego and its defences you need to get quiet, be brave, and listen to your inner voices. Behind our social masks lie thousands of faces. Each face has a personality of its own. Each personality has its own unique characteristics. By having internal dialogues with these sub-personalities you will turn your egotistical prejudices and judgments into priceless treasures. . . .

Examining our sub-personalities can be a tool to help us reclaim the lost parts of ourselves. First, we must identify these parts and then we must name them, then we'll be able to disengage from them. Actually naming them creates distance. [pp. 92–93]

Following Whitfield (1987), I consider it essential for us to connect with and heal our hurt "inner child selves", as experienced at different ages (perhaps visualized as in a set of Russian nesting dolls). We can then fully utilize our adult competencies and skills in everyday functioning instead of being helplessly driven by our hurt child aspects. Through play and meditation, we can develop

Figure 5.   Selves in development.

our magical, wise, and playful child aspects, since these link us to our creativity, in-tuition and inner knowing, and, indeed, to the divine being in us all: what Pert and Marriott and others refer to as our higher self, or even soul or spirit.

Identification with the oppressor

The power imbalance between a child and abusive or dismissive adults in her life can lead to her developing a very negative self-view and inhibit her exploration of her real potential. The adults' "judgement" of her may be enforced consciously or unconsciously through processes of external or internalised oppression (re-evaluation counselling: see www.michelinemason.com for a discussion of internalised oppression). These can so distort her self-perception, as in a hall of mirrors, that it may come to bear little or no resemblance to her reality.

Alleyne (2007) has developed the concept of "internal oppressor" specifically in relation to racism. She argues that, "The oppressor is an aspect of the self that functions as an inhibitor, an internal adversary and enemy. It is distinct from internalised oppression, which is the process of negative racial internalization" (p. 271).

This dynamic occurs so commonly, and usually unconsciously, in other global oppressions, such as adultism, sexism, ethnocentrism, ageism, ablism, heterosexism, etc., that it might be very difficult for a person oppressed in one or more of these ways to achieve and/or maintain awareness of her core or true self and feel liberated enough to claim her inherent right to self-definition and, therefore, self-judgement. Continued abuse or social oppression of any kind can completely distort our innate sense of who we are and what we are capable of, so leading to self-putdowns, self-sabotage and even selves-oppression.

A mother or primary carer does not have to be clinically depressed, or narcissistic, or have a personality disorder to damage or stunt the growth of a baby's true self. If a parent has internalized oppression of any kind and accepted a false judgement about himself, he is likely to hold up the same "distorting mirror" to his children (Figure 6). A common version of this phenomenon might be the harsh superego (Freud) or parental voices (Bowlby), which unremittingly attack or criticize the child self.

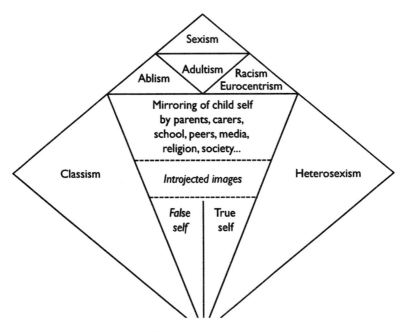

Figure 6. "A hall of mirrors": distorted sense of self.

Without informed support, it might be very difficult to see or acknowledge systematic oppression. Our false self/selves tend to be abusive to the true self in oneself or others, devaluing and denying innate self-worth and potential. Social institutions come into being which reinforce distorting images of the self and others who are similar. These maintain the status quo, which is inherently in favour of the dominant majority and, therefore, oppressive to minorities.

Language is a primary tool of oppression *or* liberation, since it can distort or clarify images of the self, and the other. Unsurprisingly, therefore, minorities of any kind are often described in unflattering terms in relation to the majority. There are few positive connotations of "black" in contrast to the multitude for "white"; similarly for feminine and masculine; gay and heterosexual; old and young; child and adult; disabled and able-bodied, etc. As neurolinguistic programming (NLP) reminds us, language is seldom neutral, being coloured by our acquired view of the world around us: "The map is not the territory".

Dissociative identity disorder

Children who are physically, emotionally, and/or sexually abused by their parents or carers are caught in an impossible dilemma, since the very person who should protect them and meet their needs is a danger to them. The child has no workable strategy to keep himself safe *and* attached to his abusive carer, and so he might develop chaotic or *disorganized attachment* behaviours.

A child in this situation might split off her needy aspects, and identify with the abusive carer against her vulnerable self and others like her. Miller (1987, pp. 281–284) and other writers on child abuse have described this common psychological defence of identification with the aggressor: unable to protect herself from abuse or invasion (physical, sexual, emotional, or psychic) or to end it, the child might learn to survive her maltreatment by justifying it. She internalizes the abuser's negative view of herself and others like her, and maltreats herself and/or them in a similar way.

If a child's persisting neediness and/or vulnerability become intolerable to her abuser self, it may then seek to punish the abused victim part of herself for continuing to hold up this "mirror". Self-splitting is, thus, a useful way to think about incidents of severe self-harm where one "self" might literally seek to punish or kill off another "self" that is blamed for the abuse suffered, because of the unbearable levels of emotional pain associated with it (Sachs, 2005).

The child may dissociate and identify with the oppressor against her perceived negative aspects so as to protect her true self from further violation and what might be experienced as a threat of total annihilation. The more severe and prolonged the abuse, the more splitting occurs, with the likelihood of multiple identities being spontaneously created by the self for survival in different threatening situations.

Gloria Steinem explains the development of multiple personality disorder (MPD), now commonly referred to as dissociative identity disorder (DID):

> As is now known, MPD is almost always the result of frequent, sadistic, erratic, and uncontrollable abuse in childhood by someone on whom the child is dependent; abuse so intolerable that children learn to dissociate from it through a form of self-hypnosis and so escape into a "different" person who does not feel the pain. Having

once split off from the core personality, this "alter" begins to acquire a separate life history, complete with distinctive manner-isms, behaviour, and social relationships, almost as if it were a person born at the moment of "splitting". Once this ability to disso-ciate has proven to be a valuable way of surviving and dealing with the world, alters continue to be born to meet different needs and demands. [Steinem, 1992]

Selves-splitting is a complex defence mechanism to which persons with DID may resort as a creative but extreme response to repeated and unbearable early trauma. Sadly, what helps their psyche to survive in their early life may be inimical to their every-day functioning later on.

Verena's story

I worked with a highly intelligent and creative young woman for several years, during which we became aware of her unconscious facil-ity for switching personae if she felt under threat of any sort. This led to "her" frequent loss of time and history when in another "personal-ity". Hearing Verena's stories of multiple abuse within her own family, and then in the care system, which totally failed her time and time again during her childhood, adolescence, and young adulthood, I real-ized how her very being had been repeatedly assaulted by adults to whose care she had been entrusted. DID became her survival strategy, her only alternative to death or going totally insane.

As I learnt more about her mother who had also been severely abused as a child, I realized that, perhaps from infancy onwards, Verena had needed to develop different personae to relate to her mother's chang-ing alter states in order to survive their murderous attacks on her core self. The wonder was that Verena was not only still alive, but had not become completely mad herself, and that, despite all her hurt, she was very strongly connected to her intuitive and spiritual selves. The self that brought Verena to therapy was a deeply wounded but very sensi-tive, empathic, articulate, clear-thinking, and compassionate person. However, she already feared having a child herself and, unawarely, treating him as she had been.

So, a victim of abuse may resort to self-harm and/or become an abuser himself if he unconsciously displaces his own justifiable rage at the abuse and his hatred of the abuser onto himself or others whom he perceives to be vulnerable and from whom he does not fear retaliation. These might include babies, small children, pets, elderly persons or those with physical or mental disabilities or other negatively viewed aspects in various oppressions, as in racism, ethnocentrism, homophobia, etc.

People with DID can switch personalities quite dramatically, and without any "central organizing consciousness" orchestrating such shifts or even being aware that other "selves" may be "impersonating" them (Costner Sizemore & Sain Pittillo, 1979; Pert & Marriott, 2006, p. 133, describing Frank Putnam's work). As a generalization, it seems that very young children, and girls in particular, might be more likely to dissociate in response to repeated and unbearable trauma, while older traumatized children, and especially boys, may be in a permanent state of hyper-arousal (Cairns, 2002, p. 61).

*   *   *

Attachment-disordered children are hypervigilant, alert to any perceived threat of abandonment or attack as affecting their very survival. Their biochemically programmed survival responses of *fight*, *flight*, or *freeze* are constantly triggered by primitive emotions that flood their whole being at cellular level, not just their limbic brain. Pert and Marriott (2006, p. 136) consider that such feelings are as powerful as drugs, with similar impact on our physiology.

This could explain such children's lightning changes in mood, behaviour, and, it seems, in personality, too, when they can suddenly switch before their carer's astonished eyes from a calm and pleasant child to a raging out-of-control house-wrecker, like a Dr Jekyll–Mr Hyde character.

I recall a small, severely abused six-year-old boy in a foster home explaining his table and chair-throwing exploits with mingled pride and puzzlement: "I am very strong when I am angry!" Foster carers will sometimes comment on how such a child might roll her eyes upward before these sudden mood swings. It is as if she has spontaneously learnt to put herself into a trance state in order to deal with what might feel like a threat to her very existence or core self. (See p. 23, above, Van Gulden, 2002, on "paratactic distortions".)

*   *   *

Roet (2000, pp. 91–92) compares the hyper-aroused states of trau-matized persons, who are constantly on "red alert", to leaving an alarm in a previously burgled house switched on indiscriminately all the time. This would be both inefficient and cause a lot of distressing noise for the occupants and neighbours.

Roet recommends the use of trance work by skilled hypnother-apists to help the conscious mind communicate with that part of the unconscious that might be stuck in time (often going back to child-hood, when the original trauma may have occurred). Roet suggests that this "part" or "self" needs updated information, based on a realistic assessment of the current level of danger and the adult's resourcefulness in the present, in order to deal more effectively with such eventualities than would have been possible for her child self in the past. This is, in effect, a rewriting of her personal narrative.

It is important to note that such work requires great care and skill and is often part of "inner child healing". This can include self-hypnosis, which is extremely powerful since—as in NLP change-work—it combines visualization, auditory suggestions, and kinaesthetic experiences, linking left and right hemispheres of the brain. Such therapy can be used to heal painful memories from childhood through the adult's revisiting the past in imagination as an advocate for his child self while having full access to his current resources and knowledge, as well as compassion for his younger self in that traumatic situation. Like other energy work, inner child healing should only be undertaken within a safe therapeutic frame-work and by appropriately qualified and experienced practitioners.

* * *

Neurolinguistic programming (NLP) specializes in emotional "change-work", which is often done in light trance. Thus, NLP offers valuable background pieces of the body–mind jigsaw puzzle of quantal healing. As children, we internalize adults' views of ourselves and our families and the outside world; these may be liberating or oppressive, e.g., critical parent voices and family mirroring. NLP gives us the tools with which to challenge mistaken or outdated thinking, boost our self-image, set goals for ourselves more consciously, and generally improve the quality of our lives, irrespective of family scripts.

NLP is the study of *how* we perceive "reality" (through our senses) and, through our acquired views and selective use of language, *give meaning to* the world and our experiences of it. Our perceptions of reality are, thus, shaped by the stories we hear about and tell ourselves, and the family scripts, values and beliefs, and role models we adopt. We may communicate positively or negatively with ourselves and others to co-create our ongoing "reality" in an often unconscious, but self-reinforcing way. Thus, our "map" might not represent at all the "territory" we seek to traverse.

The name "NLP" is derived from *neurological*: our "body–mind" and sensory processing of information; *linguistics*: our use of language and its impact on our thoughts and feelings and physiology, as well as on other people, and theirs on us; and *programming*: how we sequence our thoughts and actions to achieve our goals, consciously or not.

To achieve more challenging goals, we can model ourselves on others who have achieved them by observing how they speak and act and copying exactly what they do.

The founders of NLP, Richard Bandler and John Grinder, began by studying brilliant communicators. They sought to model excellence and resourceful states through their keen observation of the work of such geniuses as Virginia Satir, Milton Erikson, and Fritz Perls. Bandler and Grinder wished to explore whether others could replicate the results of these outstanding therapists by mimicking exactly *what* they did and said, and, most importantly, *how*: through imitating their body language, including posture, facial expression, tone, breathing, etc.

NLP emphasizes *pacing before leading*: first building rapport with the client through paying close attention to his "eye-accessing cues" and the verbal predicates used—whether mainly visual, auditory, or kinaesthetic (feeling) words and phrases—in order to establish and match his preferred mode of communication, including nonverbally. Only then will habitual language and thought patterns and behaviours be challenged to help a depressed patient, for example, to radically alter his negative thinking, feelings, and physiology (including posture and breathing) and get himself into a more resourceful state of functioning.

Indeed, the thinking behind NLP "parts reframing" and "neurological levels" change-work assumes that we all have different states or aspects, some of which may appear to be dysfunctional and even self-sabotaging. However, the *intention* behind our behaviours is usually benign and self-protective, as in the concept of defences in psychoanalysis. Van Gulden (2005) recommends working with troubled children in a way that makes them aware that they have more resourceful "parts" that they can *choose* to develop and access "if not now, then some day soon" to resolve a particular behaviour problem.

Gloria Steinem, a radical seer, reframes in a thought-provoking way the human capacity for "dissociation", noting that this can include even gender changes:

> what would happen if the rest of us could acquire for positive reasons the abilities these accidental prophets have learned for negative ones. If such extraordinary abilities can be summoned to help survive the worst of human situations, they are also there to create the best. What if we could harness this unbelievable potential of body and mind? . . .
>
> People in different alters can change every body movement, perfect a musical or linguistic talent that is concealed to the host personality, have two or even three menstrual cycles in the same body, and handle social and physical tasks of which they literally do not think themselves capable. [Steinem, 1992, p. 318]

Storytelling, myths, metaphors, and scripts

Survivors of abuse or oppression often remain stuck in their initial reactions to trauma or loss, when they experience shock, numbness, and/or denial, sometimes with somatic symptoms. This deadening response to intense pain might help them to get through otherwise intolerable situations, but they then pay the price in existing rather than living.

Weil (2002) explains that

> Traumatic experiences are stored in different areas of the brain at the same time . . . The person is captivated by the trauma. The amygdala stays extremely sensitised . . .
>
> In the area of the neocortex (front brain) coping strategies are developed, in an attempt to overcome the traumatisation by

unconsciously re-enacting measures. Those script patterns, that were developed in an attempt to cope with conflicts, are experienced as cognitive, emotional, behavioural and physiological limitations.

Beneath every basic belief of the life script lies a specific set of trauma blocks within the limbic system. Every trauma block in turn provokes processes of script formation and script maintenance within the frontal area of the brain . . . the life script can be understood as "avoidance attitudes"—motivated by the illusionary intent to avoid retraumatising experiences in the future.

To cure the script, integrative therapy must address both areas of the brain, where traumatizations are stored . . .

Meridian-based Psychotherapy and Counselling (MPC) procedures allow to directly address the limbic system. They resolve blocks between amygdala and hippocampus *and withdraw the energetic basis of the script* . . . the trauma moves to a far distance, that is, finds an adequate place in the person's history. [Weil, 2002, p. 168, my emphasis]

Story telling

A primary task in therapy is to help the individual or family to be aware of their (usually unconscious) personal or family beliefs, myths, or scripts, and decide how functional these might be and what might need changing. Erikson's use in his hypnotic work of storytelling and creating new metaphors for healing was noted to be particularly effective in accessing more resourceful states ("parts" or "selves") in his clients, since stories help to connect left and right hemispheres in the brain.

Connor (2001) explains this commonly-used NLP process:

Stories, analogies and parables are the best way of accessing unconscious resources and Erickson was a master of telling stories that not only engaged the client, but also held the key to solving their problem. He would construct metaphors where the story line paralleled the client's problem and then, as the story was resolved, the client was able to bring the resources that were suggested in the story into their own situation.

A simple use of metaphor in the Milton Model is . . . where objects are credited with powers they do not have. These are used extensively in fairy stories and legends, for example: "The walls have ears . . .". "See how time flies." "Be still and let the room tell you its secrets . . .." [p. 182]

A common way to help a survivor to move on from traumatic or disabling experiences is to encourage her to "tell her story" to a safe and supportive audience in the context of counselling or therapy or in a self-help group, where she is *not* disbelieved, or judged and condemned for what has happened. Whitfield (1987) explains that, through the experience of feeling heard, a person gets to hear the "story" herself. In then "retelling her story", she can explore different versions and her full range of emotional reactions until, eventually, she feels able to let go the hurt and to heal and move on. The client in "Verena's Story", above, would often say that she was "bored" with having so much pain, and wanted to just get on with living; this felt like her natural impulse towards health.

Cozolino (2006, p. 32) describes how, as an adult psychotherapist, he serves as "an external neural circuit or auxiliary executive system". He helps his clients to piece together their previously unarticulated stories from seemingly random clues to repressed traumatic memories and their sensory cues from the environment. Cozolino believes that "Therapy and other healing relationships utilize all levels of connection—from metabolic regulation to narratives—to alter neural network activation and balance" (*ibid.*, p. 33).

Creating shared family stories

In presenting his work with a bereft family, Byng-Hall (1995, pp. 250–257) has highlighted the importance of "telling stories" as a shared task. Since children may be at very different levels of development and understanding, he helps the family to create a shared, coherent story; in this way, even very young children can, as they grow up, learn "what happened". Byng-Hall believes that the story has to be fundamentally true, though not necessarily the whole truth. So, the story must have "room to grow" in order that the children can hear more bits of it as they get older and have increased understanding.

The story has also to be congruent with the family's culture and beliefs about death and/or other losses. So, the therapist's task is to find out what the *grieving script* is for the family, and also to construct her own story of "what happened". Such an approach can be usefully applied to doing gradated life story work with children and families.

* * *

Daniel Stern (1985, p. 110) has observed how, from infancy on, everyday care-giving rituals and interactions gradually serve to create a RIG (representation of interaction that is generalized). RIGs build up for the baby over time an internal working model (Bowlby, 1969; Craik, 1943) of how her family operate, and the particular role or *identity* she is allocated in it.

A child may be typecast, so that only certain behaviours and attitudes of hers are selectively attuned to, reinforced, or sanctioned by her parents. Gender stereotyping is common in many cultures, with girls being socialized to smile and "look happy", while boys are discouraged from crying or showing any vulnerability. Counter-identities, or other selves, may develop in opposition to such type-casting, if it is felt to be too restrictive or oppressive towards the core or true self.

Byng-Hall (1995) notes that family scripts are historical, usually intergenerational, and tend to lead to unconscious *replication* in adult life, so requiring more conscious attempts at *correction* or *improvisation* to adapt to changed circumstances.

Marcia's story

I worked briefly with a mother, Marcia, who had survived repeated assaults on her, including rape, by the father of her youngest son, Gino. Marcia presented as an independent and feisty woman with a mind of her own. She had a strong network of "sisters" in the neighbourhood, who supported her care of her children by providing regular respite as and when needed until Gino started having such violent outbursts that no one would help Marcia out any longer with childcare for him. She became increasingly ill with stress and her children then became carers for her in a reversal of roles. This totally undermined her authority as a parent over them.

Marcia had always had a conflicted relationship with her own chronically ill mother, and so she initially chose a *corrective family script* of "a strong mother" to help her to be a more effective parent to her children. However, whenever Gino showed any aggressive impulses, Marcia began to identify her small son with his violent father, who had terrorized her throughout that pregnancy. For his part, having been continually "alarmed" by his father's assaults on Marcia while in her womb and during his first few months of life, Gino was very difficult to soothe. His "fight" responses were quickly triggered by any perceived threat to his being.

By the time he was a year old, Gino had already been typecast as a budding young psychopath who would follow in his father's and grandfather's footsteps. True to role, which he could not give up without adult help, Gino began to terrorize his mother and much older and bigger brothers and sisters with his increasingly violent assaults on them whenever they teased or thwarted him.

Predictably, Gino ended up in the "care" system and went through a series of foster homes, which he disrupted through his aggressive behaviours, before being placed at ten years old in a small children's home in a different county. After a very difficult start when he continually assaulted members of staff, Gino began reluctantly to settle down and accept the unit's rigid structure. With few and far between visits from his mother, Gino could now try out new roles that were less aggressive and even quite disarming.

Marcia's projections were so powerful that, at first, it was difficult for me and other adults to separate Gino from them and see him for the sad, lonely, and frustrated child he actually was. Marcia, however, could not accept him in another role and, during her infrequent visits to the home, she would quite unconsciously provoke him into reverting to more aggressive behaviours towards her or staff. Or Marcia would get into "sick" role, requiring nurturing and attention from staff as well as Gino.

The professionals reluctantly decided to suspend her contact with her young son until Gino could feel more confident in his new non-aggressive role at the unit and engage in a more appropriate child–mother relationship with Marcia. She was offered counselling locally to help her look at how she was unconsciously *replicating* her sick mother's script and, instead, to *improvise* new and healthier ways of relating to her children, especially Gino, who was meanwhile being supported by the staff in rewriting his personal story.

*   *   *

Feinstein (2002) suggests that "personal myths function not only as biochemically-coded models of reality, but also as fields of information" (p. 99). Personal myths are "organising models that shape perception, understanding and behaviour and emerge from four sources: biology, personal history, culture and transcendent experiences" (*ibid.*, p. 100).

Feinstein believes that "psychophysiological forms and mythic fields are linked by resonance" and that new "mythic fields become established when new patterns of understanding are initiated and repeated" (*ibid.*, p. 102). More intriguingly, and perhaps controversially, Eden, who can "see" mythic fields in colour in a person's aura, describes this transition:

> When a new myth has become more than an idea and has begun to take a stable physical form, it begins to infiltrate the auric bands changing some of their colours. Its energy will be less dense and move more quickly than the energy of the old myth. As a new myth begins to take hold, at first it looks faint to me, but with time it becomes more distinct. . . . I can see the energy of an old myth doing all it can to hold on, like hot tar. If it gets stuck that way for a long period, physical illness often follows. [*ibid.*, p. 103]

Energy psychology

"Energy psychology" is a generic term given to a range of treatments of the body's energy system that address emotional difficulties and self-limiting beliefs in a prescribed format. These treatments include thought field therapy (TFT), created by Roger Callaghan; emotional freedom technique (EFT), by Gary Craig); EmoTrance (ET), by Sylvia Hartmann); and Tapas acupressure technique (TAT), by Tapas Fleming).

Pert (2005), the neuroscientist and biophysicist who coined the term "molecules of emotion", explains the interplay of mind and body:

Emotions and thoughts initiate a series of cascading chemical and cellular events—including the formation of new neurons—that are the basis of other emotions and thoughts. Some studies suggest, in fact, that meditation may cause neurological shifts that are as potent as our most effective medications for alleviating anxiety and depression. . . . Energy interventions impact the body's intricate electrochemical system as well as more subtle energies. [Pert, 2005, pp. xi–xii]

EFT, which draws on acupressure and cognitive therapy, and eye movement desentization and reprocessing (EMDR), created by Francine Shapiro, are among the newer "energy therapies" that seem to offer amazingly rapid results (Mollon, 2005).

EFT is quite simple to use and can easily be taught for self-help purposes, even to children. It is increasingly being used with children as well as adults in Europe and the USA to address "core issues" arising from early abandonment and abuse and to facilitate emotional and even physical healing sometimes, often with quite dramatic results. (See Gary Craig's website, www.emofree.com and Conference proceedings on "Psychological trauma and the body", September 2007, London, CONFER.)

EFT and EMDR are among the repertoire of therapies used in the Traumatic Stress Service at the Maudsley Hospital in London. Both therapies facilitate body–mind connections, bridging left hemispheric thinking and language functions with right hemispheric emotional and somatic processing of often repressed early memories.

It is generally accepted that, in order to heal from pre-verbal traumatic experiences stored in the body, they need to be safely recalled and articulated: "Those who cannot remember the past are condemned to repeat it" (Santayana, 1905, p. 1).

NLP and some of the newer "energy" therapies like EFT and EmoTrance seek to deal with the emotional impact of repressed memories without retraumatizing the client. As with inner child healing and other specialized forms of therapy, such work should only be carried out by skilled and appropriately qualified practitioners within a strict therapeutic framework.

Interestingly, NLP emphasizes the importance of "anchoring" resourceful states rather than painful and vulnerable ones. So, trauma work tends to be done using a technique of "dissociation" and distancing words or even numbers to represent the painful experience being talked about. The intention is to minimize the risk of retraumatizing the client, and possible abreaction.

* * *

Any therapy that can anchor more positive emotional states in attachment-disordered children, to replace their early learnt instinctual responses of terror and rage, should help to reduce their destructive mood shifts by "rewiring the brain" to create new "emotional" synapses to their underdeveloped front brain. Such optimistic views of the plasticity of the "social and emotional brain" tend to inform parent–infant psychotherapy and attachment therapies, whatever their orientation, rather than the social determinism that sometimes seems to be implied in studies of mothers' attachment styles to predict their babies' future relationship patterns.

The reality is that there are many variables which can influence the outcome: the child's temperament, genetic endowment, natural resilience, physical and mental capacity, and environmental influences, including attachments to other significant adults and siblings. The parent's recourse to family scripts (Byng-Hall, 1995), her own resources and support network, as well as her innate capacity for healing, will all contribute to shaping her developing relationship with her child.

Interestingly, meditation practice at school assemblies has been introduced in a number of primary schools in England with reportedly calming effects on pupils. (Presentation of new initiatives in schools at a Ministry for Peace public meeting at the House of Commons, London, in December 2004.) Safe massage techniques are also being taught to children in British schools through the fast-developing "Massage in Schools Programme", created by Mia Elmslater of Sweden and Sylvie Hetu of Canada. Their belief in the beneficial effects of touch on the body–mind is so great that their "vision is that every child attending school experience positive and nurturing touch every day . . . everywhere in the world" (see MISP website, www.massageinschools.com).

The global interest in traditional healing practices is already linking eastern and western medicine and complementary therapies. Energy psychology therapies such as EFT and TAT integrate acupressure with cognitive therapy. Similarly, through "tapping" on the Chinese meridian energy system, the American creators of Brain Gym describe the benefits for children, adults, and even business organizations of various simple exercises that link different parts of the brain. For instance,

> Positive Points are acupressure points located above the centre of each eyebrow. They are specifically known for diffusing the fight-or-flight reflex, thus releasing emotional stress. Touching these points transfer the brain response to stress from the midbrain to the front part of the brain, allowing a more rational response. [Dennison, Dennison, & Teplitz, 1994, p. 51]

In this way, bodywork and other touch-based and energy therapies are finding validation in the new body–mind paradigm of healing ("Power of touch" Conference, November 2007, London: CONFER). So, ironically, neuroscience research has provided a meeting ground for more traditional psychotherapists as well as complementary therapists, NLP, and the newer energy psychology practitioners who consciously work towards integration of right and left hemispheres of the brain.

CHAPTER TWO

Background to the development of CAT: a programme for fostering mutual attachment between child and carer

The story of CAT. Phase 1: 1995–1996

J ust as each family has its own complex history, with members contributing different perspectives, so do projects such as this one. The four CAT therapists involved in the pilot (Maggie Gall, Margaret Saxby, Pauline Sear, and myself) came to it with our own family stories, and conscious and unconscious motivations for wanting to make a difference to children living outside their families by helping them to form healthy new attachments.

All four of us were agreed that we wanted a *"child-centred* attachment therapy"; hence the name, CAT, rather than the adult- or parent-centred therapies that seemed to prevail at the time. This did not mean that control-hungry children should be allowed to take over, but that the carers should be supported in staying in charge as parents while respecting their child as a little person in his or her own right, with individual needs and feelings and personal and family stories.

Therefore, we felt very strongly that *intrusive holding therapies* were contraindicated for children who have already been physically, sexually, and/or emotionally abused. We agreed at the outset that physical holding would *not* be part of the therapy, unless it occurred spontaneously in a session, initiated by either the child or carer. In any case, as ℭAT therapists, *we* would not engage in such holding.

Maeja's story

I qualified as a social worker in London in 1974 and soon began to specialize in adoption and fostering work. This background experience complemented my training in the early 1990s, both as an attachment-based psychoanalytic psychotherapist with the Institute for Self-Analysis (now known as The Bowlby Centre), and as a parent–infant psychotherapist at The School of Infant Mental Health in London. What I did not know at the time was that Rose's and Emily's stories were pivotal to my professional development and interests.

I had felt greatly inspired when reading, in the early 1980s, about Fraiberg and her multi-disciplinary team's pioneering attachment work in the USA with struggling young families. Then, in the early 1990s, after watching videos of Acquarone's and Watanabe's psychotherapy with babies and mothers in London and Japan, I began to believe that negative attachment patterns formed by adults through their own childhood experiences do not have to define and limit their relationships with their own children in turn.

My own struggles as a parent made me more compassionate towards others, and I became increasingly interested in helping to foster parent–child bonding wherever possible. Like Emily, I had an "aha" moment when I suddenly realized the healing implications of helping stuck families to understand and implement the basic bonding cycle (Figure 1, p. 9).

I was very fortunate to be based at the time at a local family-finding unit where three of my Social Services colleagues—Pauline Sear, Dr Maggie Gall and Margaret Saxby—were immediately enthusiastic about putting ℭAT into practice and contributing their very different skills, knowledge, and experience to it.

Pauline's story

Pauline came to ℭAT with several years' experience of supporting struggling families whose children were considered by social workers to be especially vulnerable. In Pauline's words:

Along life's road other people also shape and put into focus things we may have not tapped into in our unaware mind. So it was for me, years ago now, when I attended an "Inner Child" workshop facilitated by Maeja. Little did I consciously know then that this day would change my life. Through work and new friendships, I realized a new passion, still with me today, to work alongside struggling children and families. These experiences provided a safe haven for my own Inner Child to heal, although of course I did not know that at the time, nor how greatly I was affected by learning about Gemma's story.

Somewhere deep inside, though, my Inner Child could identify with little Gemma's thoughts and feelings. Without being in any way conscious of how I would use my own childhood experiences to advantage years later, somewhere, somehow, a strength was forming. In a strange way, this worked alongside old hurt and anger, which provided me with the gut-essential tools to much later work alongside troubled and hurt children.

I began to assemble some bits and bobs of things in a box to start to do some direct work with children and families as a way of helping them to communicate when perhaps they were unable to say what they meant or even know how they felt. This seemed a fitting way in which to begin to work more closely with families through observing the attachment/interaction between them rather than asking direct questions, as was usually the case then for most workers involved in family work.

In some small way, this seemed to work with most of the families, and made good use of the time spent with troubled children as they dived into the box of "goodies" and made up all sorts of stories, where otherwise they would have been reluctant to talk for whatever reason. This time was both fun (especially if the parents or carers participated), moving, and spoke volumes about the children's inner self, as each child made sense of their world as it really was, without prompting or telling them what to do. A box of sand, a box of toys or "creatures" will do more than any amount of spoken words when you are working with a very hurt and/or angry child. It provides a safe haven for the child "to be", as we would discover over time.

Time moved on with my direct work with children gaining momentum. I began training at a London college in Play Therapy, and made more use of the toys and "creatures" in my day-to-day work. I was soon fortunate enough to be invited to spend one day a week at a local family-finding unit, which was engaged in preparing children for new adoptive families. As it happened, Maeja was already working there, and soon we were supporting our first "attachment-disordered" child and his parents. Serendipity or what, but that was the start of ℂAT.

Time passed until the day came when Maeja and I "set up shop" locally to provide support to foster families, adoptive families, and birth and step-families. The ℂAT Programme was now in full swing.

Maggie's story

When I first became involved in what was to become ℂAT, I was working as a Senior Social Work Practitioner at a small family-finding unit. With colleagues in the adoption team, my work focused on supporting adoptive parents post placement, and encouraging them to form strong and lasting attachments to their new family members.

At first I felt that the ℂAT Programme simply represented what I considered to be good practice: what every social worker should be doing during home visits. However, the structured ways of working and the actual way the Programme is put together makes it a unique and specialized form of intervention, one which I would later commission on an independent basis for another local authority.

Margaret's story

Margaret now lives in France and runs a guest-house there, still helping families with her generous hospitality and (in)famous sense of humour. She came to ℂAT with twenty years' experience of working with children at the family-finding unit, and supporting their new carers. Margaret soon discovered that she had a gift for such work, having started it on an informal basis; she went on to specialize in "direct work with children". Margaret is pragmatic, so her belief in ℂAT from the outset lent it a much-needed "grassroots" seal of approval.

*   *   *

The ℂAT Programme came into being initially as a conceptual framework for working with bereft children and adoptive parents, who each have to acknowledge and mourn their losses before they can move on to form positive new parent–child attachments (Figure 7a,b).

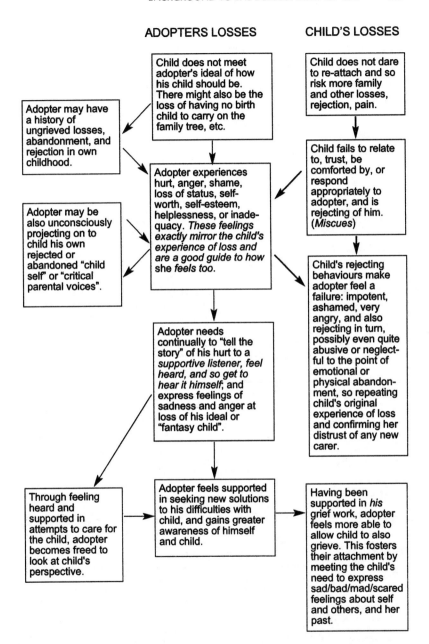

Figure 7(a).   Loss and grief work for adoptive parents of very hurt children.

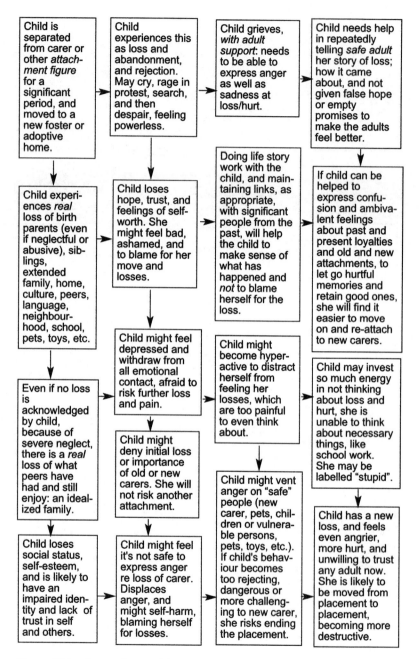

Figure 7(b).   Separation and loss issues for bereaved children. Griefwork needed in fostering and adoption placements.

Ghosts from the past: the carer's or child's previous history of relationships, can get in the way of either one being able to give the other appropriate *cues* and *responses*. Old hurts and unmet expectations from the past may distort current communication between child and carer. The child may not meet the "fantasy" of the carer, and interactions then become increasingly negative. This will force the child into false self, or people-pleasing, mode to survive, until she cannot repress her *real* feelings any longer and explodes in frustration, to her and everyone else's dismay.

Equally, the carer may not be the "fantasy parent" of the child, and so he does not get validation as being good enough. He might then reject the child and the placement could end, with the child having to move to another family, where this negative cycle starts all over again.

The timing for our CAT proposal was fortuitous: The Director of our local Social Services Department at that time was particularly interested in Vera Fahlberg's work on attachment, and CAT had freely incorporated her ideas on "positive and negative interaction cycles" (1991) and for fostering attachments. We had a new County Adoption Manager who was willing to act on the Director's interest and help our small team combine theory and practice to pilot the CAT Programme for the county. And we had agreement from our local managers to allocate precious time to developing, piloting, and evaluating CAT over the following twelve months.

We began with experiential training for ourselves by answering an abbreviated version of Main's adult attachment interview (AAI) questionnaire. This had a powerful impact and made us aware of the need to first test on ourselves any such exercise in gaining self-awareness before expecting families to do the same. It remained an important principle in our work with CAT families. I was therefore interested to learn that Byng-Hall encouraged his trainee family therapists at the Tavistock Clinic in London to do their own genogram in group supervision; "the aim is to explore the supervisee's 'caring' script—that is, the script that brought them into the caring profession, and in particular into family therapy" (Byng-Hall, 1995, p. 133).

We had initially intended that one of us would train in administering the AAI questionnaire ourselves, so that we could use it as a research measure at the beginning and end of work with each family. However, time and money constraints made this impossible. So we devised "Child and parent attachment behaviours" questionnaires for parents to complete (see Appendices A1 and A2). These were derived from Fahlberg's very helpful developmental guides to attachment behaviours (1991, Appendices).

Conceiving and co-developing the project in one year from theoretical framework to therapeutic practice was an amazing story of synchronistic events:

- a child care social worker's sudden labelling as "attachment-disordered" of a child already on referral to me;
- the recent dissemination of new learning from the USA about reactive attachment disorder by PPIAS, a self-help group of adopters (now known as Adoption UK); and
- our very useful learning from the Post-Adoption Centre in London, which had included our "attachment-disordered" child and family in their own new attachment therapy pilot project during the summer of 1995. Pauline Sear and I provided the necessary preparation, support, and follow-up to the family after their "intensive week" (see family C, Chapter Four).

These events were followed by a series of unexpected encounters with various colleagues around the county, all of whom boosted our belief in the therapeutic value of our proposed child and family attachment programme. However, during the first six months of our developing the project, Family Finders staff suffered an unprecedented number of accidents, serious illnesses, and even deaths in their immediate families. These almost totally disabled our small CAT team, since three members and our team manager suffered concurrent personal and family losses.

Nevertheless, we felt that CAT was "a gift from the universe", which we had a responsibility to develop and share in order to help families struggling with attachment difficulties. This remained our ethos through all the trials and tribulations of the following year, although I often felt I was scouting ahead through very difficult terrain on my own.

The pilot project was very small as a result, and this may have influenced our managers' views on CAT's potential, despite a positive evaluation by a senior Social Services researcher at the time.

Pauline and I then decided to offer CAT independently, and we continued to do so for the following ten years.

We learnt slowly but surely that we *had* been inspired. CAT is based on very simple attachment principles that can be easily taught to families and professionals who are willing to learn. It is a cost-effective, brief family intervention (four to six months usually) that can make a positive difference to a lot of unhappy children and parents. We have also used the CAT framework for therapeutic assessments of several struggling families to salvage failing placements, and to assess sibling and family attachments, and complex contact arrangements, in order to make recommendations to placing agencies and the Courts. (See Chapter Six.)

Dealing with loss

There were enormous gains through our making new professional friendships and the cross-fertilization of our varied learning and experience. These were, however, almost offset by the series of losses suffered by staff at the family-finding unit where CAT was based. In the first six months of the project, seven of the eleven staff members experienced a major loss of this kind through a sudden accident to, or the serious illness and/or death of, a family member. These disasters, one almost every week, became a major threat to the survival of the project right at its inception.

It was as if we as CAT therapists had to be reminded of the incapacitating effects of loss, and the need to acknowledge and mourn it, before we could move on to work with our chosen pilot families, the As and the Bs. Coincidentally, each of those two families in turn experienced the loss of a parent, which set back our starting date for the project by several weeks. So it came as no surprise to me that, when writing about CAT twelve years later, this book, too, had to be set aside for some months while I was compelled to do my own griefwork following an unexpected family bereavement.

Rationale for developing CAT: a programme for fostering mutual attachment between child and carer

Many of the children who come to Social Services' attention and are subsequently fostered or adopted, or end up in institutional care when families are no longer able to hold them, are already deeply scarred by their experiences of multiple separations, losses, rejections, and abandonment as they are moved from one placement to another. If they have also been physically, emotionally, and/or sexually abused in one or more families, their ability to trust carers and form meaningful attachments is likely to be greatly impaired. This in turn undermines the confidence, competence, and commitment of their new parents.

With ever diminishing placement resources for such children, the practical and emotional costs of yet another breakdown are considerable, both in the short and long term. Children who dare not attach need to feel in total control of their frighteningly unpredictable world and are likely to "act out" from fear in ways that are increasingly dangerous to themselves and others.

Attachment-disordered children generally grow up with very low self-esteem and might end up in abusive relationships, so perpetuating the cycle of rejection, abuse, loss, and abandonment that they are so desperate to escape. Current neurobiological research suggests that some of these adults may subsequently be diagnosed as having borderline personality disorder (Cozolino, 2006, pp. 256–268). This is a distressing condition that is not generally well understood, and which severely affects their ability to make and sustain healthy relationships.

Holmes (2004) links the psychopathology of children with *disorganized attachments* with that of adults with borderline personality disorder. In his view, both

start with:

(1) parental unresolved/traumatized states of mind;
(2) moves to the D (Disorganised) infant caught in an approach–avoidance bind, with no secure base refuge when threatened either from without, or by her own unmodulated feelings;
(3) then shifts to the controlling 6-year-old who has eventually found a security strategy based on role reversal and providing pseudo-secure base for herself [see Gino in Marcia's story, Chapter One];
(4) includes repressed terror and inability to repair interpersonal discontinuities and loss as revealed by picture completion studies;

(5) and then moves to adolescence and early adulthood in which
the individual is controlling, aggressive, unable to self-soothe
when faced with emotional turmoil and loss, liable to dissociation, and cannot extricate herself from pain-producing relationships. [Holmes, 2004, p. 183]

Emotional holding or physical containment?

Reactive attachment disorder is a *DSM-IV* diagnostic label that has
been increasingly applied in the USA to attachment-disordered children and covers a multitude of behaviours that are very familiar to
frustrated foster and adoptive parents in the UK, too. (See Chapter
One for a description of common causes and symptoms.) Attachment therapies of all kinds have developed, including the controversial and aptly-named "intrusive therapy" in Colorado, where
treatment techniques have included holding down a child physically and inciting him to express anger, as in the rage reduction
therapy pioneered by Dr Foster Cline in the USA.

However, the danger that such forceful treatment is in itself
abusive was tragically proved a few years ago during a "rebirthing"
session in the USA with a ten-year-old child, Candace Newmaker,
which ended in her death. The therapist, Connell Watkins, is
reported to have admitted to the judge during her trial in 2001 that
she herself would not have undergone such "therapy" as it would
be "too traumatic".

Anger is an emotion that abused children are often afraid to
express openly, but project on to their carers and other adults who
end up feeling frustrated, enraged, powerless, and out of control.
The rationale for holding therapy seems to have been that, through
provoking the child to express negative feelings while physically
holding him until he was too exhausted to fight the adult (thera-
pist/parent/carer) any longer, he would end up in a quiescent state
where he could finally trust a carer to safely assess *and* meet his
emotional needs. This, it was thought, could also lead to his giving
up his obsessive attempts to control the adults and everything in his
hitherto unpredictable world.

Neurobiological research on the healing effects of touch provides a theoretical understanding of why some "nurturing holding"

techniques might prove to be effective if carried out in a respectful and non-abusive manner (Seifert, 1992). Terry Levy and Michael Orlans (Post-Adoption Centre workshop in London, 2006) advocate a "holding nurturing position" which, if matched by a caring attitude, could possibly feel therapeutic to children as well as to adults who have never felt emotionally "held" by, or attuned to, a parent.

However, any recourse to invasive treatment techniques is likely to be counterproductive and give dangerously contradictory messages to the child: "We are adults and in control because we are bigger and stronger than you and can hold you down." The child may interpret this as meaning: "It's okay for me to control/hurt others less powerful than me." Since many of these children are already apt to vent their considerable frustration on smaller children, pets, and objects, this could be taken as licence to do so openly.

The involvement of their carers in invasive therapies could also be perceived by the child as betrayal by adults she is being told to trust. As Jan Hunt (see (www.naturalchild.com/jan_hunt) writes, "It can be immensely difficult for a child to regain full, genuine trust after being forcibly held—regardless of the parent's 'good intentions' or the resulting surface behaviour".

* * *

Aware of such parental and professional dilemmas, Cairns (2002) has some useful insights on the precautions to be taken during the long journey towards re-attachment. She offers very helpful "health warnings" about the need for "therapeutic carers" to feel sufficiently "held" by their own attachment network and supervision in order to provide safe and secure emotional holding for the very hurt children they care for:

Step 1: commitment

Each child needs us to commit ourselves to sharing a journey with them, a journey which we undertake in the full knowledge that it will change us forever. . . .

Some of the time, and it must be only some of the time, we will need to experience the world as the child does. This will produce a dizzying sense of dislocation, followed, if all goes well, by an expansion of perspective.

Step 2: personal support

It is essential when living and working with children with unmet attachment needs that we establish and maintain our own close, confiding, intimate relationships. This is the source of our own sanity and a resource to sustain our own resilience. The work may challenge and destroy both. It will also challenge the durability and flexibility of our own secure attachments. . . .

Step 3: Professional supervision

It is even more important that direct carers—parents, family network care-givers, adopters and foster carers—have access to professional supervision and support than it is for child care professionals whose work with the children is not carried out in their own life space . . . to provide the essential overview of the system which will reveal the direction in which we are moving, will alert us to any risks, and will propose systemic solutions which will be beyond the scope of our own vision. . . .

Step 4: Working with others to build an environment which promotes secure attachment

It will be an environment in which all those close to the child are adopting a consistent approach which meets the child's needs, adapting the approach to fit their own role with the child, but providing great consistency in the basic structures surrounding the child. [Cairns, 2002]

Salzberger-Wittenberg (1970, pp. 142–155) refers to Winnicott's concept of the mother providing a holding environment for the infant, and to Bion's view of the need for the mother to provide emotional containment of the baby's unbearable feelings of fear, rage, anxiety, and aggression. Salzberger-Wittenberg explains that:

This model is based on an infant being held both physically and emotionally by a mother. For instance, hearing her baby's terrified screams mother responds by picking up, holding and carrying the baby, her arms around him forming a cradle which expresses that he is not falling to bits, but being held together and saved. Note that *it requires both the mother's understanding of his fear and a response in terms of physical handling which meets his emotional need.* [ibid., p. 144, my emphasis]

So, in this way, endless repetition of the basic bonding cycle (Figure 1, p. 9) enables the child to internalize both physical and emotional holding by the carer; to develop self-regulation of mood, including learning to calm and comfort himself when in distress; and to grow those all-important "emotional synapses" to his brain to reinforce this learning.

CAT's philosophy

Given the fully justified controversy about some of the "intrusive holding therapies" in the USA, the question for us as attachment therapists in the UK was: can a child and family be helped to attach in a mutually respectful way? The CAT Programme was developed with this philosophy in mind.

If a child is to attach securely to a new carer, she needs to be treated with respect and her wishes and feelings validated in an appropriate way, so that she is supported in uncovering and expressing her true self. That is the only basis for an honest and mutually satisfying relationship. Otherwise, the child will conform through fear to the carer's wishes, relating only superficially with a false self/selves constructed over years of reacting to hurt and deprivation by previous carers.

The new carers of such a child might themselves require much skilled support and emotional holding by professionals while they learn to identify the child's feelings, help her to express these appropriately and claim her right to have basic needs met in a non-abusive way. Years of neglect could have left a child completely unable to discriminate between various bodily states and sensations, let alone her confusion of emotions and feelings. Like a new baby and mother, child and carer might need to be supported in learning to *give and respond to cues* about needs that the child has learnt to suppress, perhaps even from her own consciousness, because it was not safe to express them previously.

Through consistently meeting the child's needs, the carers can gradually teach the child to trust them to do so appropriately. The child might then begin to feel more secure and slowly reveal her true self and feelings, including "negative" ones like anger or sadness, which she might have been disapproved of, or even punished by previous carers, for expressing. As her feelings and needs are recognized and validated, the child learns that she too is acceptable as she is, and her self-esteem increases. The more she is respected, and so learns to respect herself, the more she will respect others, too.

Grief at her losses, and rage at what has been done to her, will also need to be expressed as part of her mourning process. Therapeutic life story work is an essential part of this, helping to clarify for the child the roles of significant people in her past. If previous carers were neglectful or abusive, the child might need help in sorting out quite ambivalent feelings about them. Birth parents may have been idealized or vilified, and carers might themselves need help in presenting to the child a realistic but compassionate picture of her family, who remain, ultimately, part of her psyche.

If birth parents are portrayed as totally evil, abusive, neglectful, etc., how will the child learn to feel good about her origins and therefore about herself, and develop a positive self-image and feelings of self-worth? The adults' denial of her parents' importance in her internal world will be likely to encourage the development of a false, compliant self that tries to conform to the new carers' expectations of her. A strong physical or temperamental resemblance to either parent, if also decried, will make it even more difficult for the child to develop a positive and integrated self-image.

The new carers might also need skilled support in rewriting their own family scripts, doing inner child work as appropriate, and grieving the loss of their ideal or fantasy child, so as to accept the reality of the child placed with them and attach to her in turn. Some parents might never have felt entitled to this child, and so will need help in now claiming her.

The power of attraction

Beth's and Rose's stories (Chapter One), as well as Alicia's story (Chapter Four), illustrate the crucial part which the infant has to play in shaping relationships, through providing *attachment cues* to attract and claim their carer.

Foster carers and adoptive parents have long believed intuitively in the potential of healthy new family attachments for healing a child's woundedness from a traumatic birth history, although it is widely accepted now that "love may not be enough" to heal very troubled children (Thomas, 1997).

As a therapist working for some years with troubled children in specialist foster care placements, I would often read their placement histories and wonder how they could ever be helped to heal from the deep hurt they had suffered through early parental abuse and/or neglect and rejection. Their unconsciously learnt patterns of interaction tended to be repeated in subsequent foster and/or adoptive homes or even children's units. There seemed to be no hope for them, given their damaging histories.

These very challenging children came from all over the UK and were estranged from their families, friends, communities, culture, and sometimes even language. They were placed with "specialist" foster carers locally because their own Social Services Departments had no more "care" resources to contain their generally aggressive and destructive behaviours. However, I never ceased to be amazed by the spontaneous healing, even without therapy, that some of these children seemed to experience within a year or so of living with a foster family who actually *liked* them. I was reminded, thus, of John Bowlby's prescription for mental health: that a child needs a continuous relationship with a carer in which *both* find satisfaction and enjoyment. (Bowlby, 1953, p. 11).

The foster carers had somehow been attracted to the child placed with them and managed to see her as being more than the "problem behaviours" that had led to the disruption of her previous placements. This helped to give the child a new feeling of self-worth and a real sense of belonging to the foster family. In brief, the carers had succeeded in helping the child to create a healthy new attachment and so to feel less rejected and abandoned and, therefore, more willing to please her new family by giving up some of her unwanted behaviours.

Parents for Children, the first specialist adoption agency in London, discovered early on from their experience of placing children with special needs that a "chemical attraction" between child and new carer is essential to the success of adoptive placements (see annual reports for 1979–1980). Other key factors include realistic expectations of the child, and willingness by the adopters to work co-operatively with the agency.

Thus, I came to recognize the innate healing potential of families, and the need for professionals and therapists to acknowledge this and work in partnership alongside them in order to help hurt children to heal through providing timely, well-informed, and skilled support as part of a *team* approach. However, re-attachment work is neither easy nor quick (Figures 8 and 9).

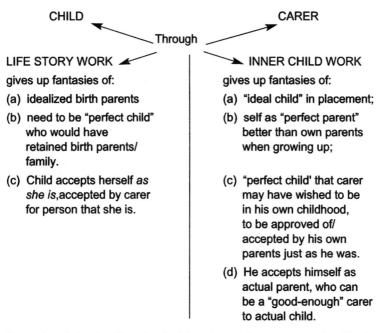

For safe griefwork with a family (*detachment* from past, real or "fantasy" losses), support and safe holding are necessary in order to undertake therapeutic life story work with children, and inner child work with carers who may have "ghosts in the nursery" (Fraiberg, Adelson, & Shapiro, 1975).

For re-attachment to new carers to occur, both child and carer will need to grieve and release emotional energy invested in child's wish to return to own family, or carer's wish to have a different kind of child.

Figure 8. Detachment and re-attachment work.

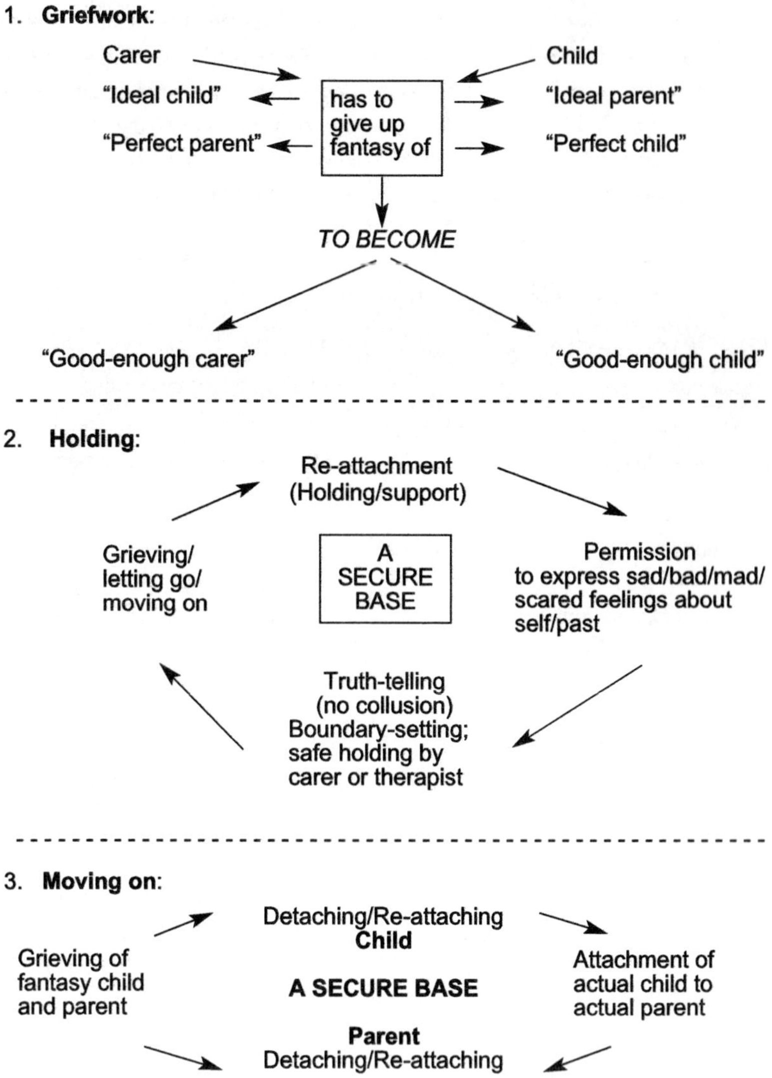

1. **Griefwork:**

Carer → has to give up fantasy of ← Child

"Ideal child" ← has to give up fantasy of → "Ideal parent"

"Perfect parent" ← has to give up fantasy of → "Perfect child"

↓

TO BECOME

↙   ↘

"Good-enough carer"   "Good-enough child"

- -

2. **Holding:**

Re-attachment
(Holding/support)

Grieving/
letting go/
moving on

A
SECURE
BASE

Permission
to express sad/bad/mad/
scared feelings about
self/past

Truth-telling
(no collusion)
Boundary-setting;
safe holding by
carer or therapist

- -

3. **Moving on:**

Detaching/Re-attaching
Child

Grieving of
fantasy child
and parent

A SECURE BASE

Attachment of
actual child to
actual parent

Parent
Detaching/Re-attaching

Figure 9. Re-attachment and grief work (detachment).

CHAPTER THREE

From theory to practice: CAT as a "working model"

A child-centred perspective

Gemma's story[1]

Born in the war-torn East End of London, Gemma spent her first three years in a house shared by two families: Aunt Doris, Uncle John, and two cousins, Ronnie and Frances, occupied the downstairs. Upstairs lived little Gemma with her Mum, Dad, and Nan. She was a happy little girl until the day she was sent to a faraway county called Yorkshire, evacuated there to keep her "safe from all the bombing", the grown-ups said. But no one ever explained to little Gemma why she was the only child in the whole family to be sent away for three long years.

Decades later, travelling by train to Yorkshire as an adult suddenly brought back to Gemma all the repressed memories of her painful exile as a small child. As soon as she entered St Pancras Station in London, Gemma had a flashback to being very small and frightened. She suddenly remembered standing all by herself on a platform crowded with crying children who were being sent away like herself, with no parents to comfort or reassure them.

Gemma hated everything about Yorkshire, especially the strange family she was forced to live with and their odd speech and ways of doing things; they even served Yorkshire pudding differently from the way her Mum and Nan and Aunt Doris did. The people in Yorkshire spoke in a strange way that little Gemma could not understand, and they then outraged her by laughing at her Cockney accent. She became self-conscious when speaking, and very soon began to stutter badly.

There were no telephones readily available then to help Gemma keep in touch with her beloved family. By the time she returned to London after the war, they were like strangers to each other. Her Nan wept when she saw the state of Gemma's neglected teeth, and heard her stammer each time she spoke. And now it was Gemma's own family who laughed at her strange accent and some of the things she did differently, so that Gemma learnt very early on that she was a misfit wherever she went, an outsider, even in her own family. Her special place there had been usurped by her new baby sister, Susan, whom she grew to dislike for that reason.

Gemma learnt to keep silent and watch the adults around her. In her words:

> We knew at an early age not to answer back, have an opinion, or talk about feelings. (I did not know the word "Feeling" at that time, of course.) Simply, that we could not half-way say how it was. So, "Button the lip, and get on with it", appeared to be the family motto, and indeed was so for many families. With men away at war, women struggling to cope, rickets, malnutrition, shortage of rations, bombs dropping, who had time to talk about the way it must also have been for the children?

> There was an ongoing time when things were uncomfortable at home. Visiting "uncles" while Mum was at work and Nan "sleeping", my innocence was taken. Who to tell, who would listen to a child who already talked too much, said the wrong thing, and wanted to but didn't argue, to get across how I felt? Suffice to say that nail-biting, bed-wetting and stuttering became a pattern that would last into adulthood. Who noticed, who cared, who did anything about it?

Little Gemma got into increasing trouble at school and once, when she stuttered while reading aloud, the impatient teacher slapped her head hard against the classroom wall. She ran home crying to tell her mother, only to be slapped again for being punished at school. Gemma stopped going into her classroom after that, and would take her books and lunch to the local marshes and read happily for hours. She was soon expelled from that primary school and then two more because of her refusal to accept adult authority any longer.

Fortunately, an English teacher at secondary school then recognized Gemma's hurt and potential; she quietly encouraged the girl to resume her studies. It was a turning point for Gemma, and she learnt to attach to and trust this teacher who understood and respected her. This provided a new beginning for her at school and in life.

The child

Many long-term accommodated children who have developed attachment-related difficulties are perceived by carers and professionals as just being disruptive and generally unmanageable at home and at school. The adults may not understand where the child is coming from, or where he is at. There may be very little intervention for the whole family to help them understand and acknowledge the dynamics of the hurt child in their care, and how they can all be supported. If the placement then breaks down, the child risks further wounding.

Such children may have a series of moves and different carers within a short space of time because of the unpredictable behaviours and negative "baggage" the child carries with her. Since she anticipates unavailability of, or rejection by, each new carer, she becomes rejecting for self-survival and her negative expectations are self-reinforcing. Before long, the child's negative internal working model of parents can bring about the very outcome she fears: her removal from this new family, too.

Such a child's negative self-view makes the likelihood of her forming secure attachments in any family unlikely, and so each subsequent placement is unconsciously sabotaged by her. The hurt child thus becomes part of the "pass the parcel" syndrome within the "care" system.

The carers

Every carer of hurt children carries with them their own inner child. When a child displays rejecting or disruptive behaviours towards them over a period of time, many carers feel unable to manage. They may feel despairing and deskilled and, at times, isolated with these feelings. Their inner child self may feel threatened and hurt, not coping, not in control of the situation; or, even worse, hurt and angry that the child in their care has rejected them before being rejected by them. The carer's hidden feelings from their own past hurts are re-awakened by the presence of the hurt, disturbed child within their current family. Like him, they may "act out" their fear and rage unawarely.

"In every nursery there are ghosts. These are the visitors from the unremembered pasts of the parents; the uninvited guests at the christening" (Fraiberg, Adelson, & Shapiro, 1975).

Without an understanding of these natural reactions, and without adequate tools to handle the situation, some foster carers give up on the child and ask for him to be removed. Or a carer may emotionally withdraw from the child, ending any chance of their forming a positive attachment (Figure 10).

In such situations these difficulties can be exacerbated if the child is seen for therapy on his own, excluding the carers who may have no real knowledge or understanding of the child's inner world. Moreover, because of their own blocked inner child feelings, or need still to grieve for their unborn "fantasy" child, the carers may feel unable to fully claim the child as their own. And when the child is seen as the one who needs "sorting out", this serves to reinforce his negative view of himself, the world, and his carers. Thus, this damaging pattern of interaction is likely to repeat itself, and follows the child through each disrupted placement.

Child- and family-centred interventions

Hurt children in placement and their carers have a right to be supported. In working through child and adult issues at the onset of behavioural difficulties, an intensive therapeutic programme of interventions should be seen as major preventive work. This can result in positive changes from previous negative patterns, and help both the child and carer to maintain their place within the family and promote their feelings of self-worth.

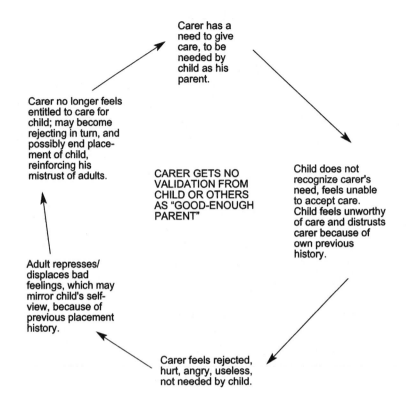

Carer has a need to give care, to be needed by child as his parent.

Carer no longer feels entitled to care for child; may become rejecting in turn, and possibly end placement of child, reinforcing his mistrust of adults.

CARER GETS NO VALIDATION FROM CHILD OR OTHERS AS "GOOD-ENOUGH PARENT"

Child does not recognize carer's need, feels unable to accept care. Child feels unworthy of care and distrusts carer because of own previous history.

Adult represses/displaces bad feelings, which may mirror child's self-view, because of previous placement history.

Carer feels rejected, hurt, angry, useless, not needed by child.

Figure 10.   Carer invalidation spiral.

In cases where children move on to adoptive parents, attachment therapy that includes child and carer can provide a framework for direct family work, so encouraging the bonding process to develop. This should include individual therapeutic sessions for child *and* carer, with inner child work for the carer, as well as joint carer/child work. Work with other children in the family, or with the carers as a couple, may also be needed.

Therapy can be carried out within the home to promote continuity of work within the child's natural environment. Alternatively, a child-friendly venue elsewhere that is suitable for such work can provide a separate "safe place" for the family to explore their difficulties together. (See Chapter Four, "Alicia's story"; and Chapter Five, "Frankie's story". In both cases, sessions carried out at home yielded crucial information that might not have been available to us if we had confined ourselves to office sessions with these families.)

The therapeutic work needs to be experienced by the family as supportive, encouraging, and enabling them to grieve over their past losses and to work towards positive objectives and forming secure attachments with the child. Since such work encompasses the child and his carers, it provides a secure base for the child to claim his adoptive parents, and for them to claim him as their son.

Reparenting skills

Children who exhibit out-of-control behaviours usually find this as frustrating and anxiety-provoking as their carers. Most of all, they need reassurance that they are loved and valued and can be contained appropriately by parents who can act as responsible adults and not let their own "child selves" get pulled into battles which no one wins.

Carers can monitor their own strong feelings (countertransference) when helping a child to deal with unbearable feelings of rage, grief, or fear at being out of control and powerless in an unpredictable and threatening world.

Verrier (1994) describes the strength of such unconscious communications:

> adoptees use projective identification, not only as a defense mechanism and a primitive form of object relations, but also as a means of communication. What that means is that anyone in a relationship with him will begin to experience his feelings and react to them. The adoptee uses projective identification to communicate what he really feels inside because he has no words to describe those feelings. The feelings originated before he had language.
>
> Adoptive parents are very familiar with the technique of projective identification, as are reunited birthmothers, although they may not have known what it is called. Those projected feelings trigger the parents' own sense of rage, hostility, sorrow, or helplessness, causing them to react in ways they consider totally out of character for them. [Verrier, 1994, 184–185]

If the carers can contain their own strong feelings and express them appropriately, verbalizing perhaps for the child how she might be

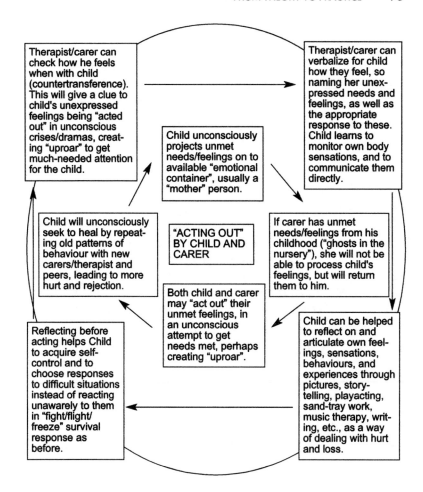

Figure 11. Helping children who "act out" their feelings.

feeling the same, they will provide a different model for her of dealing with conflict and gaining self-control.

As Jeremy Holmes explains:

> Parents who can contain and attune to their children have children
> who can put their feelings into words and who are able to resolve
> conflict. Those who cannot contain and attune are more likely to
> have children who are at risk of dealing with their feelings by split-
> ting and projective identification . . . [Holmes, 1993, p.131]

Finding safety valves in fraught situations, lowering the emotional temperature with gentle humour, and allowing a raging child to save face and self-determine through choosing from options acceptable to the carer, may defuse some conflicts (Figure 12). Networking with other parents can help carers let off steam and build up a repertoire of creative responses to challenging behaviours. (See Archer, 1999a,b; Cairns, 2002.)

The CAT approach

The CAT Programme has *three* main intertwining strands.

1.   Helping carer and child match Cues and Responses to improve their communication and strengthen their attachment.

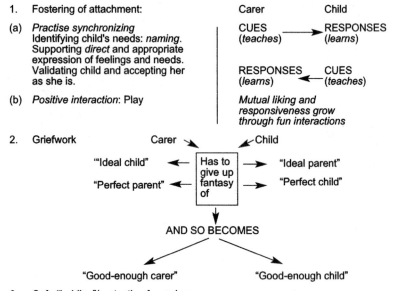

1.   Fostering of attachment:

(a) *Practise synchronizing*
     Identifying child's needs: *naming.*
     Supporting *direct* and appropriate
     expression of feelings and needs.
     Validating child and accepting her
     as she is.

(b) *Positive interaction:* Play

Carer	Child
CUES ⟶	RESPONSES
(teaches)	*(learns)*
RESPONSES	CUES
(learns) ⟵	*(teaches)*

Mutual liking and responsiveness grow through fun interactions

2.   Griefwork

Carer ↘   ↙ Child

"Ideal child" ⟵ | Has to give up fantasy of | ⟶ "Ideal parent"

"Perfect parent" ⟵ | | ⟶ "Perfect child"

↓

AND SO BECOMES

↙   ↘

"Good-enough carer"   "Good-enough child"

3.   Safe "holding"/protection from abuse

Carer/Therapist creates "a secure base" from which the child and family can safely explore fantasies of child and carer; what her real needs are; how to express them directly and appropriately, trusting that they will be met consistently and safely, i.e., predictably, by carer.

Carer finds Child more predictable, responsive, and gratifying to parent, claims her as own, feeling entitled to protect and care for her, so minimizing the risk of child "acting out" to provoke care/protection from strangers.

Figure 12.   Child-centred attachment therapy work.

2. Griefwork for the child (life story work) and carer (inner child and child loss work).

3. Play-work with child and carer to build up their fun-time together and promote mutual liking and understanding.

Fostering mutual empathy and honest communication between carer and child

This helps them to identify and synchronise their cues and responses, and practise care-giving/care-seeking behaviours, so claiming each other in an attachment dyad (Figure 13).

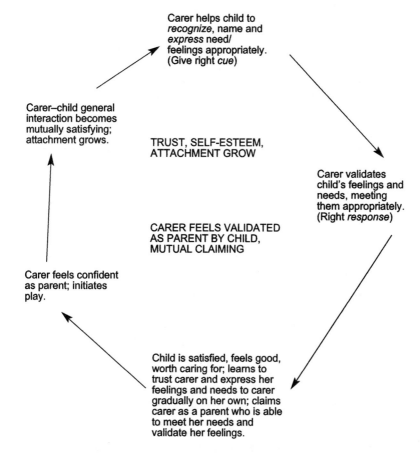

Figure 13. Carer–child mutual claiming spiral (based on Fahlberg's work).

Since a very hurt or neglected child is unlikely to have had her basic instinctual needs met appropriately and consistently, she might well not recognize her own bodily sensations as indicating a need for food, warmth, defecation, etc. Her awareness of her body may have become so distorted through abuse or gross neglect that the carer may have to treat her for a while as if she were an infant. The child may actually be unaware of why she is in discomfort, and so will need help to express what she is feeling, to name and recognise bodily sensations before and after her basic needs are identified and met appropriately by the carer.

If the child has previously had her bodily sensations and feelings discounted or misnamed, deliberately or otherwise, this process needs to include "unnaming" and *correctly renaming* what she is feeling. Through consistently helping the child to complete the "basic bonding cycle" (see Figure 1, Chapter One) the carer provides a secure base from which the child can develop trust that her needs are valid and will be met. In this way the child can learn to identify both the source of her discomfort and the remedy for it, and so ask to have her need met appropriately by the carer (Fahlberg, 1988, pp. 38–40).

In this way, as in a baby's first year of life, crucial neural connections can be made between the child's left hemisphere of the brain, which controls her thinking and language functions, and the right hemisphere, which is responsible for her emotional and physical functioning.

Recent neurobiological research suggests that mothers also grow new "emotional synapses" in their brain through engaging in natural bonding interactions with their babies after birth such as "'eye contact, facial expressions, soothing vocalizations, caresses, and exciting exchanges" (Cozolino, 2006). This process helps the mothers to grow in empathy and stay attuned to their babies, and it might also apply to other primary carers of children who feel very strongly committed to them (Cairns, 2002, p. 67).

*   *   *

Attachment-disordered children may never have felt safe enough with previous carers to express anger or negative feelings about hurts or losses *directly*. In their often unconscious frustration at this, they may vent their aggression on less threatening "objects", such as smaller children, or pets, or the furniture. The child who insists "I don't know", when asked to explain destructive acts, is probably being quite truthful, since the real cause—deep, ungrieved hurts— is safely repressed in the unconscious.

Cairns (2002) explains this process of dissociation very simply:

> Dissociation is the process by which the brain protects the organism from becoming totally overwhelmed by generating patterns of automatic splitting of awareness in response to repeated experiences of an overwhelming nature. [pp. 42; 60–61; 113–115]

When babies have no empathic carers who can attune to and contain their distress, helping them to regulate intolerable emotional states, they either dissociate from these feelings or remain hyper-aroused. From being a defensive strategy, dissociation can become an ingrained response to emotional stress and, hence, dysfunctional. So, a child who habitually dissociates from his own angry feelings is likely to find himself surrounded by very angry adults.

Hurt children may project their unbearable feelings into a receptive carer, who becomes the unconscious "container" for their hate, anger, and destructive feelings. The carer may already be feeling bad and useless as a parent because the child placed does not resemble her fantasy or "imagined child" and will not accept care from her. The carer's feelings of frustration, inadequacy and helplessness may then mirror the child's fear and rage at not being in control in a world that she perceives as being hostile to her.

Moreover, if the carer has not digested similar feelings from her own childhood, never having had these contained and metabolized (Bion, 1978) by her parents in turn, she may end up projecting them on to the child placed. This is in addition to not being able to process what she has received from the child in the present, and so returning it undigested. The child might then end up with a double dose of bad feelings about himself, and have no help to process them. (See Figure 4, p. 27.)

The carer can start to recognize the child's emotional state by monitoring her own powerful feelings in countertransference. If the carer can be supported in containing these safely, and not retaliate by "acting out" angrily on them towards the child, she may be able to go on then to process ("metabolize": Bion, 1978) the child's unpalatable feelings and return them detoxified. Thus, the child is supported in exploring feelings that were previously too unbearable or unsafe to "reflect on" and could, therefore, only be "acted out" unconsciously.

Griefwork is essential for helping both carer and child to identify ungrieved hurts and losses of the past, to express their sadness and anger and hurt, and move on through repeated "telling of their story of what happened" to a supportive listener (Whitfield, 1987). The grieving cycle (Figure 14a,b) can be seen as a necessary counterpart in Attachment work to the basic bonding cycle (Figure 1, p. 9). (See also Figure 7a,b.) As Miller (1987) teaches: "Mourning is Nature's way of healing".

Griefwork for the child is encompassed in skilled and sensitive life story work, carried out at a level appropriate to her age and understanding and kept up to date. *It needs to include her carers, whose support is essential for her to undertake such painful work.* This will help the child to express her confusion of sad and angry feelings about what has happened to her, clarifying her understanding of her past, the roles of significant persons in it, and her probably ambivalent feelings towards them. Ultimately, whether neglectful and abusive or not, her birth parents remain part of her psyche and need to be portrayed with both realism and compassion if she is to develop a positive self image, thus reclaiming their good aspects for herself.

Griefwork with the carers can be more complex as they may need to exorcise "ghosts from the nursery" (Fraiberg, Adelson, & Shapiro, 1975), so as to disentangle from their current relationship with the child placed their own ungrieved experiences of hurt and loss, rejection and abandonment, from *their* childhood. Inner child work may be needed to help them get in touch with their unconscious child selves (both hurt and creative aspects), to mourn appropriately, and so to move on to reclaim the positives of *their* pasts, thus "rewriting family scripts" (Byng-Hall, 1995). Mourning *their* loss of an idealized parent or childhood may help carers to empathize with the child's need to do the same, and support her in doing similar griefwork on her past. (See Figures 8 and 9, pp. 65, 66.)

The carers, whether they have other children or not, might need to mourn the loss of the ideal or fantasy child they dreamed they

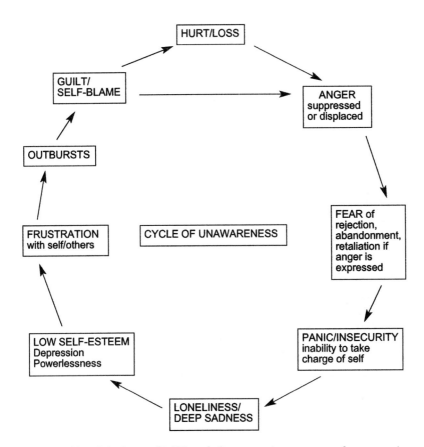

Figure 14(a).   Grieving cycle. When feelings remain unexpressed, we remain locked in this cycle of hurt/angry/sad/fearful feelings until, in extreme frustration, we explode verbally or physically—only to blame and hate ourselves more, 'acting out' even more dramatically on our unacknowledged negative feelings of hurt and or loss.

would parent, and perhaps even ritually say goodbye to this imagined child. Only then can they totally accept the reality of the child placed as she is and so derive satisfaction from matching *her* actual needs for care, empathy, and positive interaction, instead of rejecting her for not being the child they longed to have, or of being themselves to *their* critical parents.

Play work with carer and child can help both to get in touch with the origins of the child's unconscious angry feelings. Just as

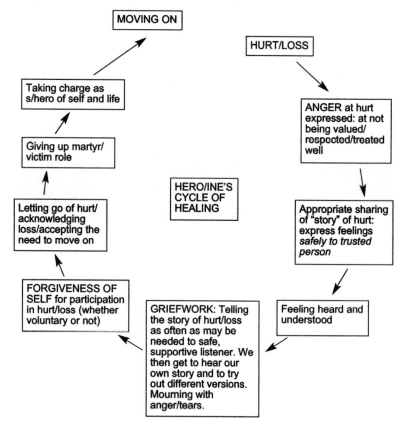

Figure 14(b). Griefwork and moving on (adapted freely from concepts in *Healing the Child Within* by Charles Whitfield [1987]).

inner child work can help the carer to identify and separate his own hurt child self feelings. Otherwise these may be expressed inappropriately towards the child placed, so undermining the carer in his role as a responsible parent who needs to take charge as the adult in the situation. CAT therapists prefer the use of the term "taking charge" to "taking control" of a frightened, raging child who needs to be helped to acquire *self*-control. (See "'NLP four pillars of childhood", Chapter Eight)

Playing together, or having fun time together, is such a simple healing practice for families in conflict that Theraplay™, developed in America, now has a worldwide following (www.theraplayinstitute.com). Theraplay™ is a body–mind therapy that has four main dimensions: structure, engagement, nurture, and challenge. Through specific "play" programmes, Theraplay™ helps carers attune to the unmet infant needs of non-attached children and facilitate the bonding process in a more relaxed and boundaried way.

We all know that when we get on well in an adult relationship we want to spend time together with our partner or friend, to please each other and do things that both enjoy. All this strengthens our attachment. The opposite occurs when we are not getting on well, since we no longer want to spend time with our partner (who is now not regarded as our friend). We cease to do fun things together, and we are then more likely to drift apart in a downward "spiral of negative interaction", with increasing time to dwell on each other's failings.

The same applies to parents and children in conflict. They do not want to spend any quality time together, and the rift between them grows, often to the point of the placement disrupting. No matter how busy a carer might be, investing time in doing something that both child and parent enjoy is a pre-requisite to building a mutually satisfying relationship. Playing or having fun time together is a rewarding way of *completing* the basic bonding cycle (see Figure 1, p. 9). It provides a necessary balance for the carer, who has so much of the time to contain the child's anger and hurt, listening to her pain and acknowledging her feelings of hurt or loss, even if her expressed need cannot be met in the present.

Winnicott believed that psychotherapy was about two people "playing together", and that where patients are not able to play, it is the therapist's task to help to bring them into a state where they can do so (1985, p. 44). Many hurt and neglected children are described by their carers as unable to play, and having no imagination or sense of humour. Most probably, these children take things literally because of their early experiences of deprivation and abuse. It is the carer's task, as in therapy, to help the child to learn to relax and play and smile and laugh. These are all spontaneous baby behaviours that have been inhibited in the child by abusive or non-attuned carers.

It makes sense that an abused child will constantly be on "red alert", hypervigilant to any signs of threat from people around him or the environment, since that has been his early experience, triggering "fight, flight, or freeze" survival responses even when he is with new carers. Laughter may not be part of his repertoire of learnt behaviours, except in bravado or at hurt to others. Constant reassurance, treating such a child with respect, and gently joking with him (laughing with, and not at him), playacting, miming, and telling playful stories (perhaps those intended for a much younger age group), can all help him to start to relax and learn that it is safe to have fun and to develop his innate creativity and imagination.

There is enough research currently to show how emotionally and physically healing such playful behaviours and laughter are, even for adults, in releasing endorphins that make us feel good, so helping to create new pathways to our emotional brain and boosting our positive mood and immune system. (Robert Holden's Happiness Project—visit www.happiness.co.uk. There are dozens of websites for individuals and organizations on the importance of laughter in reducing stress and promoting health.)

And so, through playing and spending fun-time together, a child might begin to trust the carer enough to then open up and begin to express her pain or discomfort and real needs and feelings, revealing more of her "true self". Carers sometimes notice that a child will start suddenly to disclose painful experiences from the past, perhaps while engaged in other activities, as when looking out through the window on a car journey. Or, in the middle of a crowded market or shopping centre, a child will confide something significant to the adult she is with, as if testing to see how the carer will respond to her disclosure. Such moments, if handled well, can lead to further time spent quietly later on in talking and listening, cementing their new and growing attachment.

Fostering entitlement to the child[2]

So much is expected of adoptive parents. They have to deal with so many outside pressures, as well as trying to bond with a complete little stranger who has already learnt that trusting adults can be a painful experience. The adopters have to deal with sometimes quite extreme behaviour, and the rewards are often small. And all this without the lovely cuddly years of baby cuteness!

In the first few weeks of a new placement, professionals need to indulge the adopters in their acceptance/rejection of birth parents. We cannot expect adopters to claim both the child and her family straightaway. Adopters have to go through a process of "owning" and claiming their child, and it is difficult for them to also include the birth family until they feel attached to their new child. Otherwise, it may feel to them like "kidnap" of the child, if the birth family is perceived by them in very positive and accepting terms.

That is not to say that adopters will continue in this mode, but time is needed to readjust until they can comfortably embrace the positives of the child's birth family and truly enable the child to feel positive, too. Especially where a child is expressing anger and hurt towards their birth family, the new protective feelings of adoptive parents towards the child will help them to "own" and attach to her.

Adopters become the "everyday" parents, but initially have no legal parental responsibility for the child. The adoption process can feel very disabling, especially if legal proceedings are contested and long drawn out. Sensitivity has to be shown to the adopters' need to embrace "their" child, if the split between good parents/bad parents is not to be made by themselves as well as by the child.

Previous foster carers who may have become very attached to the child will also need help in letting him go "with a blessing" and permission to attach to new parents. Otherwise, adopters may have great difficulty in ever claiming the child as being truly theirs to parent. See "Edward's story" (Chapter Four), where Mr and Mrs C felt they had "stolen" their little son from the family he really belonged to, his foster carers.

Notes

1. The part of this chapter from "Gemma's story" as far as the section headed "Reparenting skills" is contributed by Pauline Sear.
2. This final section of the chapter is contributed by Maggie Gall.

Phase 2 of the CAT programme (1996). Brief evaluation of the pilot project: our learning from adoptive families

Our local Social Services Department accepted an initial proposal to pilot CAT, over a six-month period in 1996, with two adoptive families in the north-east and two in the south-east of the county. However, almost immediately there was a change in plan as the north-east team had staff changes and withdrew from the project. The CAT team of four therapists in the south-east, based at a family-finding unit, worked in pairs with families A and B, with the intention of then taking on a further two families for the pilot.

This plan proved to be untenable since three of the workers had recently suffered bereavements, as had their team leader. Each of them needed time off to deal with their grief. Where this was not fully acknowledged, the worker herself then became ill, so that subsequent work with the CAT family had to be carried out at a slower pace to allow her more time off for grieving.

Grief work cannot be rushed

This was such important learning for CAT that we did not get it at first, despite the many family losses through illness, accidents, and death that staff at the family-finding unit had suffered from the outset of the project. We reluctantly postponed for a few weeks the start of work with our pilot families, but only because, coincidentally, Mr A and Mrs B had also suffered parental losses, which meant the additional loss of a grandparent for the children in their new families.

Writing this twelve years later, after recently experiencing an unexpected family bereavement, I am much more aware of how intrusive grief is. The reviewing and reworking of lost relationships can become a major preoccupation, making everyday living and work or study seem a distraction from the griefwork that demands its own process and pacing. When this learning is applied to work with bereft children in new families, the need for flexible timing and support for child and carers by skilled and empathic therapists cannot be overemphasized.

What we have also learnt through experience is that the loss of a "conflicted attachment" is likely to stir up a much more complex mix of emotions. It might require a far longer period of mourning and reworking of the past than relationships that have been relatively straightforward and mutually rewarding. However, this mourning, though perhaps more painful, can ultimately be just as transformative and enriching.

Life story work is an ongoing process

Griefwork can be done through therapeutic life story work (Figure 15) with child and carer. It will need to acknowledge the importance of the child's often "conflicted attachments", and his probable confusion of emotions and preoccupation with the past, *before* he can start to settle in his new "family" and feel safe enough to trust and form new attachments there. (See Figures 8 and 9, pp. 65, 66.)

Life story work should carry a "health warning": carers need to be prepared for the possibility that, because such griefwork is so painful, their child might regress in behaviours and act much worse before things start slowly to improve. The carers might need to be reminded of our reactions as adults to reviewing painful events and losses, and our natural reluctance to undertake such work. Indeed, for adults to appreciate the magnitude of the task we expect bereft children to

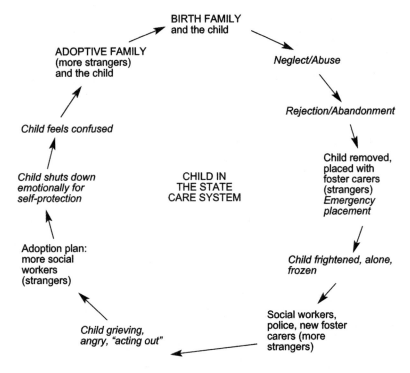

Figure 15.   Life story work.

undertake, we would have to compare, if not the loss of our own parent, that of another much loved adult, whom we are now expected to replace with a complete stranger, and not of our choosing.

If such work is done sensitively with children and their adoptive parents, it can really help to build their attachment. Ironically, this is a circular process, as shown in Figures 8 and 9, pp. 65, 66. For a child to feel safe enough to undertake such painful griefwork, she will need to feel sufficiently settled and supported, with her new family providing a secure base. Moreover, in order to foster her beginning attachment to them, she will need to "detach" to some extent from previous carers, or even her birth parents, in order to review those relationships and, if appropriate, to withdraw some of the emotional energy she had invested in previous attachments.

The timing is, therefore, crucial when starting life story work, and there are different views on this. The manager of the family-finding unit commented at the time of the CAT pilot project:

It has raised many questions for me about why children suffer such attachment difficulties when they have lived in their present homes for a considerable time. Therefore, is it the right answer to deliver this service when the child is in a permanent home or should a part of the work be completed either at the rehabilitation stage or to help children to adjust in foster homes? It has also reconfirmed a strong view I have that ALL children should have a "life story book", regardless of whether they are moving on or returning home. And that all social workers need to be aware of its value and to actively promote the use of this book in order to prevent children from having gaps in their background history due to the lack of continuity suffered in placement.

Ideally, life story work should be able to draw on background information and photographs provided by the birth and extended families and previous foster carers. This helps the child to piece together where he has been previously and why he has had to move, with so many losses of people and places, including neighbours and school friends and perhaps pets, too, that were special to him. (See also Appendix B.)

Life story books, when prepared by a child care social worker or adoption or other specialist worker, are often regarded as the *be-all and end-all* of therapeutic work with a child and might be "frozen in time", so that there is no ongoing link to the child's current life with a new family. However, these books can be excellent tools for undertaking griefwork with the child, with support for him being provided by the new parents, who should in turn be supported by professionals through this often quite painful process. If members of the birth family can also be involved, there could be some mutual healing.

Some workers organize "A life appreciation day", when significant people—family members, foster carers, and professionals—are invited to come together to share their memories of a child and significant information about her background to add to her story in a *celebration* of her life. A video or other recording of this day can then be added to the child's "Treasure Chest" of memories. It would be prudent to make a copy of any such recording for everyday use, as indeed of life story material, since these precious and often irreplaceable treasures might be attacked and even destroyed by the child in a fit of temper or self-hatred.

Life story work with Alicia

Family B, who had adopted Alicia as an abandoned baby from an institution abroad, made every effort to obtain as much information as they could about her family and her homeland. They took videos of her in the institution on their first visits to her there, as well as after she joined their family in Britain. Despite the language barrier, they managed to locate her parents and travelled to meet with them, taking precious photographs of them and her older siblings. These became very important to share with Alicia as she grew older.

Although reluctant at first to bring up a very painful past for Alicia, Mrs B prepared a life story book during our work with the family. We were interested to note that she had integrated photographs of Alicia's birth family and her homeland with those of the child in her new home and adoptive family. So, although not chronologically in order, the book was current and relevant and able to be more easily spoken about and shown to Alicia from a very young age. In recent years she and the Bs have revisited her homeland, giving her, as a teenager, a much-needed opportunity to learn at first hand about its culture and language and people, and so to form a better sense of who she is and literally where she has come from.

A manager's perspective

Following the pilot project in 1996, the manager of the hard-pressed family-finding unit had commented:

The CAT Programme has been a pulling together of theories, hopes, and ideals that often lie dormant for many workers. Most practitioners want to improve their own practice and, likewise, Local Authorities want to maximize on the skills and commitment of their workers, thus providing a quality service.

If ideas are to be developed, the best way is through practice rather than theory: using techniques that have been tried and tested as well as trying out complementary innovations. In the Family Placement Service there is probably more opportunity to take an overview of the whole of the Services for Children, as, sadly, we are most often dealing with the effects of less than ideal parenting and children who have been both traumatized and damaged by their experiences. The Adoption Agency has the unique opportunity to look at the whole of the child's life, including periods of being "accommodated" and living with birth families.

It is with regret that I have to say that there have been, and are still, times when I consider that the Service to Children can be unintentionally abusive because it is thought that there are no local resources to meet the individual needs of specific children. The Department has then made placements with specialist Agencies at enormous cost when it could provide those services "in house". I have experienced at first hand children returning from expensive "out of county" placements where the marketing of facilities and skills far exceeds the actual return for the child. The question that this raised for my team centred around the notion that it was also because there is often insufficient recognition of the skills of the workers as well as a lack of confidence on their part as individuals to challenge the "experts".

The CAT Programme has, on the positive side, focused thinking, raised morale, and challenged many ideas. It has also given the workers the confidence to recognize their skills and to use them in a more creative way that is both child-centred but also time-limited. I am aware of similar work that is ongoing with an adult focus, but not one which specifically focuses on the child.

The reverse of this has been the need to constantly remind the CAT team that there is a lack of time that can be specifically allocated since the Programme cannot take precedence over our responsibility to also fulfil the other statutory functions of the Adoption Agency.

As a manager, it has been difficult to grapple with the changes that are an inevitable part of such a project, and to constantly assess and fine-tune what is an incomplete Programme at this stage, due to the small number of cases that have been involved. [The team, consisting of two pairs of CAT therapists, were unable to work intensively with more than two families during the six-month pilot project.]

I have no doubt that the Programme will be of benefit to many families and that the workers in turn will continue to grow in confidence as CAT develops.

Learning from family A[1]

When we became involved with the CAT Programme, the couple that we chose to work with had actually had their children in placement for six months. So, in a sense, the study for us has been retrospective. When children are placed for adoption, work begins immediately within the new family group, so we saw the Programme as being preventive, as well as curative of any attachment problems. Using CAT preventively, we consider its importance lies in helping parents view attachment problems as a difference in family dynamics, given the new relationships, rather than pathologizing the child placed.

During the standard "Form F" assessment, prospective adopters are encouraged to look at their parenting capacity; once children are in placement, the theory, so to speak, is put to the test. When providing post-placement support, we encourage adopters to look at their perceived parenting skills in relation to the child or children's actual behaviour and responses. For new parents it is very often "trial and error" in working out how to handle behaviour problems. Through helping parents to isolate particular disturbing forms of behaviour, and concentrating on those, small goals can be set and are seen to be achievable. Star charts include both parent and child interactions.

Observing children with new parents, and particularly children with attachment difficulties, it is important for parents to acknowledge that the children newly placed cannot be expected to have a sense of belonging to them, and that a lot of the child's anger and hurt, often expressed through bad behaviour, belongs more appropriately to previous carers, including birth parents.

We encourage parents *not* to take the misbehaviour as being personally directed at themselves, but to deal with it on a more practical level: certain thought-through responses to a particular behaviour. Placements are then less likely to fail because the adopters do not feel so overwhelmed and rejected on account of the child's chaotic behaviour.

The CAT Programme helps parents to identify specific responses to various "non-attached behaviours". They can then explore with the worker ways in which they can create a sense of trust in their child by responding positively and encouragingly, rather than with anger and rejection. It is also very encouraging for parents to look back and acknowledge their parenting skills and to witness positive changes, however small, in their children's behaviour.

We see the elements of the ℂAT Programme as essential in work with families post-placement. We feel that by building on the already established skills of their adoption workers, all families could be offered this type of intervention with varying degrees of intensity.

Further thoughts on ℂAT²

Looking at attachment research, and understanding how any break in the early "bonding cycle" can cause such destructive interactions, helps to focus the work with both the child and the parents. The beauty of this intervention is that it combines assessment with treatment and involves the whole family in a potentially healing experience since it promotes communication and mutual understanding.

Chloe's story

Family A, with whom we worked on the ℂAT pilot project, had a recent adoptive placement of two small, very damaged, attachment-disordered siblings. Chloe and Darren were chaotic and would quite happily have gone home with me or the postman or anyone who was nice to them! They had no sense of danger and their sensory development was stunted. They were beautiful children but demanding and exhausting.

We had started the pilot project by giving a questionnaire to Mr and Mrs A to complete (see Appendix A1). They scored the children very low on "attachment behaviours", as demonstrating little or none. This questionnaire proved to be a lifeline for the adopters, since it was updated every few weeks and they could then identify small changes in the children's behaviour that would otherwise have been missed. Mr and Mrs A could now positively identify change, however little. They were learning to read the cues their children presented to them, and their responses (Appendix 1B) became more and more appropriate, further encouraging their bonding with the children.

I could give many examples, but the following one always sticks in my mind. I was reading a story to Chloe (aged three), a pop-up book about insects. On one page there was a beef-burger with lettuce in it, and inside the lettuce was a caterpillar. Darren, at five, was delighted to see this and immediately started to frighten his little sister. Chloe's face crumpled. She began to cry, scrambled off my knee, ran over to her adoptive mother's lap and snuggled up to be comforted.

Mrs A was too concerned with Darren's teasing to appreciate the significance of Chloe's spontaneous behaviour, so I asked her, "What do you think happened there?" "He's such a wind-up," she replied. Mrs A was amazed and tearful when I pointed out that Chloe had sought comfort from her and not cuddled up to me, as she would previously have done. Chloe now identified Mrs A as a source of safety and comfort, evidencing her growing attachment and trust. It was such a simple thing, but the adoptive mother had missed the cue. Her response was directed towards the offending sibling, rather than holding this precious moment of bonding with her distressed daughter.

One of the most valuable aspects of CAT has been that it teaches *all* family members to be aware of cues and responses, since if cues are misread, they can inhibit attachment rather than foster it. It sounds simple, but how many times do parents say, "I just don't understand them!"; or children complain that their parents do not understand them, or are unfair. If *cues* are read correctly, *responses* become positive and mutually satisfying.

Within the attachment dyad, if interactions are not mutually pleasing, the relationship breaks down. Parents need to feel needed and loved just as children need to feel secure, safe, and loved. If parents get nothing but negative responses, the gap between parent and child grows bigger so that mutual distrust and rejection become the only way each knows how to respond to the other. (See Figure 10.) If this pattern can be interrupted and a new cycle of mutually satisfying behaviours engendered, the relationship can be healed and parents become protective of their children who, in turn, start to feel more secure and trusting.

The CAT Programme works with family members individually and jointly, as needed. Many therapists work with the child only, simply feeding back to the parent, or sometimes giving no feedback at all. Our belief is that there aren't "problem children", but "families with problems". The parents must be part of any therapeutic work that seeks to modify challenging or negative behaviours, because unless the parents change the way they respond to their child, i.e., reading cues successfully, the child will be unable to break the negative interaction cycle on their own. Even if the child's behaviour can be changed, repeated negative responses from the parents will prevent true healing.

When I worked with CAT families, we would look at cues and responses in the context of the family's dynamics, since the child was never "*the* problem" on their own.. Incorporating any stranger into your home is difficult, and each member of the family needs to be aware of their role in it and how they view other members. *Sculpting* is one very visual way of letting families see how relationships actually are: where family members position themselves in relation to others, how they perceive each other's roles, and what their expectations are of each other. These must be open and understood for family life to succeed and healthy attachments to form.

The CAT Programme takes everyone's views into account and feeds these back, however painful for the parents to hear, so that defensive stances and beliefs can be explored and rectified. The therapeutic work is intensive and often difficult, but it really does move families forward.

During adoption assessments, couples/families feel they are under the microscope and that their very souls are laid bare. This is a cathartic process, and essential if parents are to be able to foster attachments to emotionally damaged and distrustful children. Adopters need to fully understand how they have come to be the people they are and why they hold certain values and beliefs. Adults who show an ability to form and maintain secure attachments themselves will be more successful in parenting emotionally hurt children. The CAT Programme spends time with the parents and helps them to see how their own upbringing can impact on the way that they then go on to parent.

Parents often repress difficult feelings and memories of the past that have never been dealt with. These may suddenly be re-awakened when they themselves become a parent (Fraiberg, Adelson, & Shapiro, 1975). So, adults who have never had satisfying parenting themselves might find themselves being expected to provide just that! The negative responses they received when young are then more likely to be unconsciously transferred in *replicative scripts* (Byng-Hall, 1995) to their birth or adopted children, often with devastating consequences.

The attachment cycle also becomes a sort of inheritance line, with dysfunction passed from one generation to the next. This is amplified where adopters take on already damaged children with conflicted attachment histories. This can lead sometimes to further risk of harm, since insecure attachments negate the feelings of protection normally felt by parents with strong and healthy attachments to their children. (See Figure 4, p. 27.)

Learning from family B[3]

Alicia's story

Alicia was referred to CAT at three years old because of her "irrational violent responses", attributed to the severe neglect and ill treatment she had experienced during her first eighteen months of life, lying confined in a cot in a hospital abroad. When Mr B had first visited its "Abandoned Children's Ward" he had chosen Alicia to be their adopted daughter. She was only six months old then and, of all the babies in the ward, she had been most responsive to him (cues and responses). However, Alicia subsequently lost her early developmental gains because of the gross neglect she experienced in that ward over the following year.

Videos taken by Mr B during his two visits to Alicia in that hospital over a ten-month period confirmed a general deterioration in her state. At sixteen months, Alicia was barely able to sit up without support, let alone pull herself into sitting or standing or even crawling position. She made no eye contact and stared at her hands with a vacant look, just like a "Spitz baby". Alicia seemed now to be also visually and hearing-impaired, showing no reactions to overtures or noises. She sought no attention and, unlike the other babies in that ward, she did not ask to be picked up whenever strangers appeared. She had, in effect, given up hope of interacting with a caring and responsive adult.

The medical director of the hospital described Alicia to the Bs as "mentally handicapped", and indeed their video pictures suggested institution-induced autism or "hospitalism" (Spitz, 1945). The Bs did not know if this were reversible or whether their toddler was already too brain-damaged by her first year and a half of privation to ever catch up developmentally.

I already knew the Bs, having carried out their adoption assessment during the previous year. So within a few days of her joining her new family in Britain, I visited Alicia as her "welfare supervisor" for the purpose of the adoption proceedings. She could now sit in a high chair and maintain eye contact with the Bs, but she looked through me as if I were invisible. There had been concern about her hearing ability, since she had seemed impervious to the noise of crying babies and the loud voices of the staff in the institution when the Bs had visited her. Now, they speculated that Alicia's apparent non-hearing and non-seeing were self-protective, to shut out the constant impingements on her sensitive self in that harsh environment.

On subsequent visits, I observed marked gains in the toddler's development. Alicia was bright and able to understand simple instructions; although she had no speech as yet, she could communicate her needs non-verbally. She was friendly and approached me at once when I visited, even though I was a stranger. Alicia began to relate to me directly, lifting her arms to be picked up. Standing on my lap, she would then minutely examine my face, neck, and hair, turning my head this way and that, as if I were a doll, and she were still a baby.

Alicia's global developmental delay necessitated a lot of one-to-one attention and teaching by the Bs. Her eye contact and interactions steadily improved, as did her physical co-ordination and progress. The Bs' early concerns that she might have cerebral palsy or autism soon proved to be unfounded. Alicia learnt to sit up on her own, then crawl, stand, climb, and, in time, to walk and even run, always showing great curiosity about everything. She loved being outdoors, as she had been confined for her first eighteen months in a hospital cot with very little besides cockroaches on the wall to observe.

Alicia was obsessed with creepy crawlies, skin blemishes (like moles), spectacles, and rings worn by people. She had to be taught by the Bs that she could not have people's spectacles, if they were being worn, or their rings! She would try to pull mine off, treating my hands as if they were objects that were not attached to me. Alicia refused to be confined by a seat belt when travelling by car, and she preferred to wear no clothes. All of these behaviours could be linked to her early experiences of prolonged confinement, but they were exhausting to the Bs.

Within fifteen months of Alicia's arrival, Mrs B admitted to having severe problems in managing the little girl's behaviours to the point where she felt that their new daughter was destroying their family. Alicia's almost miraculous progress with the Bs and her lively and responsive personality had masked the increasing difficulties they were experiencing in dealing with her wilfulness and mega-tantrums.

Alicia was, in brief, controlling and very aggressive, especially towards Mrs B. She was indiscriminately affectionate with strangers, with a tendency to wander off at will. She was unable to comply with simple requests for co-operation by the family, draining them all with her prolonged screaming outbursts from morning till night.

Knowing the Bs were very experienced in child care, I was at first surprised to learn that this charming little girl could cause such havoc in their previously well-ordered household. Nearly three years old by now, Alicia did not speak any English but clearly understood it and was frustrated by her inability to express her feelings and wants verbally. Her explosive tantrums would begin from 5 a.m. when she woke up; they sometimes lasted all day. Her frustration often centred around Mr B, whose sole attention she demanded whenever he came home from work, effectively "capturing" him, to the detriment of their other family relationships (Byng-Hall, 1995, p. 163). Alicia was correspondingly quite dismissive towards Mrs B, who felt increasingly rejected by, and angry with, the little girl and Mr B for his greater tolerance of her misbehaviours.

CAT interventions

We identified with the Bs that the major issues for them were currently:

- *effective management of Alicia's escalating tantrums*, including a consistent approach, since there was a tendency by Mr B in particular to be very permissive with her, perhaps in an attempt to compensate for her eighteen months' confinement in a hospital cot;
- *Alicia's primary attachment to Mr B*, who had chosen her from the many babies in the hospital ward, needed to be shared with Mrs B, who had full time care of her;
- *Protection*: the child's reluctance to accept any restraints when outside, and her overfriendliness with strangers, put her at risk of harm.

We felt there were other issues for the family which included:

- *losses*: these were multiple for Alicia (family, culture, language, country) and for the Bs (the need to extend their family through adoption because of their second son's hereditary illness, and the recent death of Mrs B's mother). All these losses needed to be acknowledged and mourned.

We co-worked with the family over a six-month period: in individual, couple, and parent–child sessions, and, through discussion and play-work, in weekly two-hour sessions either at their home or at the family-finding unit.

Play-work, with boundary-setting, proved to be crucial to the success of our work with Alicia and Mrs B in particular. The little girl seemed intuitively to know that the play sessions were her "special time" with her mother, not to be encroached on by adult preoccupations. She would shush us if we spoke! As a play specialist, Pauline was quickly able to engage with Alicia, maintaining clear boundaries, and gradually drawing in her mother into nurturing play that the little girl spontaneously initiated. Mrs B was able to see Alicia in a different light, and therefore to offer her appropriate nurturing and a chance to regress to baby behaviours before expecting her to move on as a three-year-old.

In Pauline Sear's words:

Ground rules were established at the onset of the sessions within a boundaried play space which afforded Alicia containment in a non-threatening environment. This boundaried area provided a safe inner haven for the little girl which, over time, proved that Alicia was able to explore and accept limitations in play. This led to increased positive interactions with her mother who was able to observe and respond to her daughter's requests for nurturing (cues).

Alicia enjoyed exploratory play, often in silence, while she chose which toys she would use. She appeared to have a great need to be nurtured, and showed this in her play with baby dolls. Alicia could be very loving and needed close physical contact with her mother, but she was also very demanding if she wanted something NOW! If her demands were not met at once, she would tantrum like a much younger child.

As the weekly sessions progressed, it became evident that Alicia was able to play happily, with very few tantrums. The joint play with her mother was managed within the same ground rules and limits. Shared, spontaneous play initiated by Alicia was reinforced by Mrs B, who felt "freed" to enjoy and encourage this positive side of her daughter. Early on in one session, after wrapping a small blanket around herself, Alicia sought the comfort of Mrs B's lap, curled up, and went to sleep for the duration of the session.

Mrs B was then able to use this time to explore her own unacknowledged inner child feelings about this little daughter who was now being given special time and attention in a way that she, as an eldest daughter in her own birth family, had never had the luxury of enjoying. I felt that Alicia had intuited her mother's need and so allowed Mrs B "special time" with me while she slept.

Subsequent sessions were then geared for Alicia and her mother to play together, for instructions to be given and understood, and consistency to be maintained. Mrs B was able to observe the toys that Alicia chose, how she used them, and how she was able to communicate her unspoken needs. The mother was encouraged to focus on some of Alicia's demands and to change negative patterns of interaction in which they had both been stuck.

Mrs B was thus able to see the value of this special play-time with Alicia in building their attachment as mother and daughter. Alicia also learnt to cope with frustration in the sessions, e.g., not being allowed to take a pair of sunglasses from the toy box away with her, or Maeja's rings. This, too, provided modelling for Mrs B.

Family work. Relationships had, almost inevitably, become skewed in this family, given the very different and competing needs of Alicia and the B's two teenage sons; one was totally disabled and the other extremely capable. The Bs had been mentally prepared for a smaller version of their disabled son, but not for the volatile, aggressive, and lively little girl that Alicia had turned out to be. Mr B now felt very guilty about so burdening his wife and sons. Having spent three weeks on his own with Alicia while abroad, he had developed a close relationship with her. This made it much more difficult for Mrs B to take over the mothering role with the little girl, who kept pushing her away (miscues and responses. See Figure 4, p. 27).

Both parents were very aware of Alicia's history of privation and physical restrictions, including being routinely swaddled in her cot. They had, therefore, been reluctant to apply normal restraints when she misbehaved, as she increasingly did with them. However, their lack of boundary-setting provoked even more alarming behaviours by Alicia, including running away, in her unconscious attempts to elicit secure holding by them. Caught in an increasingly "negative spiral of interaction", these previously confident parents had become quite bemused by the confusing cues Alicia was giving them both.

We therefore focused on helping the family to reinforce normal boundaries of behaviour. We also encouraged Mr B to relinquish the "mothering role" to his wife and to support her in setting limits for Alicia.

The Bs did some very sensitive life story work with Alicia, using videos taken of her while abroad to begin to tell her story during one of our home visits. Despite her limited vocabulary, the little girl seemed to understand a little as, silently, she watched herself on screen in the institution and then with the Bs both abroad and later in Britain. We all recognized this was only the *start* of ongoing work that the parents would need to do with Alicia over the years to help her understand more and more of her story as she got older.

Making positive changes. The Bs were in crisis over Alicia's escalating tantrums when they agreed to participate in the CAT pilot project. Their willingness to try new strategies soon helped them to take charge appropriately as adults and "hold" Alicia both physically and emotionally. This assisted her, in turn, to acquire much needed self-control and social skills. Joining a playgroup also greatly helped, along with her acquisition of a growing English vocabulary to communicate her feelings and needs more effectively than throwing tantrums.

The B's elder son, William, aged fourteen, proved to be an excellent ally in this family work, since he could be more objective than his parents, who got caught up emotionally in Alicia's tantrums. William himself pointed out the need for Alicia to be treated consistently, regardless of the context (e.g., car travel), so that she knew what to expect and felt more secure. (Alicia was brought by car to Britain from abroad by the Bs, who were strangers to her. At an unconscious level, therefore, she might have associated car travel with confinement and being taken away by strangers. She might also have had an unconscious resistance to learning a "foreign" language, since she was three years old by now but barely spoke any English.)

Mrs B fed back that she had found some of our CAT interventions intrusive, and she questioned our linking of issues from the past with their difficulties in parenting Alicia more effectively in the present. However, Mrs B acknowledged that participation in the project had helped to change their attitude to discipline as well as her own to "growing closer through play in a peaceful environment" with her forceful little daughter.

Mrs B also acknowledged that her now altered expectations of Alicia's behaviour in potentially problematic situations did make some difference to the outcome. It seemed likely that Alicia herself felt safer since her mother was taking charge of the situation as a parent, instead of being undermined by her tantrums and perhaps then responding inappropriately. (See Chapter Seven.)

Learning from "control group" families C and D

It was enormously helpful to us in this pilot project to compare the effectiveness of brief focused therapy with CAT families A and B and that of ongoing work with two families, C and D, not included in the project, but with whom we were involved over a much longer period.

Work with family C

Edward's story

Edward was only seven when we first met him, but he already had a history of playgroup and infant school failures. As a bright five-year-old, he had been expelled from his first infant school after only three weeks there, since he could not be safely contained in that setting. We learnt that the large classroom was open plan in layout which, not surprisingly perhaps with hindsight, added to Edward's own anxieties about being contained there safely.

His behaviours were soon deemed to be too disruptive to be managed in an ordinary primary school setting, and he had no schooling for almost a year before spending a few weeks in a small educational assessment unit. It was then decided that Edward had "special educational needs", and so he was placed in a school for children with "moderate learning difficulties". This assessment was based on Edward's behavioural and emotional presentation, despite his considerable intelligence and an innate resourcefulness.

Edward had been removed from his mother's care soon after birth because of her gross neglect of his older brothers and sisters. He was placed shortly after with experienced foster carers, and Mr and Mrs C were introduced to Edward when he was just eleven months old. His adoption by them, heavily contested by the birth parents, had taken four years to finalize. This prolonged period of uncertainty about Edward's future with the Cs seemed to have left the new family in an emotional limbo. We learnt much later that the adopters had indeed never felt able to claim Edward as their son. He had been so attached to his foster carers when the Cs met him, they almost felt that they had stolen him.

The teachers, like his parents, were having considerable difficulty in containing this seven-year-old, who kept running away, at every opportunity it seemed, from school as well as from home. Edward disliked changes of any kind, and, if not properly prepared for a new situation, he would simply run away. Edward had also begun to shoplift, and, as he ran further and further away on his own to local parks, his sexualized behaviour raised considerable concerns for his safety during these escapades. Edward was verbally and physically aggressive towards his parents, teachers, and his peers, and he quite often posed a danger to himself and others.

The police were frequently involved, not only because they were called out when Edward went missing, but also because he had begun to dial 999 himself from public call boxes and would usually ask for the Fire Brigade or another emergency service. The parents and school were naturally annoyed and embarrassed by Edward's constant raising of an "alarm" to professionals of one sort or another, and there was much blaming of each other for his misbehaviours.

In his drawing of a house for us in an early session, Edward made sure it included a burglar alarm and had strong fences, indicating his general feelings of insecurity at home. Mr and Mrs C then informed us that they did not feel safe in their neighbourhood. Edward had clearly picked up their anxieties about living there.

The parents' inability to "metabolise and contain" (Bion, 1978) their own anxious feelings had led to a role-reversal for Edward, who felt unheld by them.

The Cs felt with increasing despair that they were the wrong parents for Edward and, unfortunately, the school had come to the same conclusion. After his every misdemeanour, the head would call the parents to task as if they were naughty children who needed correction, just like Edward himself. The Cs were a modest and unassuming couple who felt increasingly undermined and deskilled in their parental role. They were completely unable to predict what Edward would do next to alarm or shame them further. They believed that the whole neighbourhood knew about their inadequacies as parents.

Pre-CAT Pilot Project work

The Cs' anxiety about not being the right parents for Edward began to transfer itself to us, too. Were they able to protect him? Were they committed to his placement with them, or was it near breakdown because of his ongoing misbehaviours? Why was he acting like this anyway in "a nice family", which, if anything, over-indulged him as their only child. We had yet to learn from our CAT work with family B about the crucial importance of boundary-setting to help a child feel safe and contained.

The Cs then described to us how, on a recent day trip to London, Edward had not only refused to sit with them when travelling by tube, but then began to play a game where he would get off the crowded train on his own when it stopped at each station before jumping on board again just before the doors closed! The parents remained seated, doing nothing to intervene, as they had felt so mortified by Edward's earlier vociferous rejection of them. They seemed unaware of just how dangerous his behaviour was, or that they were failing to protect Edward by not claiming him publicly as their son and holding him firmly, despite embarrassment at his likely protests.

As with Family B, it was the parents' over-permissiveness which alerted us to the absence of the attachment–protection dynamic in Edward's case. Like Alicia, he was running further and further afield and putting himself at ever greater risk in a desperate and unconscious attempt to provoke safe containment by the Cs. However, in their feelings of shame and inadequacy, they distanced themselves even more from him.

We learnt much later that the couple had had very little time to grieve over their inability to have a child of their own before

Edward was placed with them The Cs themselves had only recently been helped during their intensive "attachment therapy" week at the Post-Adoption Centre in London to grieve over the loss of their "ideal child". This, they had imagined, would have been a quiet, blonde, blue-eyed little girl, whom they felt would have been the perfect match for them.

Instead, Edward, as their "real child", was stockily built, dark-haired, and boisterous. The Cs had never been able to claim Edward as their adopted son. They thought from the start that he did not fit into their family. They still felt he belonged to his foster parents, who had cared for him from soon after birth.

We later learnt that even using his name had been problematic for the Cs, since a disliked relative was called "Edward". However, they did not feel entitled to give their new son a different name since he had been known as "Edward" for eleven months already. The positive aspect of this was that the Cs had been able to empathize with how confused the little boy might have felt about the sudden and simultaneous loss of his name and identity as well as of his foster family and home and all that he was familiar with.

We could now better understand why Edward found changes of any kind so difficult. Finding Edward too much to manage on her own, even in his first few months with them, Mrs C sought to address the problem by taking him to three different mother-and-toddler groups each week. The constant change in environment and people must have been overwhelming for this sensitive little toddler, who, more than anything, needed stability and security. Edward reacted with tantrums to any change, alarming his worried adopters even more. His increasingly challenging behaviours since placement had fully taxed all their resources.

Meanwhile, the Cs remained highly ambivalent towards Edward throughout the protracted adoption proceedings, believing—perhaps even unconsciously hoping—that he would soon be returned by Court Order to his birth family. After a last-minute courtroom drama involving his very angry and distraught mother, the Cs could scarcely believe that they were Edward's legal parents at last and now fully responsible for him. It seemed that their thought of "losing" Edward in the contest for him with his birth parents had got in the way of their attaching fully to him and claiming him as their son.

The Cs' thinking may also have been conveyed unconsciously to the little boy, who proceeded to "act out" being lost by frequently running away from the puzzled adopters. In what had become a negative spiral of interaction, they felt more and more rejected by Edward and less and less able to claim him as their son and protect him appropriately, containing him physically and emotionally as he so desperately needed.

Nevertheless, Mrs C must have retained some hope for Edward, since she persuaded me quite early on to refer the family to "experts" for treatment. She had heard that the Post-Adoption Centre in London was offering attachment therapy, and they accepted the Cs in their pilot project in August 1995. Pauline Sear and I got some useful learning from our observations there, which helped us to design our own "child-centred" model of attachment therapy.

CAT-influenced work with family C

Mrs C had found the intensive week of treatment at the Post-Adoption Centre in London very helpful and empowering. However, we still needed to continue to support the family locally. Pauline and I learnt, through working in this way, that careful planning and preparation for intensive therapy, with a routine follow-up period to reinforce new learning, monitor progress, and provide skilled support, are essential to the success of any programme of family intervention.

The Cs disclosed that they often felt undermined as adults by Edward's challenging behaviours, so they would end up responding to him quite inappropriately in child self mode. This was not surprising, and we later heard the same from his headmaster and a very experienced respite carer who knew Edward well. His forcefulness, logic, and constant challenges to adult authority tended to wear down otherwise competent and confident adults, including his teachers, in their belief that they were right in any conflict with this seven-year-old child.

The Cs increasingly ineffectual *responses* to Edward's miscues (see Figure 4, p. 27) had the effect of reinforcing his very early feelings. These were of being frighteningly out of control in a dangerously unpredictable world where any change was alarming.

Edward, therefore, sought to control every aspect of his life, while treating his parents as other children whom *he* needed to look after (see Holmes, 2004, p. 183).

This was very poignantly illustrated by Edward's behaviours when the Cs suddenly decided, quite foolhardily we thought, to take this runaway child on a week's holiday abroad. They reported no major incident until one morning when Mrs C's parents, who had accompanied them, remained in the hotel while the couple and Edward strolled to a nearby shop to buy a local paper. As they were about to leave the shop, the skies opened and there was a sudden and very heavy downpour. Before they could decide what to do, Edward had disappeared.

Frantic that he could easily get lost in a foreign country, Mr C went in search of him while Mrs C hurried back in the rain to the hotel to tell her parents that they would all have to go searching for him. But Edward was already back, desperately trying to convince his bewildered grandparents that he needed a large towel to run back with to the shop so that he could provide shelter for his parents from the rain! Edward could not have expressed more eloquently how much he loved his parents, but also that he perceived them as rather inept children whom *he* needed to protect. He had indeed claimed the Cs, but not in a *parental* role!

Play-work

Pauline's play-work with Edward was invaluable in helping the parents to set appropriate boundaries to hold and protect him. We continued to see the couple jointly for a year in all to support them in *taking charge as his parents*. In Pauline's words:

> Edward presented as a chaotic child when he first came in for play sessions. He was unable to settle for even the shortest time, choosing instead to walk and run around the play area. He did this for the first two sessions, and his anxiety seemed very high. He spoke little to me then, but would pick up various toys and quickly put them down again, barely looking at them.
>
> After Edward gradually began to settle and look comfortable, I scheduled weekly sessions for the following two months. I structured these very carefully in order to establish a secure base for

Edward, maintaining firm boundaries, consistency, and ground rules so that he would have some sense of containment within the session.

We then moved on to indirect, less structured play within a tight therapeutic framework. This enabled Edward to gain in confidence and make choices, as he developed a growing sense of "self". He began to recognize his positive and negative choices, to change direction in his play, and his behaviours, too, over time. Edward then began to communicate his feelings verbally. Previously, he had "acted these out" quite negatively and often very dangerously, as when he would run away from school for long periods at a time and cause his parents and teachers great concern for his safety.

The picture that emerged over time was of a strong-willed, but sometimes scared young boy who was often confused by his parents' and the school's somewhat inconsistent holding. Edward needed firm boundaries to correct the role reversal that sometimes occurred in his family, with him acting as "controlling parent" and Mr and Mrs C responding in "helpless child" mode. The Cs were encouraged to participate in some joint work with Edward, taking charge verbally and non-verbally as his parents, and setting clear rules. This helped to relieve him of his perceived responsibility for them, and to enjoy being more of a child himself.

Making positive changes

Life story work. Pauline supported the family in doing a new life story book with Edward to include his seven years with them, since his original book had been prepared by a social worker before his move as a baby to the Cs. This time, Edward could choose what went into his book, and he decided to *exclude* all photographs and references to his birth family. He wanted to belong to his adoptive family and was not yet ready to tolerate the ambivalence inherent in the adoptive child's position of straddling two families.

Mr C needed reinforcement in his role as Edward's father, and to support his wife in her mothering of this very challenging young child, who could still "act out" his anxieties quite dangerously at times. However, Mrs C's more relaxed and creative responses to Edward made a considerable difference. His teacher, too, learnt to deal with his disruptive behaviours at school by de-escalating conflict. Edward proved responsive to greater structure in his life and clearer boundary-setting by his parents, as indeed he had been in play sessions with Pauline. As with Alicia in family B, Edward knew what he needed and had been unconsciously "acting out" his anxieties to elicit this containment.

Pauline and I decided that further involvement by us with this family was contraindicated, since Mrs C was expressing the family's dependence on us for functioning well, although in reality she and her husband had always had to deal with their child's recalcitrance and consequences. We ended work with the family a year after their intensive week's therapy at the Post Adoption Centre in London. We were now confident that the Cs had the resources to continue to parent Edward more effectively. A twinkle in her eye at our final session made us realize that Mrs C had benefited from having so much professional attention, although she actually enjoyed rising to challenges herself.

As a postscript to Edward's story, we learnt a few years later that Mr C had a sudden heart attack one day, soon after leaving their home with his wife and son. It was Edward, now just eleven years of age, who recognized the signs from watching medical dramas on TV and rushed to a neighbour's house to ask her to call an ambulance at once. Edward undoubtedly helped to save his father's life by getting him immediate treatment.

Learning from family D

Donna's story

Donna was a single parent with "moderate learning difficulties". I had worked with her for many years, initially as an adoption worker in helping to place her baby, and later through psychotherapy to help her grieve her many child and family losses. When Donna became pregnant again, old childhood and adult hurts resurfaced. My increasing concerns about her ability to care safely and effectively for her new son prompted me after some months to involve Pauline Sear in working with both mother and child. This period overlapped with our starting work on the CAT pilot project, so that we became increasingly clear about our objectives in working with Donna, and how to set about achieving these.

In Pauline's words:

Donna and Charlie, aged one, began play sessions with me because of concerns about the baby's delayed development and the mother's seeming inability to meet his needs.

Donna had received very little positive parenting herself, and she had difficulty in coping with Charlie in a calm and encouraging way. I sought early on to engage Donna in interactive play with her baby, but she did not seem to know what to do. Her anxiety about appearing "stupid" might have been transferred to Charlie, who would pick up toys and simply throw them around. Embarrassed, Donna would then tell him off sharply, and Charlie would start to scream, confirming her in her feelings of failure as a mother.

In a following session, Donna ventured to play with the dolls house and small family figures on her own. I encouraged her in this "free play", and gradually included Charlie in it to help them interact more positively. As her own "inner child" needs began to be met, Donna would laugh out loud when Charlie began to share toys with her. Simple ball-rolling across the floor gave both a great deal of pleasure.

On her first visit with me to a local park, Donna felt too anxious to allow Charlie the simple pleasure of walking on grass; she chose instead to carry him between the different play facilities. Her anxiety might have communicated itself to Charlie, who screamed for a couple of minutes, without tears; he only quietened after being put by her in a baby swing and rocked gently. Later, she was able to let him toddle around a little on his own.

We then learnt that Donna could only ever remember being taken once to the park as a small child. Her mother died shortly after, and she was put in a local children's home while the rest of her family emigrated. An abandoned child herself, she did not know how to meet her real baby's needs. Donna responded reluctantly to my firm expectations about her parental role, and was very slow to engage in nurturing and stimulating play with her son because of her fear of failure.

With hindsight, this intervention with mother and child may have been much more effective if condensed into a very focused and time-limited programme of our co-working, with ongoing therapeutic support from me for Donna's learning much-needed parenting skills from Pauline, since I had already established with her a relatively "secure base" from the years we had worked together. What I learnt now was that, while my previous psycho-therapeutic work with Donna had been boundaried and containing, I had somehow drifted into relatively woolly social work mode since the birth of her baby.

As Donna had no childcare support, I sometimes saw her with the baby and at other times he was looked after by a worker down-stairs. We had no agreed focus for our work together at this time and, being less boundaried now, I could not contain her own anxi-ety or mine about her actual parenting capacity. I slowly and painfully learnt that the more I responded in "helpful" mode to Donna's learnt helplessness, the angrier and more disabled she felt. Caring for a helpless baby had brought up all her own disabled, abused, neglected, and rejected child self issues, her "ghosts in the nursery" (Fraiberg, Adelson, & Shapiro, 1975). Afraid of being shown up as stupid, Donna refused to learn new, playful ways of interacting with her baby, or how to parent him more effectively.

Salzberger-Wittenberg (1970) describes the predicament of the caseworker in such cases and recommends:

> It is important to strive to do as little as possible, for any active intervention tends to infantilise the client, lead to inertia, to resent-ment and persecution as well as to promote despair about not being able to cope oneself. The worker has constantly to sort out whether she is being manipulated, drawn into fitting in with the unrealistic wishes of the client, colluding with his destructive parts, and/or helping him to avoid facing inner conflicts by externalising his problems. In all these instances, she would not be helping the client to cope with anxiety and would undermine the struggle towards growth. [p. 159]

Conclusion

For a short while, it had seemed that moving from helpless, hurt, and bereft child self mode to developing her more competent adult potential was greatly boosted by Donna's own healthy wish to learn how to be a better mother to her new baby. Realistically, however, even with more focused and sustained therapeutic support, this may have been too big a task for Donna, given her own learning impairment and the child's greater need for stimulation because of his global developmental delay.

My increased expectations of Donna, and the everyday demands made on her as a parent, were more than she could cope with. Our work together ended when I introduced her to a HomeStart befriending scheme for local support. Sadly, we later learnt that Charlie, too, was removed from her care and placed for adoption, since she was not able to meet his developmental needs.

I might have needed to acknowledge much earlier that Donna was so badly damaged by her childhood and young adult experiences of repeated rejection, abandonment, and abuse that she could not offer safe parenting to her own children. In that case, CAT could have been used for necessary "detachment" work to help Donna prepare for the loss of this son, too, and carry out further griefwork.

Contact with Charlie after adoption could also have been negotiated in a way that would have been beneficial to both him and his mother, but these are all after-thoughts. We were no longer in touch with Donna and so, sadly, we were unable to offer her any further support.

Overall learning from the pilot project

The CAT team, like the County Focus Group of senior adoption practitioners, which had met bi-monthly to reflect on the work carried out with families A and B, learnt a great deal about the potential of attachment therapy even in the limited timescale of six months for the pilot project.

1. From a co-ordinator's point of view, I realized how important it was to set aside a consistent time each week to carry out such challenging work and to reflect on it with colleagues afterwards. Monthly consultation with Dr Stella Acquarone, an experienced parent–infant psychotherapist, had fortunately been agreed from the start. Her insights were invaluable in helping us to understand the family dynamics when we felt

stuck. Thus, we were able to make important breakthroughs to help the parents move on.

2. From a management point of view, and with hindsight, more time should have been allowed for the pilot project to include provision for peer supervision and CAT team meetings, as well as the inevitable holidays, sick leave, and other contingencies that arose. This would have facilitated our intensive family work, and the planning, preparation, and reflection that were needed to carry it out effectively. The concurrent family losses experienced by four of the five CAT team members meant that additional time off was needed for bereavement work by the workers themselves before we could attend to the pilot families' losses and help them with *their* griefwork.

3. We learnt that, for effective work, the family have to be equal partners in our joint venture. We have to share information honestly with them, thus providing a secure base from which to explore the perceived problem(s), and foster trust and attachment and shared learning (Figure 16.)

4. Firm holding of personal, professional, and family boundaries is crucial in this work, which often uncovers child protection issues.

5. We realized more clearly the interdependence of the different quadrants of the attachment–protection cycle (Figure 17): the *direct* expression of feelings by the child; consistent and appropriate meeting of her needs by the carer to create a secure base, with firm holding of boundaries. This helps the child to feel safely held, worthy of protection, and so to act more predictably, giving and receiving appropriate *cues* and *responses* to have her needs met. In turn, the carer feels validated as parent, and entitled to provide care to this particular child; so he claims and protects the child as his own, thus providing safety for the child and the whole family.

6. We learnt—through comparing our longer and more open-ended work with our control group families C and D—about the value of doing focused time-limited work, since time is also an important boundary. This counteracts the tendency for individual or family work to otherwise be more woolly and drift indefinitely, with fewer long-term benefits for families in crisis and overburdened workers.

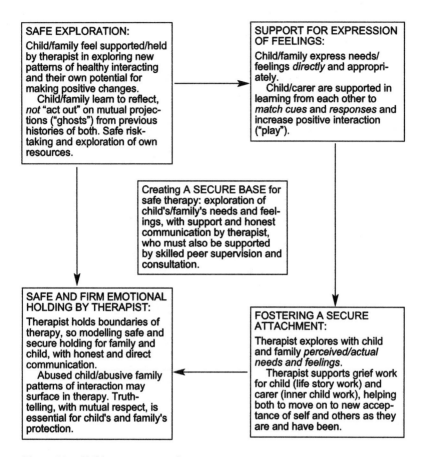

Figure 16. Child protection in therapy.

7. The child's overt problem may indicate the focus of work needed with the family. In the case of family B, the child's unmanageable temper tantrums were the original reason for referral to CAT. Work with the family helped Alicia to express her feelings and needs appropriately, and this was facilitated by her learning to speak English. However, we were then left with the underlying issue: the parents' inability to speak for themselves. They had so much unexpressed grief, as she did, too, and unconsciously they might have projected their inadmissible feelings and needs on to Alicia, which she then had to express for the family without language.

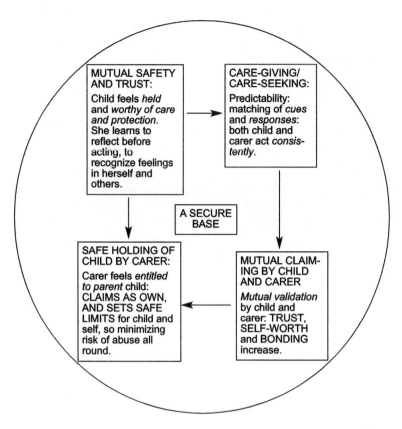

Figure 17. Attachment–protection cycle: creating "a secure base" and safety.

8. We learnt from Edward and his parents that life story work is an ongoing process, which requires the workers to be attuned to the changing developmental needs of a new family, and to support the child's growing attachment to them. In this way, his necessary mourning for the loss of his birth family and previous foster carers could be supported by his adoptive parents at a more opportune time for them all in the future.

9. When considering the griefwork that needs to be undertaken with hurt children who suffer multiple family and other losses each time they are moved to a new "home", there are enormous resource implications for providing timely and skilled therapeutic support for them and their carers (Figure 18).

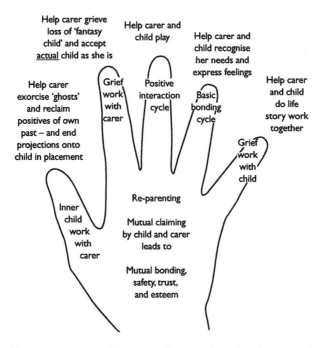

Figure 18. Holding, attachment, and nurturing development (HAND). Therapist/carer provides emotional holding: a secure base.

10. I had worked with the Cs over a period of two years, the second year overlapping with our involvement with the CAT pilot project. Inevitably, there was cross-fertilization of learning and insights from the Cs and our pilot family B, which informed and enriched our work with both families. What was most helpful in changing our approach to working with Edward and his parents was our learning from the pilot project to do time-limited and focused work with them, too. This helped us to wean the Cs off dependence on us, since, in reality, they were a competent and resourceful family.

Notes

1. This section of the chapter is contributed by Maggie Gall and Margaret Saxby.
2. This section of the chapter is contributed by Maggie Gall.
3. This section of the chapter was co-authored with Pauline Sear.

CHAPTER FIVE

Phase 3 of the project (1997–2007) CAT as an independent attachment therapy with birth, extended, foster, and step-families: our further learning from families

CAT as therapeutic assessment

Our pilot project with adoptive families taught us that truth-telling is an essential boundary in our therapeutic work with children, adults, and families, keeping both them and us safe. (see Figure 16 and Chapter Six). They could otherwise find themselves in potentially abusive situations through our collusion with their parenting failures or "acting out" of old unconscious scripts in response to the child's learnt behaviours.

Our ongoing work with our control group families C and D (described in Chapter Four, above) highlighted these points of learning, as we realized that the CAT Programme could easily be adapted to meet the needs of birth, extended, foster, and step-families too.

Indeed, the "child protection" element integral to attachment work suggested that CAT could be used very effectively in "therapeutic assessments", by helping struggling families to safely contain children who might otherwise have to be removed from them because of Social Services' concerns (see Chapter Six).

Family E's story

Our thinking about therapeutic assessments arose from our involvement quite early on with family E, who separated after allegations were made by an older adopted daughter against the father. She was moved to a foster home near her birth family, from whom she had been removed as a small child after severe sexual abuse by them.

Mrs E immediately left the marital home with their younger daughter, whose weekly contact thereafter with Mr E had to be supervised by a social worker, who happened to be me. I became increasingly aware of the family's distress after they were referred to prominent psychiatrists for protracted child, parent, and family assessments. These, like the Court proceedings, dragged on for well over a year, while Mr E got more and more depressed living on his own. The deterioration in his state and living conditions seemed to be taken as evidence of his guilt, which we were not able to comment on.

What became clear to us was that assessments for the Court, like any other intervention, can be therapeutic or not. The moment we begin to ask questions, memories that are called to mind and shared are already being reflected upon and altered, consciously or not. We therefore decided very early on that, in our joint explorations with families of their stated difficulties, CAT would combine assessment *and* treatment from the outset. This then led to our offering "therapeutic assessments" where children were at risk of harm (Figure 19).

The schooling of families

Frankie's story was educational, in more senses than one.

Frankie's story

Mr N, a legal executive, came to our first CAT session carrying two huge files. They were filled with correspondence with the local education authority about what he regarded as the school's failure to meet his adopted son's need. This was countered by the school's views about the parents' failure to curb Frankie's disruptive behaviours in class.

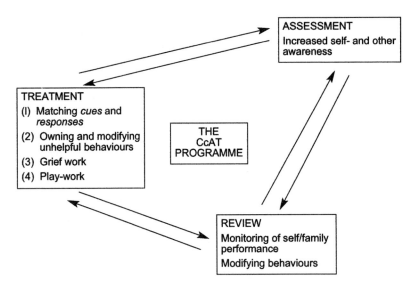

Figure 19. CAT as an assessment, treatment, and review in partnership with the family.

The parents had also got into a "negative spiral of interaction" with Frankie at home, where he was totally unco-operative. As we worked with them, we realized that Mr and Mrs N had no effective boundaries to contain Frankie safely. He seemed very immature for thirteen, and showed little potential for change. However, for the third session, we made a home visit, and then saw Frankie in literally a different light.

In an aside to Mr N about a forthcoming parents' evening at school later that week, and the need for him to obtain appointments for them with each of his teachers, Frankie warned his father, "And you'll have to be on time—it's a school rule!" We all listened in astonishment to Frankie, whose stated problem was that he seemed incapable of following rules either at home or at school. It was now evident that the problem was home-based, since Frankie had learnt that the school stuck by its rules while his parents did not abide by theirs.

We knew that, if Frankie could follow rules in one setting, he was capable of doing so in another. The work that needed to be done with the Ns was to help them to prioritize their needs as a family and do some simple rule-setting with Frankie that they could all follow. Feeling more securely held at home, his behaviours improved both there and at school.

Family-generated solutions can work better

Families have innate healing resources that can be accessed by them to create new solutions to old problems. These solutions, because they originate from within the family, are more likely to be congruent with its culture than those suggested by professionals, and therefore more acceptable to its members.

We discovered early on that some of the foster carers had a perhaps unconscious vested interest in our suggestions *not* working for them. The reasoning seemed to be that, if we succeeded where they had failed, they would be shown up as less than effective parents. So, the child whose placement was near disruption tended to be pathologized, and our efforts to help the family would be rubbished outright or simply ignored.

We had to learn how to help families access their own creative resources, and our teachers were family J.

Ben's story

Mr and Mrs J were older, experienced foster carers with grown-up sons and daughters and young grandchildren. They had offered a home some months previously to Ben, the younger brother of a teenage girl, Gilly, whom they had cared for since she was little. We already knew that Ben had been through multiple placements, and seemed likely to add this one to his list of disruptions. He was aggressive and unruly at home, and had joined a group of delinquent boys at school. Ben was unsettled in the family and very jealous of Gilly's long-standing relationship with the carers, who were over-protective towards her because of her learning difficulties.

Mr J had traditional views on child-rearing. His sanctions for the children, and Ben in particular, included getting them to write 1000 times: "I will not do (the offending behaviour)". Since the subconscious mind tends to ignore negatives, this punishment seemed more likely to reinforce the offending behaviour. Indeed, Ben often ended up being given 5000 lines to write before he had even set off for school in the morning. This would undoubtedly have left him in an unco-operative mood and more likely to misbehave for the rest of the day.

We were curious to know what actually occurred to cause these early morning upsets, and we soon discovered that the family had got stuck in a negative spiral of interaction. Mr J would wake the children up early and they would start arguing from then on: over their choice of cereals, where they would sit to watch television, jostling each other to get first through a doorway, and then insult each other as they ate their breakfast.

The teenagers also fought physically, and Ben was invariably blamed for hurting Gilly, who quietly provoked him, unknown to the parents. There were other issues of safety, too, since both children had been sexually abused while living with their birth family. We had to encourage Gilly and Ben to maintain firm personal boundaries, including in their bedrooms, as neither currently had any privacy from the other.

We did not seem to be getting very far with the family. Whatever we suggested, Mr J's immediate response would be that they had "been there, tried it, and it did not work"! Then Gilly herself suggested a variant of the usual "behaviours" star chart they had previously tried and dismissed. Her idea was accepted: that they be given two gold stars for each time she and Ben said something nice to or about each other. This was a turning point for the family who started to reinforce positive behaviours instead of focusing on negative ones.

Ben was allowed to find his own place in the family, instead of having to fight with Gilly to share hers. Their sibling rivalry diminished, and they became good friends, protective of each other.

Like Edward in family C (see "Edward's story" in Chapter Four), Ben went on to help save Mr J's life a year or so later. He ran to call out a nurse who lived nearby when the foster carer had a heart attack and needed immediate resuscitation. Waiting for an ambulance to arrive would have been much too late. A hero in the family now, Ben settled down at school, too, and later went on to college, just as the J's older children had done. Ben was now happily following the family tradition and Mr and Mrs J were immensely proud of his achievements. They had claimed him as their son.

Mrs J generously attributed the success of Ben's placement to CAT, but each family member had to play their part in working towards making positive changes and maintaining them.

Marital difficulties might be the real problem

We worked with some families where, although the concerns expressed were about the child, the real problem lay in the parents' marital relationship.

Molly's story

Molly was thirteen when she was referred to ᛒAT, as her long-standing foster placement had disrupted. The carers stated their concerns for Molly's safety, both if she remained with them and if she returned to her still chaotic and emotionally abusive birth mother in another part of the country. Molly kept running away to be with her mother, just as her older sister had done the previous year. She would get unsettling telephone calls from both, and she was painfully torn between her conflicting loyalties to birth family and foster carers.

Molly was very clear-thinking and articulate, but we were unable to do any family work since the carers would not engage honestly with us. We then discovered that they themselves were at crisis point, as their marriage was ending. They did not want to look at their own difficulties, which had contributed to the breakdown of what they described as a previously stable and mutually rewarding placement.

Child protection concerns can be exacerbated in situations of marital conflict

Rico's story

Mr and Mrs F were professionals from abroad and had referred their three-year old son, Rico, to us as they were concerned about his social withdrawal. They believed that he was autistic and had been sexually abused by the caretaker at the nursery he attended. However, we were not clear whether their complaint had been investigated.

Rico was difficult to engage in interactive play, and he did seem to be obsessional: he kept miming a lift going up and down, with doors opening wide and closing; later, we wondered if this play represented hope appearing in, and disappearing from, his young life.

Mr F spoke English well, but his wife did not. So Mr F acted as interpreter in our early sessions, and conveyed in a matter-of-fact way what his wife said, including that he was deliberately making her mad. She seemed obsessively jealous and to suspect him of having girlfriends everywhere, at college during the day and in their block of flats at night. He added casually, as a further indication of her irrational thinking, that she also accused him of sexually abusing Rico. It was not until we spoke to Mrs F on her own in a subsequent session that we realized she meant this.

We advised her to contact her local Social Services—which she did. We had been misled by Mr F's apparent openness as spokesman and not realized in time that they were actually seeking help to be a safe family for their son. Following Social Services involvement, the family split up and Mrs F returned to her homeland with Rico. Mr F remained in England to complete his college studies. We were not informed of the outcome of the Child Protection Investigation in this case, or whether the parents were offered any therapeutic support, separately or together.

The child referred may not be the only one in the family who needs help

This situation occurred frequently, so that we were constantly shifting attention from the identified child client to others in the family who also needed help, or were somehow maintaining the problem. So much so that, if a child was described as the only one in the family with behavioural problems, we would take it as a cue to explore how the better-behaved siblings were contributing to this situation.

In "Ben's story", above (see family J), Gilly used to quietly wind up her brother to get him into trouble with the carers, because she had resented his joining their family and her then having to share their attention with him. As the family work progressed, Gilly's temper tantrums became more frequent and we offered her some individual sessions to help her express her feelings. Despite her inherited "learning difficulties", Gilly was emotionally intelligent and able to articulate her frustration at not being listened to by Mr J in particular. We were then able to address this issue in family sessions and help them to communicate better.

Some of the carers we worked with, however, were not willing to end the scapegoating of a particular child and to look at our sometimes serious concerns about other children in the family. Family G was among those unwilling to commit themselves to such painful exploration with us, although the wife went on to train in marital counselling.

Christy's story

Mr and Mrs G were experienced foster carers. They had adult children from their previous marriages and a teenage daughter from this one. She was the same age as Christy, who had been referred to CAT for ongoing behavioural problems. Christy was another displaced young person, exiled from her birth family, community, and county, as she was moved from one disrupted placement to another.

The Gs were genuinely fond of Christy and wanted to help her to settle in their family. However, our sessions soon revealed that the Gs' own daughter was depressed and also needed help. The parents were unwilling to address her difficulties, and so Christy had become a scapegoat for the family's malfunctioning. Predictably, her placement with the Gs soon ended, although she was able to stay in contact with them and seek their support when she became pregnant not long afterwards.

Birth families, like family T, can demonstrate the same dynamic.

Rachel's story

Rachel was thirteen and referred to CAT by her mother for increasing behaviour problems. In individual work with Pauline, and a joint family session, Rachel was able to convey her view of the family difficulties clearly and calmly. It seemed that an older brother, reported to be adversely affected by her misbehaviours, contributed to these, but Mr T did not want to hear this. He would not attend further family sessions, leaving the burden of change to rest on Rachel's young shoulders. She saw Pauline twice more on her own.

Mrs T was torn between conflicting loyalties to her husband and daughter. Without the parents' commitment to making positive changes that would have benefited them all, Rachel could not succeed on her own. As with so many mislabelled children, her "naughty" behaviours were an unconscious cry for help for the family.

Johnny's story

There was a happier outcome for this adoptive family.

Johnny was only ten years old when he was referred to CAT for severely disruptive behaviours at home and at school. We learnt that he had mega-tantrums that would often end in his throwing some of his bedroom furniture downstairs, while his adoptive parents help-lessly telephoned Mr M's elderly parents for adult reinforcement. Increasingly, that did not work for them, and they now resorted to summoning the police for help in containing Johnny. We heard that it had taken six adults to restrain him in a recent outburst, although Johnny presented as a pleasantly spoken and quite playful child, easy to engage with.

We were intrigued when we learnt that Johnny was in a swimming squad at school with early morning training sessions starting promptly at 6 a.m.; if he got there even a minute late, he was not allowed to join in. Yet Johnny readily accepted the coach's tough discipline, reminding us how Frankie N (see "Frankie's story", above) had been able to follow school rules while remaining unruly at home.

Mr and Mrs M were very family-centred and worked well as a team. They needed to do so in order to chauffeur Johnny to his daily morn-ing or afternoon swimming sessions or the regular Saturday "swim meets" in which he took part; as well as transporting their older son, Daniel, to his scouting activities. The Ms were a mild-mannered couple who did not seem able to take charge as parents and enforce clear boundaries. Daniel was a sensitive and intelligent boy who had appar-ently been well behaved until recently. He was now vying with Johnny for negative attention, perhaps jealous of his younger brother's swim-ming prowess.

The parents had adopted the boys as babies, and did not seem to know why they had now become so aggressive. Daniel's joining Johnny in tantruming behaviours seemed to be new. The older brother was type-cast as the "good, quiet child" while Johnny had always had the role of "naughty boy" in the family. In fact, Daniel was quietly provocative of his brother's over-the-top outbursts, and Mrs M often sat between the two boys on a settee to stop them kicking at each other! We had to demonstrate to her that they were quite capable of sitting next to each other and playing a game together quietly, and that this was our expec-tation of their behaviour on our premises.

We then learnt that, as a child, Mrs M had dreaded going home after school since she could not stop her older brothers from fighting in the absence of their mother, who was at work. So, Mrs M had begun to revert to helpless child mode whenever she saw her two sons now in conflict. This gave them an increasing sense of power over her, and Mr M often had to leave home late for work in the mornings in order to ensure that both boys were in the car ready to be driven to school by their mother. This meant he returned home too late in the evenings to have any leisure time to spend with the boys then. Thus, Mrs M had little respite from their continual squabbling, and was both physically and emotionally exhausted.

With so much daily hassle, the Ms did not find their sons rewarding to care for and the boys were equally unhappy. They attended a church-run school where bullying was the norm, as were insults about pupils' mothers. For an adopted child like Johnny, who had never known his birth mother, this was like holding up a red rag to the bull. He was in constant fights and resulting trouble at school. The Ms felt so badly about themselves as adoptive parents, they seemed unable to claim their sons as their own and be strong advocates for them in this very unsatisfactory school situation.

It took several sessions of individual and joint work with the whole family before the situation eased at home and both boys were able to sit together in the back of a car without coming to blows. In one family session, when we asked them to draw a picture of themselves having a day out together, their isolation from each other was poignantly depicted in their drawings. The pictures showed them sitting quite separate from each other, even at the picnic meals drawn by the boys and their father. Mrs M drew a seaside scene, with her and her husband sunbathing on deckchairs while the boys played separately on the beach; this was the most positive of their pictures.

Things did get better over time. Johnny felt heard by us and his parents and his behaviours gradually improved both at home and at school, where he had become a swimming star. Daniel developed an interest in computers, and the boys squabbled less.

Mrs M was considering taking up part-time work. We encouraged this, as we felt it would improve her self-esteem and give her a much-needed sense of achievement. She had been a full-time mother since the boys were babies, and had felt a failure in this role once they had grown older. Mrs M needed permission to be a "working mother", as her mother had been, and not to be worrying about the boys always fighting, as her brothers used to; in effect, to withdraw from Johnny and Daniel her child self projections of her violent brothers.

Mr M now returned earlier from work since he could leave home on time in the mornings. He was able to go on cycle rides with the boys and generally spend more "fun-time" with them, reclaiming his role and authority as their father. This freed Mrs M further from feeling totally responsible for Johnny and Daniel, and their interactions with each other. She began to explore her own potential as a person.

Siblings can help each other

We had some moving sessions where siblings were helpful to each other.

Leonie's story

Family O were referred to CAT because of their concerns about their two unrelated adopted children, Andrew, who was eight, and Leonie, who was just five years old. Her placement was near disruption as Mrs O could not manage her tantruming behaviours at home and seemed to regard the child as a little monster. Both children had been removed from their respective birth families because of severe neglect of them as babies. They had each been in foster care for a while before being placed separately, when toddlers, with the Os. There were still medical concerns about Andrew, who was very underweight.

In one session, while we were talking to the parents, we noticed that the children were quietly playing "mummies and babies" together. They had pulled together cushions to make a "bed" on the floor and Andrew lay on this, covered by Leonie with a light baby blanket. She then came to ask Pauline Sear to fill a baby bottle with orange squash, and proceeded to give this to Andrew. He drank it contentedly, while Leonie held the bottle to his mouth as if he were a baby. The little girl had known intuitively that he needed nurturing.

We suggested that Mrs O do the same for Andrew at home, giving him a bottle of milk each evening. Despite his father's embarrassment that Andrew should be encouraged to regress in this way, Mrs O clearly enjoyed the nurturing time that she had missed out on with her son when he was a baby. She was then able to offer Leonie the same for a while, too, which improved their relationship.

It seems appropriate to end this section with our learning from family L.

This was a birth family of four siblings who had survived gross neglect in their first few years of life with their alcoholic and often violent birth parents. Daisy, at four years old, used to steal money from her sleeping mother's purse to buy milk and bread for her starving brothers, especially the baby who was "failing to thrive". Daisy continued to be fiercely protective of him in contact meetings, once they were removed from home and placed separately in foster care because no one carer could cope with all of them.

The siblings continued to look out for each other during these family contacts, and remained loyal to their birth father, who underwent counselling and rehabilitation in order to reclaim his children. Four years later, after each child had gone through a series of disrupted placements and Daisy's frenzied attacks on adults could only be contained safely in a children's home, Social Services was able to acknowledge the damage done to the siblings in the "care" system.

The Department supported the return of the two younger boys to their father's care.

Their hope was that Daisy would be placed in a local foster home where she could see her beloved father and brothers more often, too. The eldest brother, just twelve years old, chose to remain in his latest foster home where he could appreciate having undivided care and attention from a very committed carer.

We felt that, with ongoing individual and family therapy and practical help, Mr L would probably manage better with his children now than anyone could have foreseen.

Further thoughts on CAT work with families[1]

Over the past several years, many children and young persons came through our door. The patterns and behaviours of their struggling families were all different and yet the same, it seemed. Their attachment, or perhaps the lack of it, provided us with many insights as to how and why some families really struggled to make it work. Always the same thread of "detachment", in so far as the real relationship between child and parent manifested itself. This was more so when a fostered or adopted child felt isolated, somehow not really fitting in, maybe treated a little differently to birth children. This difference was experienced at the very core, or soul, of the child, and it demonstrated almost every time where the real difficulties lay in the families we worked with.

If the very soul of a child is not nurtured, and she feels unwanted, unloved, misunderstood; if the child is not "fed" love and nurture, then a negative cycle of interactions between child and adult will become the norm. This could lead to the breakdown of the placement. (See Figure 4, Chapter One.)

So it was with the struggling families we worked alongside, trying to change the stuck negative patterns that had brought the family to crisis point in the first place. Most of the families who came our way were in this very situation, scarcely understanding how things could be so bad when the "bonded" family members always got along so well: that is, until the difficult child arrived. Now, it seemed, the family and household were in constant turmoil.

"Normal/OK" families will interact naturally between one another. When a disadvantaged child, or children in some cases, enters the family, the dynamics change considerably. Everyone needs to adjust, and this applies even more to the fostered/adopted child or children. These children will, in most cases, have had several moves, each family different in some, or often many, ways from the placement before. The child feels him/herself already to be the outsider, once again having to "fit in" with a new family.

We all take our day-to-day family life in our stride, saying and doing what we have always known, without giving it a second thought. However, the "stranger" child entering the family has no concept of how *this* particular family behaves at mealtimes or bedtimes; their bathroom routines; socializing norms; whatever. All this is often utterly bewildering and fraught with anxiety to the newcomer, and "acted out" in misbehaviours, with the child feeling left out and not really belonging. It becomes just another placement in which the child has hardly begun to settle in before she is moved on yet again.

It may seem less rejecting to such children if they consciously or not disrupt the placement through their misbehaviours, rather than wait to be rejected by yet another family. No wonder, then, that these children carry heavy baggage, being moved around like "pass-the-parcel" in the "care" system for most of their young lives.

Many of these children speak the same silent language of sadness and despair, expressed in difficult, often abusive behaviours to themselves or others. And so, the scene will already be set: a constant round of "'Getting to know you"; "How long will I be here?"; "I'm the odd one out"; "They all talk and act different to the last family"; "What do I do, who will I ask? *Can* I ask?"; "Who am I in this family?"; "What am I?", and so on.

If only grown-ups would listen, really listen, to children, really identify with how a child might be feeling. Listen at a deep level, not simply at the words spilling out, but recalling for ourselves a feeling or experience when we were young to identify with how it might be for that child. How the child may not have the adult words to articulate and explain . . .

Often, we came across families who really cared, who would pull out all the stops to make a foster child feel like part of the family, often sacrificing their own family needs in order to assure her that she was liked and welcomed. Of course, this sometimes had the reverse effect when the family members perhaps said and did things unnaturally for them *because* there was now a stranger living with them.

The knock-on effect could often be negative reactions by all, despite the good intentions at the outset. A pattern then evolved from the natural core element: attachment or the lack of it. The child's core self feels unnurtured, misunderstood, threatened. Foster carers struggle to be natural, to like and, ideally, love, and to understand this strange child. It is an unnatural struggle to achieve what should be perfectly natural: the most basic interactions between parent and child fuelled by attachment.

From an adult viewpoint, having grown up in an "OK family", it may be easy to assume that most children "in care" ("looked after" or "accommodated" children, in current Social Care terminology in England and Wales) would adapt to their new family after the usual honeymoon period. The real test, of course, is when that time is over and reality kicks in. Experience taught us that, for these fostered children, "normal" did not mean much, if anything to them. What, after all, was normal? Each placement had differing expectations, with few being met.

Most adults expect some reward for taking in such hurt children when, instead, there is often a price to pay for their disruptive behaviours. Such children punish before being punished; run away so that their feet, not their tongues, do the talking; lash out before being hit; and are even abusive before being abused, either verbally, emotionally or sexually, or all three.

In all cases, the very reasons CAT became involved was because some or all of these factors were prevalent—the older the child, and the longer he had been in the "care" system, the more hurt and angry he was likely to be.

And what about the child's birth family? Most of the children referred to CAT, while recalling how awful it had been at home, nevertheless wanted to return to their "natural" family. Where children in the care system had contact with their birth families, the very act of leaving them each time to return to their foster homes became an issue, as they were torn between divided loyalties: "Do I belong here or there?" Some children had had a series of family moves before reaching adolescence. How can such children have formed secure attachments to any one carer from early childhood? It would appear instead more like abuse within the "care" system.

* * *

Putting CAT into practice. There were, in many cases, a real hope and expectations that we could work alongside and support some of the families to better understand together how to help children in these circumstances. I like to think that our Programme offered a unique, tailor-made package of support for each family, since no two families had exactly the same issues. It did not always go according to plan on either side, I am sure. However, there were very few families who did not respond to our way of working.

The CAT sessions were generally for two hours per session and, depending on the seriousness of concerns, held at weekly or fortnightly intervals. We used each session as ongoing assessment and treatment, and shared our overall findings with the child and family at the tenth session, inviting their feedback, too, so that we could then incorporate it in our final report, and learn from them.

Each session would usually start and end with our seeing the child and parents jointly, or the whole family together for about half an hour. In between, Maeja would work with the adults, while I would engage with the child or children in "play" sessions for an hour.

As with Mrs B in our pilot project, and family D in our control group, I sometimes involved the parents, too, in nurturing play with the child.

Afterwards, we would talk through with the child and parents about their and our understanding of what had transpired, with myself acting as advocate for the child and supporting him in presenting his point of view to the parents. It is often the child who can pinpoint the exact difficulty, as well as the solution. This usually requires a change in behaviour on the part of the adults, which they are not always willing to consider. They might then rubbish what the child says, as well as ourselves as therapists.

All was not gloom and doom, despite what must have been very difficult for some families, airing their hurt and anger and frustration in public, so to speak. And how much more frightening for the children, who were labelled "naughty" and/or "difficult" or "unmanageable"? These children, who perhaps had never been asked an opinion before or deemed worthy of acknowledgement, were now faced with having to be "theraped". They were expected to tell all in "play", although this was often referred to as "a waste of time" or "only for little kids" by sceptical parents and sometimes even the older children.

Our aim was to establish a secure base with the child and family over a number of sessions. We encouraged each to contribute very honestly their own thoughts and feelings about the difficulties at home and more realistic expectations of change. An achievable goal for child and parents would usually then be agreed on, with them all reporting on progress in the following session. We found, as might be expected, that the most successful outcomes were related to the full engagement of the child and family, with them proposing their own creative solutions to the problems they experienced.

Informal family meetings held at a set time each week at home, to agree rules and sanctions and monitor progress, often proved to be very helpful in improving their communication all round. The children would often remind the parents about these meetings, and the ground rules for them, including speaking one at a time and respecting each person's opinion. Once over the immediate crisis, such meetings could incorporate "fun-time" too, e.g., playing a board game together or doing something else together in play.

Over time, our work did have many lighter moments, as families interacted with greater ease and trust in us. Sometimes, for longer lunchtime sessions involving observation of sibling and family attachments and mediation of contact arrangements, we would suggest that the adults brought food to share and we would also provide some.

Sharing food symbolizes the "breaking of bread" together and mutual nurturing. It was very revealing how some individuals and families interpreted this activity, and whether they were willing to share or not with the other party. Some brought lunch only for themselves and "their" child or children, and were unwilling to taste anyone else's food. Others generously brought food for all members of the group, indicating their more inclusive attitude to child-rearing. The packed lunches provided also revealed the children's regular school diet, whether this was healthy or not, and, in any case, their own obvious preferences for certain foods, usually sweets and crisps and chocolate!

The children's play was also very meaningful. Often they spontaneously began to reveal little nuggets of their untapped inner selves, as sad and not-so-sad memories surfaced in sometimes silent play. The souls of even outwardly tough children seemed to be touched in such play through their unconscious knowing. A slight shifting by hand of a small toy or animal in the sand tray, a change of toy scenery in what might be a war zone or zoo would be so telling (without any words) of how that particular child has perceived, or still perceives, her world. This silent communication, sometimes with an invitation to me or another observing adult to participate, speaks volumes. It goes a long way in telling us how it is for that child without anything being said.

To be allowed to enter a child's world is indeed a privilege, and must be respected as such. Put another way, how often, as grown-ups, do we expect children to enter our adult world with our demands, and without our paying any attention to whether the children fully understand what exactly we mean. We know, but do they? A wrong word said here and there can alter the whole interaction between child and adult, but do we ever take the time to ask this of ourselves? When once we have said the word, issued the order, as far as the adult is concerned, that is that. There will usually be no concern as to whether the child, in his young mind, understands exactly what we mean, and do we really care at that moment?

On the other hand, how often have we heard the words of a child "You don't understand". Easy for adults to dismiss what the child is communicating when we are so intent on getting our own views and instructions across. Taking time, then, to enter the child's young world is a giant step to gaining trust, understanding, and the attachment so necessary in making adult–child relationships work. This actually takes no more time, in fact much less time than the endless back-and-forth in arguments and residue of negative feelings.

In summing up attachment or the lack of it for "accommodated" or "looked after" children, one is left to reflect on the reality for many within the "care system". So many of these children still do not have a voice that is listened to. We expect so much from our children, their capacity to "fit in", to behave and settle into whichever families are prepared to take them. These children instinctively know that, in many cases, they are merely tolerated, not loved as they deserve to be.

We, as adults, also have a responsibility, which is to ensure that all vulnerable children in our care are listened to on all levels; that they are understood and are fully included in our family, warts and all.

Further learning from children

Yvonne's story

Years ago, when I first started doing play-work with children, I began to visit a five-year-old girl in her adoptive home as the parents were experiencing difficulties with her tantruming behaviours. I did not know about reactive attachment disorder at the time, and that one of the common traits is having "very angry parents"! Yvonne had a nice, caring, and seemingly "normal" family and home, but why were her parents so angry with her all the time? It only occurred to me much later that this was probably due to a displacement of her negative and therefore unacceptable feelings. Yvonne's anger and frustration were transferred on to the nearest available emotional "container", usually her much put-upon adoptive mother.

Yvonne was a pretty little girl, very bright and articulate and with a delightful sense of humour; the sort of child that caring social workers often said they themselves would want "to take home" and adopt! Again, I only learnt much later that this, in itself, was a warning sign that the child was splitting: being very charming to professionals and outsiders, while revealing all her hurt aspects to her new parents, usually the person in the "mother" role, because of all the rejections and disappointment that the child had experienced in the original birth family.

Yvonne's birth mother had been very young and mentally ill. She had grossly neglected her baby until Social Services intervened and took the child away, placing Yvonne in a foster home where she was much loved and well cared for. A year or two passed while attempts were made to rehabilitate Yvonne back at home with her mother, but little had changed there and, once again, the child was removed on an emergency basis, even more hurt and neglected this time.

Placed with "emergency" foster carers who could keep Yvonne for only a few months in their very busy household, she was lost there and her needs unnoticed. By three years old, and her next "bridging" placement, Yvonne realized that she could only get attention if she screamed and fought and bit the other small children in the foster home. The foster carers were experienced in dealing with such misbehaviours, but were also very glad to have Yvonne on a temporary basis only, while permanent adoptive parents were sought for her countrywide.

A local family, seeing her picture in a Be My Parent publication (BAAF), were immediately drawn to Yvonne's pretty face and winning expression. They already had three young sons and desperately wanted a daughter too; Yvonne seemed perfect for this role. A year or more later, the bewildered parents were asking themselves why they had ever thought this. Yvonne came into their lives like a whirlwind, creating chaos and consternation in their hitherto calm household. A sturdy tomboy rather than the feminine little girl they had dreamed of, Yvonne was jealous of the older boys. She fought with them, broke their toys, tantrumed constantly, pushed the exhausted mother away, and was generally unco-operative, so that this placement, too, was now near disruption.

Not really knowing what to do about all this, I intuitively offered to play with Yvonne, with the intention of observing her behaviours myself. I set up weekly sessions at her home and followed her lead in indirect work with her. For a while, I could not really understand what the family's problem with her was. Yvonne was delightful, and only occasionally a little challenging towards me as an adult.

Then, in our fourth session, bored with our usual activities, Yvonne said she wanted to play a particular board game, one that I was not familiar with. She said it belonged to her brothers and she offered at once to show me how to play the game. Yvonne could not read as yet, and would not let me read the rules myself, so she dictated how the game was to be played. Even according to her own changing rules, Yvonne cheated constantly, leaving me feeling unusually frustrated at losing however I played. I was even more put out by her triumph at this. Since I am not usually competitive when I play with children, I was puzzled by my strong reactions to her winning all the time.

Reflecting on this session later, I realized that Yvonne had unconsciously given me an experience of what it felt like to be her: being moved from one family to another to another, with the adults making up rules she was not aware of or did not understand, so that whatever she did she ended up being in the wrong. Was it any surprise that Yvonne should then tantrum and become so controlling in this, her fifth placement? It was very powerful learning for me that a small child could convey so eloquently, and quite unconsciously, through play what her living experience was like.

Harry's story

Harry was just five years old when we met him and his adoptive parents after his placement with them disrupted; they were no longer sure that they were the right family for him. We heard that, while still only four, he had told his social worker that he did not need parents. We were less surprised at this when we learnt that his predominant memory of his warring teenage parents was of himself, little more than a toddler, standing between them and shouting at them to "Stop!", while they threw saucepans at each other in their kitchen.

Like Edward in family C (Chapter Four), Harry genuinely did not see the difference between adults and children or why he should do as he was told to by grown-ups. As far as he could see, the only difference was that the adults were big and he was still very small. So, all he had to do was to grow bigger as quickly as possible. He could then return home and look after his birth parents. Clearly, they had not known how to look after each other or him, which is why he had been removed from their care when little.

We then noticed that Harry seemed to be growing taller at such a pace between our fortnightly or monthly sessions that we began to comment on it. Each time, his adoptive father, who was tall and strong, would respond by laughingly pressing Harry's head down as if to squash him and keep him from growing up. It turned out that growing big quickly was a burning issue for this little boy, who had not been able to stop his battling parents from hurting each other when he was only two and still living with them. His adoptive parents had generously told him that they would help him to find his birth family once he reached the age of eighteen, so all Harry wanted to do now was to grow big as fast as he could.

What we then realized was that both Harry and his adopters were allowing his birth parents so much emotional and mental space in his young life that he could not relinquish them and claim his new parents. The adopters, in turn, did not feel they could claim Harry as their son, which led to a whole new spiral of negative interactions . . . and the eventual ending of another placement for him.

Note

1. This section of the chapter, as far as the sub-heading "Further learning from children" is contributed by Pauline Sear.

CHAPTER SIX

Re-evaluating CAT: its potential in child protection work

Risk assessments in child protection work

There are unrealistic public and legal expectations that the risk of child abuse and/or severe neglect can always be accurately predicted by social workers and/or medical, health, and/or psychological experts. These unremitting outside pressures highlight fundamental concerns and contradictions in child protection and fostering and adoption work:

- workers' personal, professional and social values and accountability;
- the wish to give vulnerable children an optimal experience of family life, even if this means placing them with complete strangers;
- the impossibility of ever being sure that an abused child will not be at risk again, either within his birth family or with new carers who have been assessed as being "safe".

Social workers have a duty to protect children from suffering "significant harm" through severe neglect or abuse by carers who may well have been exposed to the same while growing up. Such parents might even themselves have been in the "care system" when young. Despite the Department's best intentions and endeavours, they may not have been adequately nurtured or even protected from abuse and/or neglect while in foster care or children's homes.

Awareness of our contribution as professionals, however involuntary, to maintaining this tragic intergenerational cycle of neglect and abuse may spur us to ever greater efforts to ensure the long-term safety and well being of the children of such parents. This has quite often meant their removal from the birth family when young, or even soon after birth, to protect them from parents already known to be failing. Of course, the younger the child is, the easier it is to place her for adoption, and professionals often seem to share the adopters' fantasy that this fresh start in a new family will wipe out the child's chequered birth history. For the same reason, all meaningful contact with parents and family members is often quickly severed, as if to avoid ongoing contamination by them.

The sad reality is that "substitute families" are not always that much safer for such hurt children. About twenty years ago, a children's charity in the north of England (Barnardos, Humberside) discovered that a large percentage of the sexually abused children they had placed were being re-abused in their new families. It was such a shocking finding that the agency rigorously overhauled its assessment procedures to screen out potential sexual offenders. However, even experienced adoption workers and panels cannot totally predict safety or successful outcomes of placements. The most sophisticated preparation and assessment procedures will not guarantee these.

Without blaming the victim, it seems that an already abused child is very vulnerable to further abuse, not just by adults who deliberately set out to exploit his known vulnerability, but by better-intentioned carers who might get drawn into abusive interactional patterns which the child has internalized (see Figure 4, Chapter One).

In counselling adult adoptees who wish to trace their birth families, we repeatedly hear how placements, described as "successful" at the time the Adoption Order was made, have turned out very differently in reality following inevitable family changes: the birth or placement of another child; the break-up of the adopters' marriage; the illness or death of an adoptive parent, etc. Quite often, mutual bonding and claiming by child and adopters were not strong enough to survive these blows, and the adoptee was rejected and abandoned again, left with no family to turn to, except the ideal of a birth family whom she now seeks in desperation, despite being informed that she was grossly maltreated by them when young.

Of course, changes can occur in the birth family, too: the support of a new partner or "significant other", increasing self-awareness, greater maturity and competence, improved self-esteem, and positive models. All these help a parent labelled as "inadequate" or abusive to become more nurturing and protective towards other children in the family. Indeed, the resilience and resourcefulness such parents need to overcome their own adverse childhood experiences tend to be taken for granted, so that risk assessments often stress parenting deficits rather than coping strengths.

Assessment is an intervention that, in itself, can be therapeutic or abusive to the child and family. Crisis theory (Caplan, 1964) suggests that families are most open to change when they are in crisis, and attachment theory indicates that families are more likely to develop an attachment to workers by whom they feel listened to and supported through such difficult times (Fraiberg, 1981). This can earn much-needed trust by the family for further painful work, including possible acknowledgements of abuse or neglect by a perpetrator. Moreover, where harm to the child cannot be proved, the investigation itself might be so traumatizing that the family will need skilled and sensitive support afterwards to regain normality for themselves and their child in their community.

Instead, what often seems to happen is that, following the initial Child Protection investigation, the social workers involved do not undertake any ongoing therapeutic work themselves with the family. The case may be passed quite quickly to a "continuing care team", where the child care worker may or may not feel able to undertake such skilled work.

The burden of accountability in child protection cases can feel overwhelming and quite deskilling, with more attention being paid to carrying out bureaucratic procedures ("ticking boxes") as an unconscious defence against organizational anxieties rather than promoting the actual well being of the child and family (Menzies

Lyth, 1988). With a high risk of burn-out in such work, and the constant turnover of staff in Child Protection Teams, young and/or relatively inexperienced child care workers may be left to carry the brunt of responsibility for the child's safety. They can end up feeling incapacitated with anxiety about the risks involved, and therefore unable to offer any of their learnt social work skills in helping troubled children and families to explore the pain of their situation and grow together through it.

Instead, an initial referral may be made to a local family centre for "observation and assessment" of parent–child interactions, rather than any therapeutic support being offered to the parents. If family centre staff feel similarly deskilled through anxiety in high risk or controversial cases, a referral may then be made to outside named "experts" to carry out "risk assessments" of the family. These are often more acceptable to the Courts in contested care proceedings, but the emotional costs can be high, especially for the child.

A family might go through assessment after assessment, sometimes with contradictory conclusions, for a year or longer, with intermittent Court hearings for directions about rehabilitation attempts or permanent removal of the child from the family. Meanwhile, the subject of all these protection procedures—the child herself—might be increasingly abused emotionally by default. While lengthy assessments and adversarial proceedings follow their course, the child and her family are often left without therapeutic support to help them deal with what has occurred.

Such assessments may run consecutively or in tandem, thus extending beyond many struggling parents' endurance the period during which they are observed or remain "on trial". Ironically, the disempowering and deskilling impact of protracted assessments and legal proceedings can actually increase the risk for some children, who may incur their immature parents' wrath for being the "cause" of such stressful investigations. Failure to stay the course might then be interpreted as evidence of the parents' incapacity or lack of commitment to care for the child safely and well enough.

There is also a view that counselling or therapy could reduce the chances of achieving a successful prosecution against perpetrators of abuse. So, parents who deny responsibility for the initial abuse or neglect suffered by the child might have to undergo this whole process without even social work support. Counselling or family therapy is likely to be offered only to parents who acknowledge their guilt, and/or with whom rehabilitation appears to be a realistic option for the child.

Thus, those families most in need of therapeutic help are least likely to get it, so placing any other children they may have at even greater risk of harm. Furthermore, even severely hurt children might want to renew contact at some time in the future with their birth families. These, however, could still be stuck in what is very often an intergenerational cycle of abuse and neglect.

The more severe the harm suffered, the greater the risk of it occurring again, either within the birth family or with new carers, because of the child's learnt patterns of behaviour and interaction. Life-changing decisions about a child's future placement with foster carers or adoptive parents, rather than supporting rehabilitation with birth parents, are often based on the opinions of experts in the field. They have to weigh up the risks of each option and might tend to favour the unknown: the child's capacity to heal from harm already suffered and to form healthy new attachments to complete strangers. However, these new parents are likely to have their own "ghosts in the nursery" (Fraiberg, Adelson, & Shapiro, 1975) that might surface once the placement is made.

As a social worker, I, too, have believed in giving hurt and deprived babies and young children a fresh start in life through adoption or "permanent" foster care. It was only after I began to work as a therapist with older children whose adoptive and long-term foster placements had broken down, entailing several more moves and multiple losses for them, that I realized how strong the pull remained to their birth family, no matter how damaging or damaged they might have been.

Some of them had come from unsafe communities where children were introduced to drugs very young, and were even bribed to steal cars to fund their addiction. One endearing eight-year-old I briefly worked with was already a gang leader on his council estate, and notorious for terrorizing elderly visitors to the local general hospital. His response to being put in foster care was to keep running back home, several counties away, to make sure that his young mother, a drug-user, was all right. Like other professionals working in this field, I heard many such sobering stories of role reversal, with even small children worrying about their failing parents' safety and well being.

Of course, the very strength of the child's bond with the birth family, however insecure her attachments to them might have been, would have inhibited her from being willing to trust new adoptive or foster parents and risk putting down roots in her new family.

Robert's story

Robert, a young boy in foster care, expressed this pull to birth family most poignantly to me: "You don't know what it's like . . . when other children at school ask you: 'Where's your family?' It's like a hole here" (pointing to his stomach). "It will never be filled up unless you can live with your family again when you are grown up."

Robert and his five siblings had been removed some years previously from a home where the father terrorized and routinely abused, both physically and sexually, all the children, from the smallest one up, as well as their mother. She was completely unable to protect herself or them from her husband's almost daily assaults on his petrified family. Nevertheless, all Robert wanted was to return home to his mother's care while placement after placement disrupted because of his inability to settle in a new family, as well as his increasingly sexualized behaviours towards younger children.

Robert was sent at thirteen to a psychiatric unit for disturbed adolescents, for containment until he was eighteen. It is unlikely that any therapeutic work was undertaken at any time with either of his birth parents, who had long separated and gone on to have new relationships. Robert's older sisters already had young children of their own. These were also considered to be at risk of ongoing abuse by their grandfather who, despite a Court injunction to keep away from his family, kept stalking the children whose local whereabouts he knew.

Helping struggling families to heal and move on

Phase 1 of the CAT pilot project clearly showed how attachment and protection are inextricably linked: Parents or carers need to feel able to *claim a child as theirs to protect* in order to set appropriate boundaries to keep her safe. Such claiming and protection can be learnt through fostering mutual attachment: child and family are "held" therapeutically by skilled workers who can facilitate safe exploration of past and present through necessary griefwork. This may involve doing life story work with the child and carers, as well as inner child work to exorcise "ghosts in the nursery" (Fraiberg, Adelson, & Shapiro, 1975) from the parents' own troubled childhoods (see Figures 16 and 17, pp. 113, 114).

During the 1970s, Fraiberg (1981) and her colleagues developed an innovative attachment therapy programme with failing parents in the context of child protection work in the USA. This offered a skilled and compassionate team approach to both assessing *and* treating the family *from the point of referral onwards*, usually starting in the hospital where the child had been admitted because of injuries or severe neglect.

The multi-disciplinary team stressed the importance for parents in crisis of continuity in "attachment" to a therapist to provide *a secure base* for what is inevitably very difficult and painful work where there has been or may be further "significant harm" suffered by the child. In the UK, Cullen and Batty (1996) brought together British social work, legal, and medical perspectives with the aim of therapeutically supporting the child and non-abusing parent, instead of simply focusing on offenders.

However, the reality for most hard-pressed Children's Services is that opportunities for doing such crisis intervention work are usually not utilized to the full because of the lack of suitable in-house or local therapeutic resources. The nature and/or extent of harm already suffered can feel so overwhelming that workers, managers, and/or the Court will rightly regard an assessment of further risk as the highest priority before the child's future placement is determined, within or outside her family.

However, this can lead to the children, as in Family E and Family L (Chapter Five) being left in a legal and emotional limbo for months, if not years, while the parents' capacity to protect and care adequately for the child is assessed. A series of outside "experts"—psychologists, therapists, psychiatrists, as well as independent social work consultants—may be engaged in an ongoing effort to predict the level of risk if the child remains with, or returns to her family.

Where Social Services can realistically honour their public commitment to keep a child within her nuclear or extended family, it seems far more cost-effective to offer adequate therapeutic resources at the point of the initial child protection investigation. If structures can be put in place to safeguard the child at home, or in an existing foster care or adoptive placement where the child has begun to put down her roots, it makes more sense to build on any existing healthy attachments and so increase the carer's capacity to claim and protect the child effectively.

The value of CAT in carrying out brief therapeutic assessments

We have long believed that "therapeutic assessments" in some Child Protection cases could be more beneficial to the child and family than what seems to be the norm: protracted assessments by experts before any diagnosis can be made, with appropriate treatment facilities then needing to be identified and funding for their use agreed by the local authority. Starting from the premise that attachment and protection issues are inextricably linked, our stance has been that families who are not *too* damaged themselves can heal and learn to attach to a hurt child, claiming and protecting her as their own (Figure 20).

Sophie's story

> Our belief was severely tested when we were asked to carry out an assessment of the sibling attachment and placement needs of two little brothers with a failing prospective adopter, Sophie. She had already been informed that they would most probably be removed from her care, since she seemed unable to meet the boys' physical, emotional, or developmental needs, despite having been offered a lot of post-placement support by experienced and competent social workers. Indeed, our hearts sank when we first visited Sophie's home and realized that Social Services' concerns were fully justified.
>
> Over a three-hour visit, we mainly listened to Sophie, attempting to build rapport with her before suggesting any changes in her management of the children. She was very angry at being judged by their social worker who was "not a parent himself and had no idea" of the

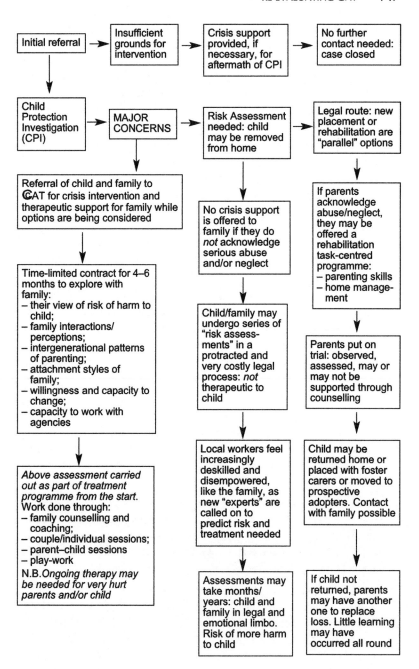

Figure 20.   Application of the CAT Programme to child protection work.

considerable pressures she had been under since the boys were placed with her the previous year. She had fallen ill soon after and had a series of setbacks, while her hoped-for network of support disintegrated. All this had left her feeling depressed, hopeless, and totally unable to prioritize the children's needs. If Social Services had not already been carefully monitoring the children, we would have needed to express our own concerns and perhaps even suggested ending the placement straightaway.

We tried hard to look for positives in the home and Sophie's strengths, as these must have been evident in the past when she was being assessed for adoption and had obviously led to the placement of the two brothers with her. Sophie was known to be a competent business-woman, but she was clearly not a housewife. And she was only just learning how to be a mother to two very needy little boys who had already suffered neglect in their previous foster placements and birth family.

Jack, aged two, was overfriendly and interacted with us at once, show-ing no inhibition even though we were complete strangers to him. He was barely walking and talking, while Joey was nearly four but had only recently begun to attend playgroup regularly. He was very anxiously attached to Sophie and found separations from her for any length of time extremely distressing.

My co-therapist, Anne Wardrop, a former Child Protection worker, and I strongly disagreed about Sophie's and the children's potential for positive change in what was such a sensitive period for their develop-ment. Anne felt very concerned about both children, while I took heart from reports by the health visitor and playgroup leader who were both very encouraging towards Sophie.

A month later, when we next visited, there were a few visible improve-ments in both children and in Sophie's demeanour. She may have felt heard by us and was feeling physically stronger. Joey was tantruming a little less, while Jack was now more mobile and Sophie was getting some respite care for him and time to herself at long last.

However, Sophie's responses to both boys' demands during our second session were still far from satisfactory: She tended to "baby" Jack, spoon-feeding him on her lap, and she kept him confined in his high chair or in a buggy for much of our visit, before putting him in his cot upstairs for a post-prandial nap. Jack seemed too passive to protest, and only kept calling out good-naturedly for a long time before even-tually falling asleep. By our third session, however, Jack was literally all over the place, refusing to be confined or shushed by Sophie. He was now also getting in the way of his exasperated big brother and competing for Sophie's attention. We had to regard this as progress for Jack.

Sophie had obviously bribed Joey to "be good" for us, but then withdrew the reward he thought was his already when he kept demanding it. This led to further tantruming by him and more punitive responses by Sophie. Feeling quite helpless, Anne and I witnessed the distress of both mother and child at being locked in this "negative attachment cycle of interaction". Joey's hyper-aroused state was matched by Sophie's increasing anger with him, and they would then connect briefly in mutual remorse and "have a cuddle" before his next tantrum began.

After a while, Anne went to an adjoining room and sat on the floor to engage with Joey, who still seemed to be quite distressed. However, he was responsive to Anne's overtures and gentle speech, and he seemed to feel understood by her. I focused on Sophie, mainly listening to her tirades against social workers and other professionals (including ourselves), and for being on trial for well over a year. I sought to reinforce the positives we had noted in both boys' behaviours, and in her own functioning, before suggesting a few changes.

Sophie would not attend any parenting group, but she had found her own resource: a correspondence course in child development. Knowing that social workers were also visiting her and the children regularly, we could relax a little and continue to encourage Sophie in the small steps she was taking towards parenting them more effectively. We realized that she, too, was painfully aware of her failings and, despite her anger, making real attempts at positive changes.

Anne and I continued our debate about the likely damage to the boys if they remained with Sophie or were moved to yet another placement with strangers after a year of starting to form new attachments to her. We seemed to be mirroring the split among other professionals involved with this family. My countertransference to Sophie left me at the end of each visit feeling bad, inadequate, and isolated, while Anne continued to feel very identified with the little boys and sad and upset for them, as did their Child Care Worker, who had known them since they were babies and was very committed to them both. However, she had continued to monitor their placement instead of handing over "welfare supervision" to the Adoption Worker, who was less critical and more supportive of Sophie. Needless to say, these workers did not get on!

Anxiety about the boys' well being remained high both in our office and in Social Services. We maintained close communication with the social workers as well as with the health visitor and playgroup leader, who were also monitoring the children's progress. Despite our widely differing perspectives, we managed to work as a "team" to hold this placement, although it still felt very near disruption.

We visited Sophie twice more at monthly intervals and, despite some remaining concerns, felt able to recommend that both boys remain with her provided she was adequately supported by a package of care, including a local therapeutic service and respite care as needed. Nine months later, Sophie informed us with great pride that she had been allowed to adopt them.

Writing about this family now, it seems incredible that Sophie managed such a turnaround in just a few months. I believe that our main contribution was to contain the social workers' anxiety about the children's well being by working through our own splitting on the case, which reflected splitting by the other professionals involved too. Anne provided a child-centred perspective by acting as advocate for the children, while I continued to believe in Sophie's potential for change. Most importantly, Anne and I communicated honestly and respectfully with each other and the other professionals, and so functioned as a multi-disciplinary "secure base" to hold the family during this crucial period when their future together was at stake.

The timing of our assessment was felicitous in that Joey was attending playgroup regularly for the first time in a year. He could now engage in more age-appropriate activities and separate from Sophie in a healthy way, while Jack was able to have "special time" with Sophie for the first time on their own. This helped their bonding, as we noted when she commented on his little achievements and "cheekiness" with pride. Sophie was also now getting more positive comments from her family and others on the boys' progress, which reflected well on her parenting ability and increased her self-esteem. Most importantly, however, she had new hope of success.

Groopman (2005, p. 193) has researched "hope" for years, and its effect on his cancer patients. He distinguishes hope from optimism, which he believes is not based on reality. Groopman quotes Richard Davidson in describing hope as having two components: cognition and feeling, which are not separate in the brain but interweave and modify each other. Neurolinguistic programming (NLP) has long taught that, to effect positive changes in our life, we need to change either our thinking, or our feelings, or our physiology: changing one will lead to changes in the other two ("Mercedes model").

The role of social workers and other professionals in influencing the outcomes of children's placements would be an interesting subject for research, since self-fulfilling prophecy—either positive or negative—is seldom considered to be a contributing factor. Yet carers, especially if they are inexperienced and lacking in confidence as new parents, can be enormously affected by professionals' criticism or encouragement of their parenting.

As that very wise and experienced family therapist, Byng-Hall, notes, "*I have observed more important shifts in family functioning arising from praising the family's struggle to manage better than from any other intervention. This is especially important for parenting skills*" (1995, p. 200, my emphasis). Byng Hall emphasizes that any "positive labelling" must be genuine and is a necessary first step to then helping parents to reflect on and change dysfunctional and possibly dangerous aspects of their behaviour.

> The general rule that whatever is focused on is likely to be reinforced, while whatever is ignored will fade is a useful one. Competent aspects of family behaviour can be noted and labelled. The dysfunctional aspects can be acknowledged, but the focus remains on the strengths. . . . It is easier for parents to talk about those painful issues for which they were expecting criticism if they discover that instead their parenting skills are being supported in front of their partners and their children. [*ibid.*, p. 205]

The reality remains that, whether child or adult, we all respond more positively to genuine praise than to blame and criticism, which simply put us on the defensive. Feeling unheard, we may then continue to seek to justify our behaviours, however reprehensible these may seem to others. Encouragement, however, softens our resistance and makes us more open to looking at options, leading to safer and better ways of functioning.

As Dr Andrew Taylor Still, founder of osteopathy, taught, "To find health should be the object of the doctor. Anyone can find disease."

CHAPTER SEVEN

CAT therapists' learning and users' perspectives; professionals' perspectives[1]

A local authority perspective

When I left the family-finding unit where CAT had been developed, I did independent work using the same principles to help adoptive families facing disruption. The results were positive and, by stripping relationships back to the bare bones, families learnt to reappraise their ways of reacting to each other. In 1999, I was appointed as a local authority Permanence/Adoption Manager. In this role, I commissioned the CAT team to work with some of the adoptive placements near breakdown. The team were also invited by the child-care team to do family assessments for the courts where parenting was not considered to be "good enough" to keep the child safe.

The CAT philosophy offered struggling birth mothers a chance to explore their own experiences of being parented when young. Rather than just assessing their current parenting skills, which were poor, by allowing mothers the opportunity to address long buried traumas in their own childhood, the team helped these mothers to recognize the reasons why they felt and acted as they did. Abuse, bereavement, domestic violence, dysfunctional family life, and poverty; we all know these create vulnerable young adults but, when they go on to have children of their own, we somehow expect them to parent well! Social Services will often commission psychological or psychiatric assessments of failing parents, often in tandem with parenting assessments, but such assessments do not equate with *treatment*. That is the uniqueness of the CAT Programme.

CAT is co-worked by two therapists: one who does "play-work" with the child, and the other who works with the parent/ carer(s). After about an hour of such individual work, the parent/ carer(s) and child come together and are supported in communicating what each has discussed or demonstrated individually with the therapist. These meetings can be painful, but they are safe and contained and enable family members to face each other's expectations and failings. Strategies for management are agreed and the families are then seen weekly or fortnightly, as appropriate. The Programme is intensive to start with, and families are then weaned off dependence on the therapists by having later sessions at longer intervals, followed by a review at the tenth session of the work done together.

The feedback we received on CAT from families was generally very positive, and we saw major changes in the way the families interacted. For example, one family was brought back from the brink of disruption, and a young birth mother had her toddler returned to her after a year in foster care, although adoption had long been planned by the Child Care Worker. Without CAT involvement, these two outcomes would have been very different.

From a commissioning point of view, referral to CAT led to an immediate offer of an appointment to families in distress, usually with them being seen within two or three weeks. There were no lengthy waiting lists or daunting assessment procedures, whereas with referrals to hard-pressed local Child and Adolescent Mental Health Services (CAMHS) clinics, the wait could be up to a year before even an initial assessment was made. The assessor would then decide what sort of intervention was to be offered, if any. Then it would be back to the waiting lists to see a therapist. Often no therapeutic work was offered until the child was considered to be settled, in a "permanent placement". By then, placements would most probably have broken down and children moved on, suffering further losses and damage. The "care system" fails so many young people and families.

My experience of the work and philosophy of the CAT team has been one of growing appreciation. As a practitioner, I see it as an effective way of working, as it has a clearly identifiable impact on family interaction. For adoptive placements, it hugely increased the chances not only of success and stability, but also of mutual satisfaction and deepening relationships which endured. For birth families, it represented the possibility of changing the dysfunctional inheritance line, and preventing children coming into care due to protection issues. It could not always effect change in extreme cases of attachment disorders, but it did enable carers to understand their task and to ease their expectations and help them to appreciate very small changes.

A fostering agency's perspective

As an organization, we have used the CAT Programme over the years with some of our foster families, as well as for individual work with children and young people placed with them.

Many children placed in foster care are traumatized and, as such, their development is impaired. CAT therapists have helped several such children on referral to our agency to come to understand their feelings of loss and bereavement, and to move on to make healthy new attachments to their foster families. We have worked together with local authorities in situations where the CAT Programme was used successfully with families where placements were at risk of breakdown. Such help is invaluable where children would otherwise have to be moved on again.

As well as offering individual therapy and the CAT Programme, Maeja has offered experiential workshops to foster carers on "Attachment, separation and loss". Reflecting on their childhood and adult experiences in this way helps new foster carers to empathize with the children placed with them, as well as reintroducing more experienced carers to this essential topic. Staff and our sessional workers have also found this training to be of great value. [Linda Folwell, Regional Development Manager, Futures for Children]

Users' perspectives

The researcher undertaking an evaluation of the CAT pilot project (see Chapter Four) in late 1996 noted the following.

Family A

In assessing the children's development at the beginning and at the end of the project, the workers noted marked improvement in their schooling, linguistic, and motor skills. Moreover, whereas initially Chloe had inappropriately attached herself to total strangers, by the end of the project she displayed appropriate attachment behaviours to her new parents. She was now more circumspect in her affections towards strangers and extended family members. All these changes were confirmed in the evaluation interview with Mr and Mrs A.

The couple recognized their tendency to "indulge and spoil" the children because of their traumatic past. They were also able to allow the children to regress. The interactive play sessions with both children and parents, therefore, became important in helping to establish firm boundaries.

Life story work enabled the parents to be more open with the children about their family background. Just one year after placement, they were able to have an open contact with the birth family in which Mr and Mrs A "could stand back and allow the birth mother to have her day".

Family B

At the beginning of the project Mr and Mrs B were very aware of Alicia's tenuous attachment to them. Despite his closer relationship with the little girl, Mr B did not *enjoy* parenting Alicia, while Mrs B did not feel *entitled* to parent her newly placed daughter.

By the end of the project the couple acknowledged that their attitudes towards discipline had changed. Mrs B also felt that she and Alicia had grown closer as a result of the play sessions. A beneficial change in family interactions was noted as Mr B assumed more responsibility for setting boundaries for Alicia, while Mrs B felt more able to relate to the little girl as her mother.

Although the couple initially resisted the idea of doing life story work, they came to appreciate the need for Alicia to learn about her past and her country and culture. Mrs B then produced a beautiful book, integrating the child's past and present. (In recent years, they have revisited Alicia's homeland to give her, as a teenager, a personal perspective of her history and culture.)

Through "inner child" work, Mrs B could acknowledge how her caretaking role in her family of origin had led her to taking on too many responsibilities, even as an adult.

Mrs B's own view of participation in the pilot project was unequivocal:

> You can't imagine what it was like. If Maeja had not suggested the programme I don't know what we would have done. Something had to happen. I could feel myself getting more and more depressed. I used to dread each day, which has never happened to me before. But I could feel myself getting so depressed and I couldn't understand why it was happening. We are both such experienced parents and I've given so much advice over the years to my friends. It never occurred to me that we would be unable to cope.

> It was affecting everyone in the house. Even my oldest son was upset by it all and the younger one couldn't understand what was happening. He got so upset because I was with Alicia all the time. She would just sit there screaming and screaming. You felt so helpless and I used to get so frightened in the car because she started attacking me. It was like one long nightmare that you thought would never end. Each night I went to bed feeling totally exhausted and woke up the next morning dreading what would happen.

> You can't imagine the change there has been in Alicia's behaviour. She still has her obsessions and we both have to be firm with her. But all the screaming has gone and she will do what you tell her. Her language is so much better now and she is doing well at play school.

The researcher speculated that

Mr and Mrs B's positive image of themselves as "experienced and competent" parents had initially led them to deny the scale of their despair and the disruption of their family life. Arguably, it was only when the programme had ended and they could reaffirm their image as "able and loving parents" that they felt able to acknowledge how desperate they had been for help.

Reflecting now on Alicia's screaming episodes, her attempts to run away, and attacks on Mrs B in the car in particular, it is likely that the little girl had pre-verbal memories of being suddenly removed by strangers (the Bs) from her familiar setting—bleak and comfortless though the hospital ward was—and driven by car to a foreign country with a completely different language and tonal sounds.

Perhaps Alicia was also screaming at her multiple losses, which no one could understand or help her with, until she began play sessions at three years old with Pauline Sear. The Bs then began to show Alicia a video taken of her in the hospital ward that had been her home for her first eighteen months of life. The video included pictures of herself with the Bs abroad and in her new home. Painful discontinuities between past and present could now be bridged, and new connections literally formed in her brain. Learning to verbalize her feelings in English, rather than tantruming, was also a major help to Alicia at this time. Most importantly, however, the B's dramatic rescue of their daughter from institutional disablement gave her new hope of a fulfilling life in a caring family.

Reflections from families ten years on

We were aware that families in crisis might be much more positive about the benefits of CAT immediately after the programme ended, and so we wanted to know what the longer term impact was. Before writing this book, feedback questionnaires were sent to about fifty families we had worked with over the years; we got a twenty per cent response rate. (Some of these families had been due to move for various reasons after we stopped work with them, and we did not have their new addresses.)

Several of the families had two or more children who had been involved with CAT. Most were foster or adoptive families, but a few were birth and extended families, and there were some step-families, too. The latter tended to self-refer and paid for the work themselves; they seemed able to benefit from fewer sessions overall, demonstrating their strong motivation to work on their own issues.

To illustrate this last point, one step-father described the child referred as being "worried about everything in life". Contact issues with his birth father had been a particular source of anxiety to him and his mother. The family's feedback was that, during an initial session, I (Maeja) "spoke to Tyler directly and got to the root of the problem straightaway. He was then ready to take on matters himself, and so no longer needed the programme."

A long-term foster carer commented on CAT work with her warring teenagers: "The children had been in separate foster homes for some time and did not relate as brother and sister when brought together (at fourteen and fifteen) in one home again." The carer had found of particular value the "individual support and help to understand each other's point of view. Also positive reinforcement to the children that nothing was their fault—they both felt they were to blame for being in care."

CAT comment: The children had been removed from a very abusive and neglectful home situation when just four and five years old. We ourselves felt that the separate work we did with the carers had also helped *them* to reframe what they had previously seen as just the children's problems.

Another foster carer had four "short-term" children (unrelated) whom we had worked with at various times. Her comments on CAT work were:

> I think they (children) found it hard to start with, speaking to some-one about their feelings, but they felt better when they had. It was probably the first time the child and their family had sat down and talked to each other about their problems, and all feedback from the family was good. Unfortunately, only one child returned home. I feel the problems with the other children were more to do with the mothers than the child.

CAT comment: This foster carer had not seen it as part of her role to be involved with our work with the children, especially as she usually had other child care commitments at home. However, this led to her feeling somewhat excluded from the work we did; she felt "there should be more feedback, while still maintaining confidentiality."

Another foster carer, with two sibling pairs who were referred to CAT at different times, fully participated in the sessions herself and commented:

> The children went on an assessment only. We, the carers, benefited from the assessment feedback, which we felt was very useful to us.

It gave us an insight into how the children were feeling about being in care, and the discussion time after the assessment was good.

Another foster carer had three challenging adolescents referred to us at different times. One had individual weekly work over a period of months, with only a few sessions involving the carer. This was pre-CAT work, and he was a very troubled young man whose placement sadly disrupted after a few years. He chose to return to his very damaging birth family and deviant community, getting into increasing trouble with the law himself.

The other two adolescents were siblings, whose previous "long-term" placement had just broken down. The older girl (aged fifteen) was desperate to attach to her new carer, and we did some CAT work with them and her sister. This enabled the girl to return to full-time schooling and she began to do really well there. The younger sister (aged twelve) was just beginning a rebellious phase and, sadly, the foster carer decided to end both placements as she had undertaken heavy new work commitments. The carer commented that "CAT had done all they could for my placements." She was a down-to-earth carer and found of particular benefit "the kind and tactful way they helped my children cope with their feelings and situation."

A single foster carer with an extremely challenging nine-year-old, who was sent two years later to a "therapeutic community", did participate in CAT work over a period of time. She commented: "It was very beneficial to both child and carer. We worked together to improve areas that needed extra attention."

The child had attention deficit hyperactivity disorder (ADHD) and extreme post traumatic stress disorder (PTSD). He and his younger siblings suffered from severe parental neglect and abuse, and were placed in separate foster homes. The carer found CAT helpful: "being able to discuss with ease ongoing therapy and any problems."

An adoptive parent of three siblings had a mixed response: The initial CAT work had been favoured because it "made G aware of what a mother's responsibilities should be. We felt at the time that, with love and consistency, G would adapt into our lifestyle." However, the adoptive placement ended some years later as "G became resentful and harmful towards his siblings. After numerous episodes of shoplifting, drug abuse, malicious damage, and arson, we took a decision to seek Social Services help and G currently resides in foster care. His siblings remain with us. Unfortunately they have decided that they no longer wish to have anything to do with G."

CAT comment: The adopters attended only a few sessions with the children, and wished to focus exclusively on G's disruptive behaviours at home and at school. As the eldest "parentified" child in a very neglectful and abusive birth family, he had continued to feel responsible for their removal from home. G had too much emotional energy still invested in his relationship with his birth mother to attach to his new family. They therefore favoured his younger siblings, who were able to make "a fresh start" with them, and this may have angered G further.

In recent feedback from our CAT pilot project, family B revealed that Alicia (Chapter Four) continued to be a very challenging child over the intervening ten years. Now fourteen, she is at last settling at secondary school and making "real friends who genuinely like her for who she is". Mrs B commented that she was determined never to give up on Alicia, who is still scarred by her first eighteen months of institutional privation. Through consistently being there for Alicia, Mrs B has finally earned her daughter's trust. The family recently revisited Alicia's homeland with her, having actively continued her life story work over the past ten years.

Conclusion: Feedback we have received, as above, made us realize that the carers' and our focus in CAT work sometimes diverged, with the child often continuing to be a scapegoat for ongoing problems in his new family rather than being supported in feeling fully part of it, as Alicia now is in family B.

Our major learning at this point is that CAT is very useful as a brief intervention at a time of family crisis, but the attachment work needs to be *reinforced* by the carers themselves afterwards. Some children will need ongoing individual therapy for some time, while carers might also benefit from follow-up sessions—at least at annual intervals—to monitor progress and provide further therapeutic support as needed. Follow-up over the years is, in fact, essential to help families to continue to hold very hurt children.

Ultimately, however, therapists like social workers, foster carers, and teachers will never know for certain what impact they may have had on a child, not just in the short term but over a lifetime. We are all indebted to a large number of people, remembered or not, for snippets of advice, encouragement, teaching, and modelling that we have benefited from over the years. We hope that CAT interventions have planted the seeds of many new positive attachments, or helped to nourish those that already existed.

Note

1. The first section of this chapter, "A local authority persepective", is contributed by Maggie Gall.

CHAPTER EIGHT

A future for CAT: spreading the word among professionals

We had discovered early on the flexibility of CAT in work with birth, extended, foster, adoptive, and step-families. We went on to use the Programme in therapeutic assessments for Social Services and the Courts where the placement or attachment needs of a child or siblings were in question. Often, there were also child protection concerns, and/or contact, identity, and multi-cultural issues to be considered. CAT principles have provided a useful framework within which to assess any or all of these. Ironically, I have carried out some of this work in recent years with colleagues at the Post-Adoption Centre in London, whose own pilot project twelve years ago inspired us to create a Child-Centred Attachment Therapy programme for local use.

A further development was to introduce CAT in 2005 to an independent therapy clinic which was already well established in providing adult mental health services locally. As waiting lists for local Child and Family Consultation Service appointments extend up to a year or longer, we had wondered whether CAT could collaborate with the clinic and help to reduce this waiting time for children and families who might benefit from brief attachment therapy.

A therapy manager's perspective

Angela Reynolds has a BSc in Social Work and was a team manager in Social Services for ten years before going on to train as an adult and couples counsellor. A BACP accredited therapist and supervisor, Angela has also trained as a Life Coach and NLP Master Practitioner. Angela, then principal psychotherapist at the Atrium Clinic in Southend-on-Sea, agreed to explore the potential of ₵AT for their work. In her words,

> As the Clinical Counselling Manager of the Atrium Clinic and Therapy Centre, it was necessary for me to be aware of the facilities available for children, adults and families in the area where I work. In addition, as I came from a social work background dealing mainly with older people, I had an interest in other disciplines and services locally.
>
> So I was pleased when I was given the opportunity to visit ₵AT in Rayleigh, Essex, some years ago, and to find out more about this Programme.
>
> I could also recall my own experiences as a mother of an adopted child when I was a young woman. This made me curious on a more personal level to learn any new skills, any new techniques available to reflect upon, or pass on to others in a similar situation. Or, indeed, to refer them to ₵AT if it seemed that they might benefit from this Programme.
>
> The ₵AT venue was large (a whole floor), unassuming, comfortable, and fairly central for families to access. It was bright and welcoming, with many smaller rooms off a large central room. Each room had a theme for different age groups and, to me, it seemed inviting to youngsters because there was so much to interest them: toys and games, practical things to do as well as reading areas, and a place for the family to engage in therapy all together with skilled workers. It seemed interesting and rewarding both on a professional and a personal level.
>
> On that visit, Maeja and I discussed a range of therapeutic interventions favoured by the therapists. We exchanged views about the benefits of different theories that underpin ₵AT practice. These include the work of John Bowlby, Donald Winnicott, and Melanie Klein, all eminent authors and psychoanalysts who were interested in the journey we each have to make from dependence

to independence. I remember talking about my passion for neuro-linguistic programming (NLP) and how this has more recently influenced my work as a psychotherapist and life coach at the Atrium Clinic. So, our caring and sharing of resources and an interest in ongoing learning started a friendship, including our working together with some families.

CAT *training*: I have learnt a lot from the methodology used by the CAT Programme, having had the opportunity to co-work it with Maeja. So I was pleased to have her arrange a training day in 2005 at our clinic for myself and colleagues to reflect on the complexities of attachment, separation, and loss. We were a small select group of dedicated counsellors, all interested in learning about the theoretical base as well as the practical elements of this important Child-centred Attachment Therapy programme that offers hope to struggling families.

In the past, I had attended a workshop with Sir Richard Bowlby, son of Sir John Bowlby, who, through his work in the Second World War and post-war years at the Tavistock Clinic in London, became concerned about the quality of life and prospects for British children within the institutional care system. He wrote very powerfully about the effects of attachment and loss on children, and how these might affect their future relationships. Bowlby provided a positive way of conceptualizing the tendency in human beings to make strong "affectional bonds" with others, and of understanding the powerful emotional reactions that occur when those bonds are threatened or broken.

The training day with Maeja gave myself and my colleagues a real understanding of Bowlby's theories and the methodology of CAT. We considered the behaviours that could be exhibited by children with secure and insecure attachments within foster families and adoptive families, as well as from the bringing together of children from two different families. We reflected on a likely range of reactions by children, depending on disturbances in parenting or the type of relationship they have with the attachment figure.

We went on to look at the different developmental stages of children and young people, and the importance of using a variety of materials to engage them and their families in play-work. This can be a very effective, yet subtle, form of psychotherapy. Bowlby had emphasized the area of "potential space" and the overlap of the two "play areas" as being the overlap between the patient and the therapist.

We then began our own "play-work" so that we could experience for ourselves the purpose, the benefits, and the fun of creating and learning experientially through sand-tray work.

This was such a pleasure for our child selves: we were encouraged to use our imagination to indulge ourselves for a short while in our own world, and to then share our sandscape in pairs, and then with the group, analysing further what we had depicted.

My scene, I believed, was simple. I chose a green tray and covered it with a thick layer of golden sand and then, using a range of shiny pebbles, proceeded to cover the whole space with the pebbles, depicting initially my husband and myself, and my four children and their partners. I then added their children—my thirteen grand-children—choosing a different colour and size for each unique person. The whole showed the fullness of my life and the impor-tance of the family to me both personally and professionally. But the scene was also tinged with sadness at the loss of my father, to whom I had been so special when growing up, and who had instilled in me his own strong family values and optimism about life and people.

CAT family work: I remember my excitement when we saw our first children and family at the clinic. The preparation of the therapy venue was so important, and we worked to create a room that had a welcoming ambience for families. Our child selves chose stuffed toy animals to place on each of the chairs arranged in a circle. The room was bright yet relaxing, inviting and interesting, to help family members all feel at ease. We had soft music in the background, a table with a few children's books and writing and colouring materials, plus another area on the floor with assorted toys. We, too, were ready to play.

At the start, it was the family and us having fun choosing where we would sit, as this could indicate the closeness (attachment) each child felt to their parents when in "a strange situation". After introducing ourselves, we asked the children if they knew why they had come to see us. Our aim was to be open and honest with them and the family, and to model this for the parents who might have found it difficult to talk to the children about their reasons for visiting the clinic. I soon realized that my observational powers, as well as my active listening skills, would be very useful, especially when recalling the session later for debriefing with Maeja.

Liam's story

The identified child client, Liam, was eleven and still experiencing emotional difficulties a year after the family had been involved in a serious car accident. While the trauma still affected them all, the mother needing extensive surgery, Liam had been particularly affected. He had nightmares and was fearful, worried about his own and his family's safety. He was also having difficulty settling at his new secondary school and making friends. He could not concentrate at all at school and had become disruptive there. Liam was very clear that he wanted to be just like his Dad and go to work and earn money, and not go to school at all!

After our preliminary introductions, we all had a variety of drinks to choose from: tea and coffee for the adults, and juice or water for the children. Maeja then invited the children to use the play materials available in "the family room" while I took the parents to an adjoining room to chat. The doors of both rooms were left open, so that the children could access their parents if they felt they needed to.

The parents and I then got down to the real work of exploring family dynamics and considering the levels of parental and child power and control. An hour passed by very quickly as I became engrossed in hearing the couple's story, how they managed their lives, their experiences of parenting, and the roles and relationships they had with each other as well as with their extended families. I used my skills as a therapist to build rapport with the couple as we considered their parenting styles, as well as any other issues they wished to pursue.

It was clear that this family were fairly traditional, with Dad being the breadwinner and Mum the homemaker while also holding down a part-time job. They had strong values, which included being "open and honest", and they said they wished to pass these on to their children. However, family work of this nature was new to them and we had yet to see whether they could commit themselves to it.

We rejoined the children and Maeja for the final part of the session, and we discussed what they wished to share with their parents, including their drawings. We agreed small changes that family members could make individually or collectively. I really liked this way of supporting positive changes for the family in a caring and sharing environment.

Finally, when we had agreed a date for a following session and the family had left, Maeja and I discussed our recollections of the session, and our own hopes, fears and expectations for future work with them.

In a subsequent session, I was able to teach Liam and his little sister some brain gym exercises to encourage crossover between the right and left hemispheres of the brain and so aid effective learning. My favourite is "Lazy 8s", as this requires the whole body and both arms to be used quite vigorously. The children were then able to demonstrate these exercises to the parents and Maeja, so we all had a go at doing them! Doing such fun activities together helps to develop connections both in the brain and in the family. We also discussed how the parents could promote a healthy life style for the children, with themselves as role models.

For such family work, we have used a range of soft toys and glove puppets, and I always enjoy seeing the faces of the children when they first come in and the room is set out like a playroom, encouraging them to explore it all. I like the range of activites available to engage with children of different ages and abilities. These include creative play with miniature figures, crayons and paper for younger children, with board games for older children who are able to read.

A firm favourite of mine is a board game, with each player throwing a dice and moving coloured counters on the board. The numbers on the board correspond to cards with questions they must answer honestly with information about themselves, their feelings, a memory, or situation. Forfeits might include doing something silly or more challenging physically, especially for the therapists! This play usually produces a wealth of information to work with, while engaging the children in a competitive game of skills, which they often win. Parents are encouraged to join in such games with the children, perhaps borrowing one to take home for play-work and improved communication with and understanding of their children.

While Maeja worked with the child or children, I would engage with the parents as a couple, specifically to look at parenting and relationship skills. We worked initially on improving their communication, going on to the challenge that gender issues present, and then learning how to compromise and what commitment means to them, as well as exploring how they manage conflict as a family.

I have personal experience as a parent, grandparent, and great-grandparent, as well as being a counsellor, life coach, and master practitioner of NLP. This enables me to draw on different methodologies to promote improvement in parenting and communication skills and I always encourage carers to be *consistent* in using these skills. I often recommend reading resources, and might lend parents books that I think will be of help to them, for example, *The Incredible Years*, by Caroline Webster-Stratton (2006).

Or I will talk to parents about the NLP concept of "Four pillars of childhood":

1. Unconditional love.

2. Encouragement.

3. Discipline (boundaries).

4. Self control (control of self).

* * *

Reflecting on those earlier days, I know that the CAT Programme has continued to evolve, incorporating learning from therapies as varied as NLP and emotional freedom technique (EFT). I believe that ongoing learning is invaluable, and that therapists need in turn to be able to model this for parents.

While my work with Maeja has been *ad hoc* and time limited, I learnt a lot about myself through this style of working. I know that the children and families we engaged with did as well. To my mind, CAT is a tried and tested way of helping children with attachment issues as well as training the carers in parenting and relationship skills. I believe it has been of real benefit to many unhappy children and their families, helping them to manage their lives better in times of adversity while creating greater hope for the future. [Angela Reynolds]

A music therapist's perspective

Colette Salkeld has an MA, focusing on "the effectiveness of music therapy as a tool to build secure attachment in adopted children". Colette is a professional clarinettist and trained as a music therapist at Anglia Ruskin University, Cambridge, working mainly in schools for children with learning disabilities. Colette has also worked for Social Services, focusing on adopted children with attachment problems. She contributed a chapter for a book, *Music Therapy with*

Children and their Families (2008, Jessica Kingsley). Here, she comments on the ℂAT Programme.

> I have found the ℂAT Programme invaluable in my work as a music therapist within the area of post-adoption support. One of the main strengths of this therapy is the focus on the family as the catalyst for emotional healing and therapeutic change in children with attachment problems. Using this type of intervention, the music therapist facilitates musical expression of quite difficult feelings and improved child–parent interactions. Using the ℂAT Programme, music therapy sessions offer the opportunity for family members to focus on their relationships, building trust and empathy with one another. When this takes place, therapeutic change is then demonstrated within therapy sessions as well as within the home and in the child's peer relationships.
>
> Attachment problems stem from failed relationships and trauma within birth families, leaving a child unable to trust adoptive parents to be available and responsive to their needs. This can lead to negative patterns of interaction within adoptive families, as parents feel rejected by their adopted child. The ℂAT Programme fosters mutual attachment between carers and children through helping them to synchronise cues and responses and encouraging them to "play" together wherever possible. In this way, the core values of the ℂAT Programme and music therapy are the same.
>
> A central belief in music therapy, as in many other psychoanalytically informed therapies, is that it is the "evolving relationship between the client and the therapist in which changes occur" (Association of Professional Music Therapists, 2000). The thinking contained within the ℂAT Programme challenges this philosophy because the music therapist's role changes to provide "a secure base" for family work while focusing on the development of the relationship between the adopted child and their new family.
>
> The music therapist, using improvised music as a tool, enables dyads of adoptive mother and adopted child or adoptive father and adopted child, siblings and family groups, to make music together. This unique medium can then enable families who have previously been caught up in negative patterns of interaction to find healthier ways of interacting through music.
>
> Music therapy can sometimes help to recreate early mother–baby interactions, which can enable adoptive parents to bond with their

adopted child. Many of them have not had the opportunity to share these early experiences with their child. Equally, because of trauma or inconsistent parenting in the past, some adopted children may never have shared these earliest experiences with an adult. By facilitating such interactions through musical improvisation, the therapist can enable the adopted child to feel emotionally contained by her adoptive parent, thereby initiating a new and healthy attachment cycle.

Grief work within the CAT Programme is also seen as essential in order that positive attachments can be developed. Sometimes, when a traumatized child improvises within music therapy sessions, past trauma that has remained suppressed for long periods of time can come into his awareness. In some cases, it might be significant that the trauma was experienced before the child could speak. The music therapist and the adoptive parents, using improvised music, are able to contain the child's feelings, holding him emotionally as he processes his grief. In this way, the therapeutic space is safe both for the child and the adoptive parents, providing a secure base for such painful work.

Over the past few years, I have combined music therapy with the CAT Programme and the clinical results have been rewarding, as adoptive parents and their adopted children have found new, positive ways of being together. [Colette Salkeld]

An attachment researcher's perspective

Sir Richard Bowlby qualified in medical and scientific photography in 1968, and spent his subsequent career illustrating research in those fields through his photography and video productions. Since retiring in 1999, Richard has promoted through lectures and seminars, nationally and internationally, a wider understanding of attachment research. Thus, he is continuing the work of his late father, Sir John Bowlby, who pioneered research on the importance of early attachment relationships, and the long term impact on children of separation and loss. Richard's comments on the CAT Programme follow.

The CAT Programme is a distillation of personal and professional knowledge and experience which Maeja and her colleagues have intuitively combined to create a very convincing model of brief family attachment therapy.

They have fully embraced John Bowlby's belief that feelings of attachment and protection must be linked to keep children safe. CAT therapists believe that, where there is a potential for building healthy attachments, it would be emotionally and financially more cost-effective to support this in a child's existing family (with birth, foster, or adoptive parents) rather than risk moving her on to a new family in the "care system" and hope that she will transplant with ease.

CAT combines assessment with treatment from the start of work with troubled children and families. The reasoning is that, while the child's behaviours may be the visible cause for concern, it is the mutual attachment with the current family that needs to be encouraged, and which can help the child to develop new ways of reacting to familiar triggers for fight or flight survival responses.

CAT therapists have, therefore, not waited for formal diagnoses by a series of experts to be made before beginning attachment therapy with the child and family. The programme is a prompt but measured response to the client's needs. The therapists work in true partnership with families, encouraging self-empowerment and harnessing their own resources for healing, even though the families' solutions might not always be what professionals would have chosen.

CAT is based on optimism and hope that even a traumatized child can be helped, through skilled and committed parenting, to become more securely attached and heal from old wounds. It would seem that, based on the therapists' experience of working with a number of very troubled children and families, this can happen, thus interrupting intergenerational cycles of neglect and abuse.

An important question for me has been: how has CAT bypassed the formalities of referral to psychiatric and psychological experts for diagnosis? The reality is that, through word of mouth, where social workers have felt that the programme can be of benefit to a struggling child and family, referrals have been made direct to CAT, with some impressive results. As the therapists have learnt, however, some of the children and families referred have needed ongoing therapeutic support on an individual or family basis, while others would have benefited from regular follow-up.

Overall, CAT appears to offer help when it is needed most: at the time of referral, when child and family are in crisis and therefore more open to change, before mutually destructive patterns of inter-action become reinforced and need more time-consuming and costly interventions. [Richard Bowlby]

CHAPTER NINE

Overall learning from CAT: who can benefit[1]

Initial learning from the pilot project (1995–1996)

Even as early as our six-month pilot project in 1996, through our work with just four families we got increasing confirmation of our initial thinking about how CAT could work, and of our intuitive belief in its effectiveness as prevention and early treatment of attachment problems. So, to recap from our learning, following the pilot project (see Chapter Four), the following is a summary.

1. Our belief is that there are not "problem children" but "families with problems". The parents must be part of any therapeutic work that seeks to modify challenging or negative behaviours, because unless the parents change the way they respond to their child (i.e., reading cues successfully), the child will be unable to break the negative interaction cycle on their own. Even if the child's behaviour can be changed, repeated negative responses from the parents will prevent true healing.

2. Within the attachment dyad, if interactions are not mutually pleasing, the relationship breaks down: parents need to feel needed and loved just as children need to feel secure, safe, and loved. If parents get nothing but negative responses, the gap

between parent and child grows bigger, so that mutual distrust and rejection become the only way each knows how to respond to the other. If this pattern can be interrupted and replaced by a new cycle of mutually satisfying behaviours, the relationship can be healed and parents become *protective* of their child again, while she begins to feel more secure and trusting of them.

3. CAT teaches *all* family members to be aware of *cues* and *responses*, since if cues are misread, they can inhibit attachment rather than engender it.

4. When children are placed for adoption, work begins immediately within the new family group, so we see the Programme as being preventive, as well as curative of any attachment problems. Using CAT preventively, we consider its importance lies in helping parents to view attachment problems as a difference in family dynamics, given the new relationships, rather than pathologizing the child placed.

5. It is important for adoptive and foster parents to acknowledge that children placed cannot be expected to have a sense of belonging to the new family. A lot of the child's anger and hurt, often expressed through bad behaviour, more appropriately belongs to previous carers, including their birth parents.

6. By encouraging parents to *not* take the misbehaviour as personally directed at themselves, and to deal with it on a more practical level (i.e., certain thought-through responses to particular behaviours), placements are less likely to fail because the adopters do not feel so overwhelmed and rejected on account of the child's chaotic functioning.

7. The CAT Programme helps parents to identify specific responses to various "non-attached behaviours". They can then explore with the worker ways in which they can create a sense of trust in their child by responding positively and encouragingly rather than with anger and rejection.

8. It is also very encouraging for parents to look back and acknowledge their parenting skills and to witness positive changes, however small, in their children's behaviour.

9. Hurt children in placement and their carers have a right to be supported. In working through child and adult issues at the onset of behavioural difficulties, an intensive therapeutic

programme of interventions should be seen as major preventive work. This can result in positive changes from previous negative patterns and help both the child and carer to maintain his place within the family and promote their feelings of self-worth.

10. Where a child, for whatever reason, feels unattached and insecure, she is likely to seek help through unconsciously "acting out" her sadness, hurt, anger, and frustration in ways that adults perceive as misbehaviour (MisCUES).

11. Feeling rejected, the child will reject the carers in turn, so that their interaction becomes mutually ungratifying and, being painful to both, decreases. They have little or no "fun-time" together, leading to a further deterioration in their relationship and his behaviours.

12. The carers, if stuck in this downward "spiral of negative interaction", will distance themselves emotionally from the child and are then unlikely to claim and protect the child as their own. If this continues, the carers place the child and themselves at risk of developing abusive interactions. This could lead to the child having to leave the family, so suffering further losses and hurt, and feeling even less able to trust again and form healthy new attachments.

13. What is therefore essential is to *change the focus of the work from the child's stated problem behaviours to improving family communication and relationships: in brief, their attachments.*

14. We realized more clearly the interdependence of the different quadrants of the attachment–protection cycle (see Figure 17, p. 114): the *direct* expression of feelings by the child (*cue*); consistent and appropriate meeting of her needs (*response*) by the carer to create *a secure base*, with firm holding of boundaries. This helps the child to feel safely held, worthy of protection, and so to act more predictably, giving and receiving appropriate cues and responses to have her needs met. In turn, the carer feels *validated as parent*, and *entitled to provide care to this particular child; so he claims and protects the child as his own, thus providing safety for the child and the whole family.*

15 Firm holding by CAT therapists of personal, professional, and family boundaries is crucial in this work, which often uncovers child protection issues. (See Figure 16, p. 113.)

16. We learnt, through comparing our longer and more open-ended work with our "control group" families C and D, about the value of doing focused time-limited work with families A and B, time also being an important boundary. This counteracts the tendency for individual or family work to otherwise be more woolly and drift indefinitely, with fewer long-term benefits for families in crisis and overburdened workers.

17. Play-work with children and families is an essential part of the CAT Programme. It provides a means of communication between child and adult, a safe way of accessing the unconscious for both and of learning how to articulate that which could not be previously spoken about, or even thought of. It helps the adult to come down to child level, since both have to use play and imagination to depict their situation and empathize with each other. Parents are often astounded at the depth of understanding even very small children reveal through such play about how they feel and how they really view themselves in the family.

18. We learnt very early on about the value of *co-working* with every family in order to avoid collusion with either parent or child, or with couples in conflict. Having a therapist to work with the child individually, or in parent–child or family sessions, ensures that he has a "voice" of his own, and an advocate to represent his view to parents, who often do not wish to hear from a child what the underlying problems in the family are.

19. Especially where there are child protection concerns, it is imperative that we, as CAT therapists, do not get drawn into countertransferential "acting out" of the parent's childhood scripts or hooked into the child's re-enactment of his old family scenarios. This means that the therapists co-working in pairs can take on different aspects of the child–parent split and, in peer supervision or external consultation, reflect on their own feelings and biases and share these, in a more digestible form, with the family (see "Sophie's story", Chapter Six).

20. Although we had devised "Child and Parent Attachment questionnaires" as quantitative tools for use with the families at the beginning and end of the CAT Programme, we feel that ongoing self-assessment by family members is more respectful and valid. As Maggie Gall commented in her work with family A,

regular reference to the questionnaires helped the parents to monitor for themselves little changes in their and the children's attachment behaviours, and so confirmed for them the mutual bonding that CAT supported.

Further learning from CAT work (1997 to 2007)

In the ten years following the CAT Programme pilot project, we continued to learn from each child and family we worked with, individually and jointly: but mainly that families are families, whether birth, extended, adoptive, foster, or step-families, and they can be very damaging or healing in their attitudes and interactions:

Some children and families, as in "Rico's" and "Robert's" stories (Chapters Five and Six), might be too deeply wounded to benefit from a brief, focused programme such as CAT, without longer term individual and family therapy for parents and child to help them deal with their separate issues. Moreover, without the adults' commitment to undertaking such painful exploration in order to move on and heal, the child is likely to continue to "act out" the family's dysfunction in an unconscious cry for help (see "Christy's" and "Molly's" stories in Chapter Five).

Social Services monitoring is essential in Child Protection cases and has a direct impact on CAT work, depending on whether it is valued by the child care workers and management or not. In some cases, where we raised new concerns about a child's safety and well being, we were quite often left feeling that we had done something really bad, just like the child who discloses abuse in her family. We have needed to be really sure of our facts and stand our ground, especially in legal proceedings if our recommendations differed from the local authority's care plan for the child.

Ongoing peer supervision and skilled and regular consultation are essential ingredients for CAT work to succeed. These have enabled us to contain our own anxieties and provide emotional "holding" for the child and family, especially where there might be child protection concerns. As in "Sophie's story" (Chapter Six), we have had to stand back from our work and understand the dynamics in the child and family system, as well as the mirroring of these by the other professionals involved as well as ourselves.

Working in genuine partnership with the family and a "team" of professionals supporting the child helps to create a necessary "secure base" for the sensitive and often painful work that has to be done to keep him safe. The child needs to know that the adults working on his behalf can communicate honestly and respectfully with each other for his benefit, setting aside personal issues and professional jealousy.

Sharing information appropriately between child and parents, and family and Social Services where child protection issues arise— and they almost always do with damaging attachments—needs to be written into our initial contract with the family.

We are aware that some traditional child and adult psychotherapists do not work in this way, and regard what they perceive as a "breach of confidentiality" to be detrimental to their work and therapy culture, as well as a major ethical issue. We learnt that *not* to share information appropriately was collusive and could put the child and family at grave risk of harm or abuse, intentional or not, which is why "truth-telling" has had to be a cornerstone of our work. (See Figure 16, p. 113.)

Follow-up needs to be written into the contract with the family and referring agency, and not just during the twelve months after CAT work ends. Feedback from the family is essential to let us know what they have continued to find helpful or not, both in the short term and longer term. Routine annual follow-up can help to monitor the family's progress and provide timely interventions, with built-in therapeutic support and much-needed continuity of care for families at times of developmental crises.

New learning for CAT therapists

Inevitably, our thinking about CAT has evolved over the years as we have learnt more about the efficacy of certain other therapies, especially those involving body–mind or "energy" work such as EFT and Emotrance (Sylvia Hartman) as well as early precursors such as NLP and inner child healing. All these now make more sense to me as interconnecting pieces of the "body–mind" jigsaw of new "truths" gleaned from neuroscience research and their application to attachment theory.

Much of this learning has been fortuitous and synchronistic: a cross-fertilization of knowledge and experience and techniques through meeting other therapists, hearing about what has worked for them, and our own "continuing professional development". For instance, Angela Reynolds' enthusiasm about NLP encouraged me to learn about it for myself and so to overcome a long-held prejudice about its use by unscrupulous salesmen to manipulate buyers!

Coming from a multi-cultural background, I am naturally eclectic, and have always valued diversity. Increasingly, in my own work with adult therapy clients, I have been struck by the powerful healing some experience through a sudden release of repressed feelings, whether through "inner child work", visualization techniques, or EFT. This is much more than "insight", which we can all develop and still not use to make positive changes. While continuing to work with unconscious processes and communication within a psychoanalytic framework, my practice has gradually broadened over the years to include such new "body–mind" therapies with thought-provoking results.

I am reminded of Neville Symington's approach to writing about *The Analytic Experience* (1986):

> I am talking of a single reality but coming at it from different perspectives. This is the Hebrew rather than the Greek way of explaining a human phenomenon. The Hebrew way is to go round and round a subject, each time using different images to illuminate what is most profound. [p. 11]

In Symington's view,

> truth can be seen or glimpsed. When I see the truth some change occurs in me. I can never be the same again. Something in my personality has altered; a previous preconception gives way to truth, but it is in the very nature of truth that each glimpse only emphasizes the degree to which truth still lies outside or beyond. [*ibid.*, p. 17]

Hopefully, this is what we have done in our writing about the CAT Programme, using family stories and different perspectives to illustrate what we sought to achieve so that other attachment therapists can continue to build on our learning and help a greater number of children and families than we could ever hope to reach.

Note

1. Paragraphs 1–20 of "Initial learning" were co-authored with me by Maggie Gall and Pauline Sear

Epilogue

Rose's healing

Forty years on, Rose was still alone and without a family to call her own. She had briefly married a foreigner and emigrated with him to his country. But they literally spoke different languages, and so could not communicate with ease. This was a very disabling experience for Rose, who unconsciously reverted to Hurt Child mode. She found herself, as at six years old, in a strange country and culture, among people she did not understand and who did not seek to understand her.

Rose retreated into herself and would not go out of her husband's flat, so starting a self-imposed imprisonment that lasted for a very long time. Her physical and mental health deteriorated, and her husband decided to end their marriage. He took Rose back to India and arranged for her, still very young, to live in a home for the aged since she had no relatives or friends to take care of her.

Rose spent ten years in what felt to her like solitary confinement among very elderly and dying women. Nevertheless, most of the "inmates" had families who came to visit or took them out briefly. Only Rose had no one to care about her. Her family still lived abroad and, apart from occasional visits to India when they visited her briefly, she had no contact with them.

Rose felt just like an orphan, repeatedly abandoned and rejected by all those she had ever trusted. Her mother, Marie, had died without any reconciliation taking place between them, and her brothers and sisters were busy with their own lives and families. Rose grew very bitter and decided to sever all contact with her birth family.

Then, suddenly, while on a holiday in India, her older brother, Peter, fell very ill and died. Letting go of her old hurts, Rose stayed with him in the hospital, helping to care for him there. It was the beginning of a new life for Rose as Peter then left her a generous legacy. For the first time in her life, she could choose where to live and to even travel abroad on her own.

Peter's death unlocked secrets of the past for Rose and her family. Jenny and Emily at last felt free to talk to each other about the family's total abandonment of their younger sister. They decided to visit Rose in India together, and gradually shared with her their different perspectives of their family story. They made no excuses for theirs or the family's abandonment of Rose since a baby, and so they finally validated her experiences.

Rose decided to forgive her sisters and bury the past with Peter. During her long and lonely sojourn at the home for the aged, she had found healing resources for herself. These included her great love of reading and a continuing interest in the world and people outside. Rose also found spiritual practices, including meditation, of great help. And she observed how other women in the home dealt with their own adverse situations.

Slowly, Rose began to let go of her long-held childhood hurts and to take charge of her life as an adult. It was not too late to start living at sixty, instead of merely existing and waiting to be rescued by her family or others. Rose had grown up at last and reclaimed her innate ability to choose to be in charge of her own life.

CAT: child's attachment behaviours

© CAT Team, 1996

The scales listed below are from 1–4; please *circle* the appropriate number for each item:
1—a very low attachment; 2—fairly low attachment; 3—average; 4—a good level of attachment

Child's interactions with parents	4	3	2	1
1. Interacts positively with parents	4	3	2	1
2. Looks at parents when communicating	4	3	2	1
3. Expects a response from parents	4	3	2	1
4. Seeks affection from parents	4	3	2	1
5. Seeks comfort from parents	4	3	2	1
6. Seeks care from parents	4	3	2	1
7. Seeks attention from parents	4	3	2	1
8. Accepts affection from parents	4	3	2	1
9. Accepts comfort from parents	4	3	2	1
10. Accepts care from parents	4	3	2	1
11. Accepts attention from parents	4	3	2	1
12. Expresses need appropriately to parents	4	3	2	1
13. Expresses feelings appropriately to parents	4	3	2	1
14. Shows awareness of parent's feelings	4	3	2	1

15. Accepts limit setting by parents	4	3	2	1
16. Protests at separation from parents	4	3	2	1
17. Seems indifferent to separation from parents	4	3	2	1
18. Seeks comfort from parents on reunion	4	3	2	1
19. Accepts comfort from parents on reunion	4	3	2	1
20. Gives appropriate **cues**/signals to parents	4	3	2	1
21. Recognizes **cues** from parents	4	3	2	1
22. Claims parents as hers/his	4	3	2	1
23. Shows signs of pride in parents	4	3	2	1
24. Shows signs of joy in parents	4	3	2	1
25. Responds appropriately to **cues** from parents	4	3	2	1
26. Explores new surroundings with interest	4	3	2	1
27. Shows anxiety in new surroundings	4	3	2	1
28. Shows normal anxiety about physical dangers	4	3	2	1
29. Plays well on his/her own	4	3	2	1
30. Shows imagination in playing	4	3	2	1
31. Is able to concentrate	4	3	2	1
32. Seems generally relaxed and content	4	3	2	1
33. Eats well	4	3	2	1
34. Sleeps well	4	3	2	1
35. Reacts appropriately to pleasure	4	3	2	1
36. Reacts appropriately to pain	4	3	2	1
37. Reacts appropriately to losses	4	3	2	1
38. Shows appropriate awareness of bodily needs	4	3	2	1
39. Shows appropriate awareness of sensations	4	3	2	1
40. Shows a range of feelings	4	3	2	1
41. Shows appropriate attachment to toys	4	3	2	1
42. Shows appropriate feelings of joy	4	3	2	1
43. Shows appropriate feelings of anger	4	3	2	1
44. Shows appropriate feelings of sadness	4	3	2	1
45. Shows appropriate feelings of hurt	4	3	2	1
46. Engages in age-appropriate activities	4	3	2	1
47. Uses speech age-appropriately	4	3	2	1
48. Expresses likes	4	3	2	1
49. Expresses dislikes	4	3	2	1
50. Seems spontaneous when smiling	4	3	2	1
51. Seems spontaneous when interacting	4	3	2	1
52. Seems spontaneous when reacting to situations	4	3	2	1
53. Shows signs of pride in self	4	3	2	1

54. Shows signs of joy in self	4	3	2	1
55. Shows signs of embarrassment	4	3	2	1
56. Shows signs of shame	4	3	2	1
57. Shows signs of guilt	4	3	2	1
58. Takes time when playing	4	3	2	1
59. Interacts positively with adults	4	3	2	1
60. Shows normal anxiety about strangers	4	3	2	1
61. Initiates positive interactions	4	3	2	1
62. Accepts limit-setting by adults	4	3	2	1

CAT parent's attachment questionnaire

The scales listed below are 1—4; please *circle* the appropriate number for each item:

1—a poor level of attachment; 2—quite low; 3—satisfactory; 4—a good level of attachment.

Parent's interactions with the child   4 3 2 1

Does the mother:

1. Encourage appropriate exploration by the child 4 3 2 1
2. Encourage appropriate independence by the child 4 3 2 1
3. Respond supportively when the child shows fear 4 3 2 1
4. Respond supportively when the child shows anxiety 4 3 2 1
5. Initiate positive interaction with the child 4 3 2 1
6. Respond positively to interaction with the child 4 3 2 1
7. Recognize **cues** from child for care 4 3 2 1
8. Recognize **cues** from child for comfort 4 3 2 1
9. Recognize **cues** from child for attention 4 3 2 1
10. Help child to recognize and meet bodily needs 4 3 2 1
11. Help child to recognize and express range of feelings 4 3 2 1
12. Help child to verbalize likes 4 3 2 1

13. Help child to verbalize dislikes   4 3 2 1
14. Help child to make choices   4 3 2 1
15. Help child to recognize parent's **cues**   4 3 2 1
16. Help child to respond to parent's **cues**   4 3 2 1
17. Prepare child for changes/new situations
    through play   4 3 2 1
18. Talk to the child to prepare for changes   4 3 2 1
19. Explain to the child about separations, however brief 4 3 2 1
20. Reassure the child about separations, however brief   4 3 2 1
21. Encourage the child to learn new skills   4 3 2 1
22. Through play, encourage the child to learn new skills 4 3 2 1
23. Encourage the child to carry out age-appropriate
    tasks   4 3 2 1
24. Set appropriate limits for the child's behaviour   4 3 2 1
25. Act consistently, when setting limits for child   4 3 2 1
26. Explain sensitively to child about family origins   4 3 2 1
27. Show affection towards the child   4 3 2 1
28 Show liking for the child   4 3 2 1
29. Show pride in the child   4 3 2 1

Mother's behaviour/attitudes towards the child:

30. Seems to enjoy parenting the child   4 3 2 1
31. Seems to feel overwhelmed parenting the child   4 3 2 1
32. Has a positive view of self as a parent   4 3 2 1
33. Has a positive view of the world   4 3 2 1
34. Sees positive family resemblances in the child.   4 3 2 1
35. Sees negative family resemblances in the child   4 3 2 1
36. Helps the child to learn positively about her
    cultural heritage   4 3 2 1
37. Helps the child to develop a positive self view   4 3 2 1
38. Helps child to develop a positive ethnic identity   4 3 2 1
39. Shows empathy with the child's situation   4 3 2 1
40. Shows empathy with the child's birth family   4 3 2 1
41. Feels entitled to parent this child   4 3 2 1
42. Shows claiming of child as own   4 3 2 1

Does the father:

1. Encourage appropriate exploration by the child   4 3 2 1
2. Encourage appropriate independence by the child   4 3 2 1
3. Respond supportively when the child shows fear   4 3 2 1

4. Respond supportively when the child shows anxiety 4 3 2 1
5. Initiate positive interaction with the child   4 3 2 1
6. Respond positively to interaction with the child   4 3 2 1
7. Recognize **cues** from child for care   4 3 2 1
8. Recognize **cues** from child for comfort   4 3 2 1
9. Recognize **cues** from child for attention   4 3 2 1
10. Help child to recognize and meet bodily needs   4 3 2 1
11. Help child to recognize and express range of feelings 4 3 2 1
12. Help child to verbalize likes   4 3 2 1
13. Help child to verbalize dislikes   4 3 2 1
14. Help child to make choices   4 3 2 1
15. Help child to recognize parent's **cues**   4 3 2 1
16. Help child to respond to parent's **cues**   4 3 2 1
17. Prepare child for changes/new situations through
    play   4 3 2 1
18. Talk to the child to prepare for changes   4 3 2 1
19. Explain to the child about separations, however brief 4 3 2 1
20. Reassure the child about separations, however brief 4 3 2 1
21. Encourage the child to learn new skills   4 3 2 1
22. Through play, encourage the child to learn new skills 4 3 2 1
23. Encourage the child to carry out age-appropriate
    tasks   4 3 2 1
24. Set appropriate limits for the child's behaviour   4 3 2 1
25. Act consistently, when setting limits for child   4 3 2 1
26. Explain sensitively to child about family origins   4 3 2 1
27. Show affection towards the child   4 3 2 1
28 Show liking for the child   4 3 2 1
29. Show pride in the child   4 3 2 1

Father's behaviour/attitudes towards the child:

30. Seems to enjoy parenting the child   4 3 2 1
31. Seems to feel overwhelmed parenting the child   4 3 2 1
32. Has a positive view of self as a parent   4 3 2 1
33. Has a positive view of the world   4 3 2 1
34. Sees positive family resemblances in the child.   4 3 2 1
35. Sees negative family resemblances in the child   4 3 2 1
36. Helps the child to learn positively about her
    cultural heritage   4 3 2 1
37. Helps the child to develop a positive self view   4 3 2 1

38. Helps child to develop a positive ethnic identity   4 3 2 1
39. Shows empathy with the child's situation   4 3 2 1
40. Shows empathy with the child's birth family   4 3 2 1
41. Feels entitled to parent this child   4 3 2 1
42. Shows claiming of child as own   4 3 2 1

Life story work and life story books

Health warning: this can be very painful work for the child and adults involved, leading to regressive behaviours.

Compiling a life story book *without* involving the child and/or family and foster carers and other significant persons in the child's life, as appropriate, is *not* life story work, which is both *griefwork* and *celebration*. Arrange a "life celebration day" for the child.

Life story work is a *collaborative process*, which can take weeks, months, even years, to help a child or young person to understand who they are, where they have come from, why they are where they are now, and who have been the important people in their lives.

Compiling a life story book is a means to that end: it is both a *tool* and an *outcome*. Depending on the child's age and understanding, she may require more than one book—even perhaps a series of simple "graded" books/photograph albums with pictures and simple captions—to help her understand *why she is where she is at a particular time*.

There may be simpler or more informative books for her to look at on her own, or in the company of trusted carers or others important to her. At least one simple version should be always accessible to her, for when she needs to read or hear her own story, perhaps even as a favourite bedtime story when young. The child needs to be aware that the book belongs to her, and does not have to be shared with anyone (adult or child) who might misunderstand or misuse it. Looking at it together allows her to express her feelings.

More detailed or painful information about the child's past, gleaned from Social Services files, etc., can be kept in a separate book, perhaps a ring binder with plastic pockets to preserve precious documents, which she will be able to understand or need to access only when she is much older. *Do keep all original certificates, photographs, letters from parents, etc. in a safe place. Make* colour *copies, if appropriate, for a simpler version of the book for the child to look at on a regular basis.*

Sometimes a child might find the book a very painful reminder of his past, and wish to destroy all evidence, and later regret it. Some of the letters or photographs or videos may be irreplaceable. As the material is so valuable (a treasure trove of memories and information about the child's *life* and *history*), it is important to ensure that the originals are not lost at the child's whim or during a succession of placement moves.

So, what should the life story book consist of? If you were compiling one for yourself as a child, at different ages, what would *you* like to have included in it? A good way to prepare for such sensitive and emotionally-laden work with children is to first compile a book for yourself. This will help you to empathize with the child's feelings and wishes, and what she might like to preserve of herself, her past and present, for the future, when no one might be around to give her very precious information or share family memories.

Birthday and Christmas cards can be included; letters, a family tree, an ecomap; a simple flowchart to show her different moves (with dates and reasons for the move); photographs of homes, schools, her own writing and drawings and pictures cut out, and so on.

Structure of ℂAT Programme

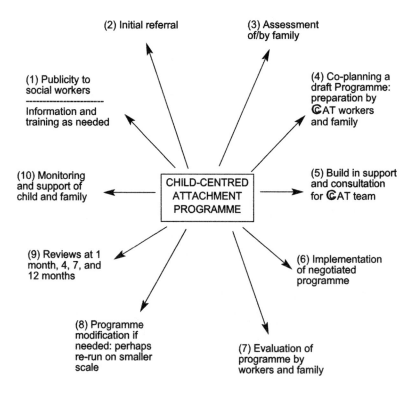

Structure of ℂAT Programme.

ℂAT work with carers

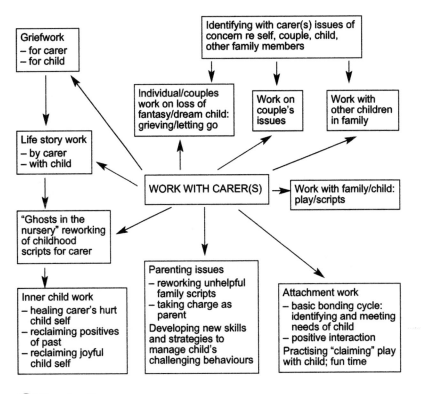

ℂAT work with carers.

Child-centred attachment work

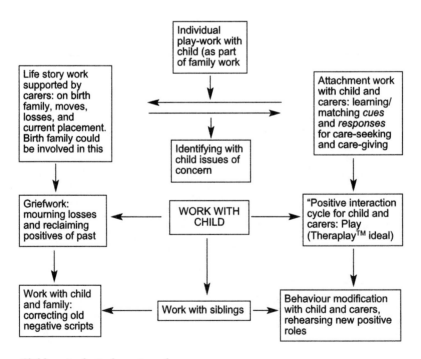

Child-centred attachment work

Ascertaining the wishes and feelings of children

New learning can be painful. It may undermine our confidence in what we thought we knew, took for granted, and leave us deskilled. We may have feelings of loss, insecurity, and feel overwhelmed by the demands made on us, before we slowly integrate new learning with the old.

We have all been a child once and so have the innate capacity to communicate with other children now. The more we are aware of our own inner child, the easier it is for us to empathize with other children.

To understand what a child is communicating to us, we need:

1. *Humility*: the willingness to suspend adult beliefs and preconceptions about a child and her situation; to really learn from the child what it *is* like for *her*.
2. *Observation skills*: practise observing children of all ages in interaction with each other and their families, but discreetly! In trains, buses, supermarkets, doctors' surgeries, playgrounds, adult environments, etc.
3. *Be aware of your own feelings (countertransference)* when observing interactions between a child and an adult. Sometimes very

painful feelings from our own childhood can be stirred up in us when we see a child being treated without respect or affection. We may *defend* against such feelings, which trigger hurtful memories from our past, by "identifying with the aggressor" (adult)—rather than with the "victim" (the child we are observing in the present, or the child we were once).

We may find ourselves making excuses for an adult's rejecting or even abusive behaviour, or justifying it, as we might have had to in a similar situation when we were young, because it was too unsafe then for us to be critical of an adult, especially if he was our parent. We may find ourselves *blaming* the child for provoking negative interactions from the adult, because the child's behaviour reminds us too painfully of our own neediness and vulnerability when we were children.

On the other hand, observing a child in play or loving interaction with a parent might stir up feelings of resentment and envy in our child selves, who might not have had such positive experiences when young.

4. *Listen to what a child is really communicating* through his words, gestures, body posture, play, stories, drawings, etc. Do not assume too quickly that you have the *full* message. The child may well have very ambivalent feelings about his situation, just as we might have felt ambivalent about our parents when we were young. TAKE TIME TO GET TO KNOW THE CHILD, SO *HE* CAN GET TO KNOW AND TRUST YOU.

5. *Unconscious communication*: one important *clue* may be the feelings evoked in ourselves when we observe a child. Do they relate to memories of our own childhood, or belong to the child in the present?

6. *Monitoring your own body sensations* during an assessment, together with good supervision and support, can help you separate what belongs to you and your past from what is being communicated to you by the child in the present, especially if there are child protection issues.

7. *Be aware of your own hurt inner child*: talk to her, be an *advocate* for her in a replay of all those hurtful childhood incidents you can recall when *you* were small, and perhaps on your own and unsupported, and totally powerless.

8. *Keeping a journal, recording dreams* and your own interpretations of them, peer counselling, can all be helpful in developing awareness of your adult and child selves, unconscious communications from one to the other, and so dealing with your past hurts and detoxifying them.

9. *Nurture your playful and creative child selves*: relaxing, having fun, being out in nature, doing creative things, are all ways of healing your inner child and nurturing healthy aspects.

10. *Be aware of child development stages* as a context for the behaviour and communications of the child you are working with. Even an infant can express her wishes and feelings through her gaze, or averted looks, clinginess to, or avoidance of, an adult, as well as to you, as a complete stranger to herself. Knowing how a normally developing child should react to carers and strangers can help you assess the interactions you are observing, and give you an indication of the quality of the child's attachment.

    DON'T JUST GUESS. BACK UP YOUR HUNCHES WITH FACTS. Vera Fahlberg (1982) and Mary Sheridan, among others, have written detailed guides to children's development.

11. *Be aware of class, religious, race, cultural and other biases in assessment.*

12. *Commitment*: once you have ascertained the child's wishes and feelings, you have to be an *advocate* for him, representing his views and best interests, even in the face of adult opposition, whether from carers or professionals.

    Children are the largest minority in the world, totally dependent on adults for their welfare and security. If they are also black, or disabled, or poor, or are members of other oppressed groups, they are even more likely to be disadvantaged. Being an advocate for an oppressed person is not easy or comfortable; you may find yourself also being oppressed. Seek appropriate support, personal and professional, for yourself when doing such challenging work with children, who are our hope for the future.

REFERENCES

Acquarone, S. (2004). *Infant–Parent Psychotherapy*. London: Karnac.

Ainsworth, M. (1982). Attachment: retrospect and prospect. In: C. M. Parkes & J. Stevenson-Hinde (Eds.), *The Place of Attachment in Human Behaviour*. London: Tavistock.

Ainsworth, M., Blehar, M., Waters, E., & Wall, S. (1978). *Patterns of Attachment: Assessed in The Strange Situation and at Home*. Hillsdale, NJ: Erlbaum.

Alleyne, A. (2007). The internal oppressor: the veiled companion of racial oppression. *Attachment: New Directions in Psychotherapy and Relational Psychoanalysis*, 1(3): 269–274.

Archer, C. (1999a). *First Steps in Parenting the Child Who Hurts: Tiddlers and Toddlers*. London: Jessica Kingsley.

Archer, C. (1999b). *Next Steps in Parenting the Child Who Hurts: Tykes and Teens*. London: Jessica Kingsley.

Berne, E. (1961). *Transactional Analysis in Psychotherapy*. New York: Grove.

Bion, W. (1978). *Second Thoughts*. London: Heinemann.

Bowlby, J. (1953). *Child Care and the Growth of Love*. Harmondsworth: Penguin.

Bowlby, J. (1969). *Attachment* (Vol. 1). London: Hogarth.

Brenninkmeyer, M. F. (2000). Assessment of attachment disorder in children: comparison of two recently developed and two established psycho-diagnostic measures. Unpublished MSc dissertation, London: City University.

Byng-Hall, J. (1995). *Rewriting Family Scripts: Improvisation and Systems Change*. New York: Guilford.

Cairns, K. (2002). *Attachment, Trauma and Resilience: Therapeutic Caring for Children*. London: BAAF.

Caplan, G. (1964). *Principles of Preventive Psychiatry*. New York: Basic Books.

Connor, J. (2001). *NLP Workbook: A Practical Guide To Achieving The Results You Want*. London: Thorsons.

Costner Sizemore, C. C., & Sain Pittillo, E. (1979). *Eve*. London: Pan.

Cozolino, L. (2006). *The Neuroscience of Human Relationships: Attachment and The Developing Social Brain*. New York: W. W. Norton.

Craik, K. (1943). *The Nature of Explanation*. Cambridge: Cambridge University Press.

Cullen, D., & Batty, D. (1996). *Child Protection: The Therapeutic Option*. London: BAAF.

Cunningham, T. (2006). *Unequal Thirds*. Calstock, Cornwall: Peterloo Poets.

Delaney, R. J. (1991). *Fostering Changes: Treating Attachment-Disordered Foster Children*. Fort Collins, CO: W. J. Corbett.

Dennison, G. E., Dennison, P. E., & Teplitz, J. V. (1994). *Brain Gym for Business*. Ventura, California: Edu-Kinesthetics.

Fahlberg, V. (1981). *Attachment and Separation*. London: BAAF.

Fahlberg, V. (1982). *Child Development*. London: BAAF.

Fahlberg, V. (1988). *The Child in Placement: Common Behavioural Problems*. London: BAAF.

Fahlberg, V. (1991). *A Child's Journey Through Placement*. London: BAAF.

Feinstein, D. (2002). At play in the fields of the mind: personal myths as fields of information. In: W. Lammers & B. Kircher (Eds.), *The Energy Odyssey: New Directions in Energy Psychology* (pp. 99–103). Eastbourne, East Sussex: Dragon Rising.

Ford, D. (1998). *The Dark Side of the Light Chasers: Reclaiming your Power, Creativity, Brilliance and Dreams*. London: Hodder & Stoughton.

Fraiberg, S. (1981). *Clinical Studies in Infant Mental Health*. London: Tavistock.

Fraiberg, S., Adelson, E., & Shapiro, V. (1975). Ghosts in the nursery: a psychoanalytic approach to the problem of impaired mother–infant relationships. *Journal of the American Academy of Child Psychiatry, 14*: 387–422.

Groopman, J. (2005). *The Anatomy of Hope.* London: Simon & Schuster.

Harlow, H. (1958). The nature of love. *American Psychologist, 13*: 673–685.

Hitlin, J. (2002). Energy therapy, edge-figures and the phases of the creative process. In: W. Lammers & B. Kircher (Eds.), *The Energy Odyssey: New Directions in Energy Psychology.* Eastbourne: Dragon Rising.

Holmes, J. (1993). *John Bowlby and Attachment Theory.* London: Routledge.

Holmes, J. (2004). Disorganised attachment and borderline personality disorder: a clinical perspective. *Attachment & Human Development, 6*(2): 181–190.

Keck, G., & Cline, F. (1992). *Hope for High Risk and Rage Filled Children.* Evergreen, CO: EC Publications.

Lifton, B. J. (1994). *The Journey of the Adopted Self: A Quest for Wholeness.* New York: Basic Books.

Lorenz, K. (1952). *King Solomon's Ring.* London: Methuen.

Mahler, M., Pine, F., & Bergman, A. (1975). *The Psychological Birth of the Human Infant.* London: Hutchinson.

Main, M., & Solomon, J. (1986). Discovery of an insecure-disorganised/disoriented attachment pattern. In: T. B. Brazelton & M. Yogman (Eds.), *Affective Development in Infancy.* Norwood, NJ: Ablex.

Menzies Lyth, I. (1988). *Containing Anxiety in Institutions.* London: Free Association.

Miller, A. (1987). *For Your Own Good: The Roots of Violence in Child-Rearing.* London: Virago.

Mollon, P. (2005). *EMDR and The Energy Therapies: A Psychoanalytic Perspective.* London: Karnac.

Parent to Parent Information on Adoption Services (PPIAS) Journal (1993). 67: 15 (Autumn).

Parent to Parent Information on Adoption Services (PPIAS) (1994). *Reactive Attachment Disorder.* Parents' and Professionals' Information Packs.

Pert, C. (2005). Foreword. In: D. Feinstein, D. Eden, & G. Craig (Eds.), *The Healing Power of EFT and Energy Psychology.* London: Piatkus.

Pert, C., & Marriott, N. (2006). *Everything You Need To Feel Good.* London: Hay House.

Robertson, J. (1952). *A Two-Year-Old Goes to Hospital* (Film). New York: New York Film Library.

Roet, B. (2000). *Understanding Hypnosis: A Practical Guide To The Health-Giving Benefits of Hypotherapy and Self-Hypnosis.* London: Piatkus.

Sachs, A. (2005). *The Psychodynamics of Self-Harm.* CONFER Lecture Series, London: Tavistock Clinic.

Salzberger-Wittenberg, I. (1970). *Psycho-Analytic Insight and Relationships: A Kleinian Approach.* London: Routledge & Kegan Paul.

Santayana, G., (1905). *The Life of Reason* (Vol. 1). New York: Scribner.

Schore, A. (1994). *Affect Regulation and the Origin of the Self: The Neurobiology of Emotional Development.* Hillsdale, NJ: Erlbaum.

Seifert, M. K. (1992). An ecological approach to attachment therapy. *Journal of Psychiatry* (1998), 155: 1718–1719.

Sills, F. (2008). *Being and Becoming: Psychodynamics, Buddhism, and the Origins of Selfhood.* Berkeley, CA: North Atlantic Books.

Spitz, R. (1947). *Grief: A Peril in Infancy* (Film). New York: New York University Film Library.

Southgate, J. (1989). Map of the psyche. *Journal of the Institute for Self-Analysis.* 3: 1.

Steinem, G. (1992). *Revolution from Within.* London: Little, Brown.

Stern, D. (1985). *The Interpersonal World of the Infant.* New York: Basic Books.

Symington, N. (1986). *The Analytic Experience.* London: Free Association.

Thomas, N. (1997). *When Love is Not Enough: A Guide to Parenting Children With RAD—Reactive Attachment Disorder.* Glenwood Springs, CO: Families by Design.

Van Gulden, H. (2002). *Living with an Angry Child.* Notes for workshop, February 2005. London: Post Adoption Centre.

Verrier, N. (1994). *The Primal Wound: Understanding the Adopted Child.* Baltimore: The Gateway Press.

Webster-Stratton, C. (2006). *The Incredible Years.* Seattle, WA: The Incredible Years.

Weil, T. (2002). Relationship-oriented meridian-based psychotherapy and counselling. In: W. Lammers & B. Kircher (Eds.), *The Energy Odyssey: New Directions in Energy Psychology* (Chapter 17). Eastbourne: Dragon Rising.

White, I. (1990). The little caretaker self. *Journal of the Institute for Self Analysis,* 4: 39–40.

Whitfield, C. (1987). *Healing The Child Within.* Pompano Beach, FL: Health Communications.

Winnicott, D. W. (1985). *Playing and Reality.* Harmondsworth: Penguin.

Winnicott, D. W., & Britton, C. (1947). *Human Relations, 1.*

INDEX